Copy This!

How I turned Dyslexia, ADHD, and 100 square feet into a company called Kinko's®

By Kinko's founder
Paul Orfalea
and
Ann Marsh

WORKMAN PUBLISHING • NEW YORK

Copyright © 2005, 2007 by The Orfalea Family Foundation

All rights reserved. No portion of this book may be reproduced—mechanically, electronically, or by any other means, including photocopying—without written permission of the publisher. Published simultaneously in Canada by Thomas Allen & Son Limited.

All of Paul Orfalea's royalties from the sale of *Copy This!* will be donated to nonprofit organizations that help children turn their learning challenges into recognized strengths.

Photographs are courtesy of the archive and personal collection of FedEx Kinko's, Orfalea family members, and Adrianna Foss.

Library of Congress Cataloging-in-Publication Data is available.

ISBN-13: 978-0-7611-4385-7

Workman books are available at special discounts when purchased in bulk for premiums and sales promotions as well as for fund-raising or educational use. Special editions or book excerpts can also be created to specification. For details, contact the Special Sales Director at the address below.

Workman Publishing Company, Inc.
225 Varick Street
New York, NY 10014-4381
www.workman.com

Printed in the U.S.A.
First printing: March 2007

10 9 8 7 6 5 4 3 2 1

To my wife, Natalie, for loving me.
To my parents for nurturing me.
To my sons, Mason and Keenan, for bringing meaning to my life.
—Paul

To my father, the original, eccentric visionary in my life.
To my husband, Johanne, for walking with me.
—Ann

Table of Contents

Foreword

WHEN PAUL ORFALEA WAS IN SCHOOL, he struggled mightily, just as I did, with reading and writing. In grade school, I relied on *Classic Comics* to understand the books that the teachers assigned, but that I couldn't read. In college, Paul used *Cliff Notes* and watched great plays on TV to survive a literature class. It's not surprising that as kids we both focused our energies outside the classroom. I sold chickens, eggs, and fertilizer; Paul sold vegetables. And we each became interested in the stock market in our early teens.

Back then, not much was known about dyslexia. All we knew was that we were different from other kids in the class, and we had to work much harder to keep up. We also didn't know that many other talented individuals went through similar difficulties in school. When he was a kid, Albert Einstein had great difficulty remembering words and written material, and was told by his teacher that he would never amount to anything. What that teacher didn't know is that Einstein's deficits shared the same brain with his extraordinary vision as a physicist—one that profoundly changed the way we understand our world.

The same is true of many successful entrepreneurs in the business world. That's why I'm glad that Paul Orfalea addresses this issue in his autobiography. Even though there have been great scientific advances in understanding how the human brain works, there is still tremendous stigma for kids and adults who do not learn in ways widely considered to be the educational norm.

I've often thought that the obstacles I faced in school helped to shape me as an entrepreneur. It wasn't until business school, when I was able to concentrate on business and economics, that I really came into my own. That experience taught me that everyone has their strengths and challenges. It highlighted the importance of teamwork and showed me that the combination of many different strengths produces a better outcome than one person working alone. That's a perspective that has had a profound influence on our management philosophy and in our relationships with our clients. As you read the engaging story of how he started and built Kinko's, you'll see how Paul Orfalea's difficulties with learning inclined him to treat his fellow workers and customers with real humanity. *Copy This!* is filled with inspiring and concrete advice to businessmen and businesswomen about how they can do the same.

The most compelling part of Paul's book, however, is the insight into the strengths that frequently accompany the challenges, and how difficulties in learning in the conventional sense often force a person to develop compensatory strategies. And that, in turn, can lead to what we commonly refer to as "thinking outside the box." The Kinko's we've known all these years would not exist were it not for the exceptional thinking of its founder.

That's a valuable message not only for businesspeople, but for educators and parents and, most importantly, for children who are experiencing problems with learning. It benefits us all to understand that we each have a one-of-a-kind brain, a special way of learning, and real strengths that are ours alone. For entrepreneurs and kids both, resiliency is a crucial ingredient in success, and there's no better way to reinforce that quality than by reminding us, as Paul Orfalea does, that being different isn't a bad thing and that we each have something uniquely our own to contribute.

Charles R Schwab

Founder and CEO, Charles Schwab & Co. Inc.

Preface

I FIRST MET KINKO'S FOUNDER PAUL ORFALEA IN 1997 while writing a story about him for *Forbes*. At the time, I had the same reaction most people do: "Who *is* this guy?" I had never met anyone like him. Nor have I since. I wanted to know a lot more, but no book existed to satisfy my curiosity. Once I began to work with him one on one, I started to feel that the words "human being" don't fully capture him. I prefer to think of Paul as a weather pattern or, as one of his partners describes him, a hurricane. Paul is a force of nature with the power to effect a lot of change in a lot of people over a lot of territory all at once.

Now, if a hurricane could talk, what would he sound like? Good question. I've done my best to translate Paul not only to the written page, but also to the linear world in which he is definitely *not* a resident. The truth is, he's always better in person; I hope you can hear him speak somewhere. I've never met a more circular, out-of-the-box thinker. It's often exhausting trying to keep up with him, as many of his partners can attest.

But, as they and I have discovered, it's worth the effort because he has an important story to tell—important not only for businesspeople and entrepreneurs who will benefit from his unorthodox and inspirational teaching, but for kids, teachers, and parents struggling with learning conditions like attention deficit/hyperactivity disorder and dyslexia. Paul's "learning opportunities," as he calls them, are a big part of the Kinko's story and of his own story.

Yale dyslexia expert Sally Shaywitz defines dyslexia as "a reading difficulty that is unexpected for a person's age, intelligence, level of education or profession." Dyslexics like Paul may not be able to decode the written word the way you or I can, but they compensate for this difficulty with an extraordinary ability to see things you and I cannot. Most people underestimate, or simply don't understand, the exceptional talents "learning opportunities" can confer on the people who have them. That is what this book is about. It's the story of how Kinko's came to be and a record of the peculiar genius behind the company.

—Ann Marsh

Acknowledgments

I want to give a heartfelt thanks to a few special people who made this book (and much of my life) possible:

Dan Tevrizian, Dan and CiCie Frederickson, and Jim Warren.

Ann and I would like to thank all the friends, family members, and the many former Kinko's partners who submitted to lengthy interviews or contributed in other substantial ways to the making of this book:

Gerry Alesia, Stuart Blake, Jerome Bohnett, Dave Bolton, Buck Brellhart, Glenn Carter, Greg Clark, Michael Cohn, Greg Combs, Render Dahiya, John Davis (from HBS), John Davis (with Stone Canyon), Chuck Doud, George and Betty Erhart, Mike Fasth, Mark Fell, Amel and Pauline Ferris, Bob Gielow, Gene Goehring, Marcus Goller, Doug Gotterba, Mark Grayson, Kyle Hanson, Jeff Harding, Nick and Lillian Heesey, Brenda Helfert, Lance and Beth Helfert, Michelle Helfert, Selma Herr, Carter Hines, Dennis Itule, Steve Itule, Hiro Izutsu, Dana Jennings, Eric Johansing, Harry Johansing, Marlene Johansing, Suzanne Nora Johnson, Todd Johnson, Mark Juergensmeyer, Christine Knight, Rich Kraus, Brad Krause, Gary Kusin, Tim LaBrucherie, Keith Lawrenz, Atticus Lowe, John Mackall, Mark and Karen Madden, Joel Maloney, Kari Martindale, John McGrath, Jeff Menecci, Melanie Minson, Bob Montgomery, Pierre Mornell, Isabel Moropoulos, Bill Morton-Smith, Louisa Murray, Tom O'Malia, Annie Odell, Todd Ordal, DebAnn Orfalea, Dick Orfalea,

Mark Orfalea, Rose Orfalea, Rob Pace, Tom Parrish, Scotty Perkins, Alan Porter, Craig Redwine, Jay Richardson, Mazen Safadi, Gary Safady, Wayne Siemens, Blaise Simqu, Phil Smith, Jacques Soiret, Judy Sonney, Karen Sophiea, Prof. James Stancill, Tim Stancliffe, Richard Tait, Dickran Tevrizian, Lisa Tuveson, Prof. Kenneth Trefz, David Vogias, Harry Waaler, Roger Willmon, Stan Witnov, Patricia Wilbarger, Bert Willoughby, Jim Wilmore, Walt Wilson, Charlie Wright, Tony Wynne, and Dean Zatkowsky.

To the many people without whom this book would never have been written, a huge thank you from both Ann and I:

Lois Mitchell, executive director of the Orfalea Family Foundation, shepherded this project through from start to finish. Our agent, Elyse Cheney, believed in this book from the get-go, as did Peter Workman and Susan Bolotin. Our brilliant editor, Richard Rosen, called forth the spirit of this book, giving it shape with both his sharp intellect and keen intuition. CiCie Frederickson, Solveig Chandler, Adrianna Foss, and Luann Alvarez meticulously reviewed early drafts and tracked down long-lost friends and facts. Mel Levine of the University of North Carolina, Sally Shaywitz of Yale University, Glen Rosen of Harvard University, and educational therapist Lee Pennington Neil shared their expertise in their respective fields. John Byrne, Nina Munk, Dori Jones Yang, Robert Spector, Catherine Fredman, Paul Brown, Alex Frankel and B.J. Gallagher shared their experience as authors. John Pollack, Erin Martin, Edward Boyle, Kelly Barron, Lisa Richardson and Scott Wenger read drafts and gave valuable input. Yanfei Shen provided dogged fact-checking. All the Marshes, Strongs, Sunds and both Jayaratnes lent unflagging support. Jim Frazier and Diane McIntee provided invaluable technical assistance. Tim Ferguson, at *Forbes*, first sent Ann to write about Paul in 1997.

—Paul Orfalea

How To Succeed in Business Without Really Reading

N OT MANY KIDS MANAGE TO FLUNK THE SECOND GRADE, but I did. I couldn't learn the alphabet. This code called reading, so easy for other students, I found difficult to break. They read as though angels whispered into their ears. They wrote in graceful curves and perfectly straight lines. I made chicken scratches. To me, a sentence was a road map with ink stains in all the critical places.

Consequently, I became a goof-off. Of the eight schools my parents enrolled me in, four expelled me. In third grade, my frustrated teachers sent me to a school for "mentally retarded" kids, housed in a teacher's residence in Hollywood. Most of my classmates suffered from Down's syndrome or other conditions of severe mental and physical impairment. Fortunately, I was given an IQ test, scored 130, and rejoined the public school system. Still, things didn't get much better. I may not have been able to read, but I could find my way to the principal's office blindfolded. My typical report card came back with two C's, three D's, and an F. A brilliant tutor named Selma Herr finally managed to teach me to read, after a fashion, using phonics. I graduated from high school, with a focus in wood shop, eighth from the bottom of my class of 1,200. Frankly, I still have no idea how those seven kids managed to do worse than I did.

My name is Paul Orfalea (OR-fah-la). In 1970, I started a copy shop in Santa Barbara, California, in an 8-foot by 12-foot storefront next to a hamburger stand. I called it Kinko's after the nickname college friends gave me because of my kinky hair. Today, there are more than 1,200 Kinko's locations across the globe. The revenues from those stores top $2 billion annually. Federal Express, our former vendor and the new owner of Kinko's, plans to dramatically increase the number of retail outlets. I am most proud of the fact that, before I retired, *Fortune* named Kinko's one of the best places to work in the country three times in a row. More than 100 of my earliest coworkers and partners are millionaires today because of what we built together at Kinko's. As someone with a condition I now know is called "dyslexia," I could have never predicted I would make my name in what is essentially the "reading business." Kinko's is not only a fixture on downtown street corners, but a fixture in the minds of millions of customers who use it to solve any number of their problems.

I teach them skills that have little to do with academics or test scores.

Today, I spend most Mondays in an unusual spot for someone with my skill set. I'm back in Santa Barbara, not far from that first Kinko's, teaching economics to college seniors at the University of California at Santa Barbara. Naturally, I use a different teaching strategy than other teachers. I don't use a roster to take roll. I take Polaroids of each student on the first day and scrawl their first names on each one. I keep this stack of photos in my pocket and shuffle through it when I need to. When I ask them for writing assignments (which is rarely), I never want more than one single page of clear and concise prose. I could care less about their grades. (I give almost all of them A's.) Instead, I teach them skills that have little to do with academics or test scores. Among other things, I teach them new ways to think about money and investing, how to present their ideas verbally, how to talk with people from "authority figures" to each other. To this end, I run an exercise to teach them one of the hardest things in the world to learn—harder than calculus, harder than economic theory, harder than fixing a photocopier.

"Peter," I say, picking a student at random. "Isn't there a lovely young woman in this class who you'd like to ask out for Wednesday night?" Nervous laughter spreads across the room. People start looking at each other or down at their shoes. They're thinking, "*This* is a world economics class?" Yes, it is.

"You want me to just *ask somebody out?*" Peter asks, incredulous. We've gotten to know each other over the past couple of classes. Now he looks at me as though I've gone insane. I am accustomed to getting this sort of reaction in life. I give him back an equally incredulous look. "You mean you wouldn't *want* to go out with one of these lovely ladies? Peter, this is your chance."

"OK," Peter says looking across at Wendy. With a toss of the head, he says, "Hey, what are you doing Wednesday night?" Verrry cool.

"No, no, no!" I say. I wave my hands in the air like a conductor. "Ask her nicely, nicely. Be polite." Have you ever noticed that kids these days really don't know how to talk to each other? Peter begins again. He sits up a little straighter. He looks her in the eye.

"Wendy," he begins, making eye contact. "Would-you-like-to-go-out-with-me-Wednesday-night?" This is a different kid entirely, both polite and courageous.

Now Wendy is embarrassed. It turns out she has a boyfriend! I ask her if she knows what she's passing up. She murmurs something and looks down. But Peter isn't off the hook. I get him to ask somebody else. This time Carol, shyly, says yes. I pull out a crumpled wad of bills from my pocket and give Peter some money, because most college kids are always pretty poor.

"Where are you gonna go?" I ask him. He hasn't thought this far ahead. "Maybe Palazzio?" he ventures. "Oh, that's a great place," I tell him. I get this pair to settle on the hour they will meet on Wednesday. By this time, there's a lot of laughter. Believe me, no one is bored. "Seven P.M.?" I confirm. "Great, maybe I'll come," I say. "I'll see you there."

I've never turned up, but I like them to think I might. Next week, I find out how the date went. Maybe I get another pair or two in class set up on dates. Sometimes the students keep dating each other, sometimes they don't. But the point is, they get a chance to learn how to talk to each other. They get to see someone navigate rejection and survive it. They get to see someone asking for something he wants or needs from another person. Sometimes that's all we need to learn to do in life.

The truth is that most of the boys are dying to ask out one of the girls. And most of the girls have an eye on one of the boys. Even if they're straight-A students, speed readers, and star athletes, they're scared half to death of putting themselves on the line. They need a push. This is one of the greatest lessons I learned from my own struggles, from my dyslexia, my restlessness, and what others call my ADHD or "attention deficit/hyperactivity disorder." (I dislike using the term "deficit"; I don't think it is one.) Doing life alone is not second best, it's impossible. We need other people. We need to know how to talk with them, argue with them, build with them, and introduce ourselves to them. We need a push. It's funny to think that human beings forget this fact, especially the straight-A types.

At Kinko's I was a tireless matchmaker among the ranks of our coworkers. I constantly urged people to fall in love and marry each other. I believed in it and I still do! Hundreds of our partners, managers, and coworkers were married to each other. I'm very proud of the fact that, at one point before I left the company, I discovered that among our 200 top people we had only seven divorces. Many of our customers used Kinko's as a dating service, as well. Thousands of them got married after meeting each other over our copy machines. Kinko's was similar to another people-oriented company I admire, Southwest Airlines, which counts more than 1,000 married couples among its 34,000 coworkers. That's a great statistic. I knew our coworkers would be stronger in teams than on their own. It's possible to go all the way through your schooling years without learning this. Given the cards I drew at birth, I never had the chance to forget, not even for a moment.

This is only one of the many gifts of my "disorders," all of which contributed enormously to the building of both Kinko's and of my life. They propelled me to think differently. They forced me to rely on other people. I was prevented from taking inspiration from books; I had to learn from the world itself, directly. I had to rely on my own eyes, a skill not enough people make use of these days. My "disabilities" enabled me to focus on the big picture at Kinko's, something I call being "on" your business instead of "in" it. My friend Tom O'Malia, former head of the Center for the Study of Entrepreneurship at the University of Southern California, taught me this concept. He told me that too many people are mired in the details of their lives. They are stuck down "in" their lives, rather than staying "on" them. They miss the larger picture; they don't face the uncomfortable questions that, once posed, can force dramatic and necessary change. My dad had a saying for this. He would tell me, "The mundane is like a cancer." He meant that all the busywork of your life prevents you from actually living.

Taking Care of Business

R unning a company in a world full of readers was . . . well, an interesting experience. I certainly didn't behave like other executives. If you opened the drawers and filing cabinets of my office, you would have seen . . . nothing. I didn't keep paperwork, files, a pen, or a computer. What for? As a nonreader, I wouldn't be using them much. In a way, the office was just for show because I didn't like spending time there. I didn't like sitting around and reading long, novelistic reports. I didn't get caught up in the minutiae of meeting minutes. (I'd rather stick pins in my eyes than sit through a board meeting.) Coworkers helped with my written correspondence. I was so avid about staying "on" my business that I was maniacal—fanatical!—about responding to my mail the same day I got it. My longtime colleague CiCie Frederickson learned to write my letters based on our brief conversations. "You figure out how to say it," I'd tell her. Later, her husband, Dan Frederickson, the president of Kinko's, also helped write correspondence for me, too. My office was empty because I had an In Box and an Out Box—but no storage box in between. I took care of business the same day it landed on my desk.

Though I couldn't avoid some writing, most vital communications were transmitted verbally, by voice mail, or in person. When I was with Kinko's, we were an oral company, a verbal company. My restlessness propelled me out of doors. How many managers do you know who *really* understand what is happening at the frontlines of their business? I did. I visited stores to find out what our different locations were doing right. Anybody can sit around in an office thinking about what people are doing wrong. My job was to get out and find out what people were doing right—and exploit it. Then, I tried to spread those practices throughout the Kinko's network.

My high school degree in wood shop belies the fact that I also have no mechanical ability to speak of. There isn't a machine at Kinko's I can operate. I could barely run the first copier we leased back in 1970. It didn't matter. All I knew was that I could sell what came out of it. From day one at Kinko's I relied on others to operate those machines, to run the store, to come up with groundbreaking new ideas, to expand our business, and to keep me and everybody else constantly inspired. The same is true today. I rely on others to run our real estate ventures, our investments, and our philanthropic endeavors. You're right if you're wondering whether or not I *wrote* these words you're reading. As with every other undertaking in my life, I relied on someone else—in this case, my coauthor Ann Marsh. Too many people think they have to do life on their own, but I've found the best way to live is to share the burdens, as well as the joys, with others. My motto has always been "Anybody else can do it better."

> **My job was to get out and find out what people were doing right.**

These days, people are quick to label others with terms like "learning disabled," ADHD, ADD, "dyslexic," and a host of other maladies. Kids often come up to me and say, "I *am* ADHD," as opposed to, "I *have* ADHD." What does that do to their self-esteem? Drugs like Ritalin and Prozac are prescribed as quick fixes. I am not against those drugs. In fact, my life improved dramatically once I started taking Prozac a couple of years back. But, before giving drugs to our kids, we need to better understand what they are trying to erase: the highly varied ways people think and process information. How many innovators, I wonder, are lost to us simply because their talents and skills cannot be accurately perceived or measured? And why are we so hung up on measuring everyone, anyway? The very bedevilment we are so eager to cure in a person may hold the key to his genius. I speak regularly to adults, kids, budding entrepreneurs, parents, business students, corporate executives, and academics and, believe me, the things I tell them are not what they learn in classrooms. When tearful parents come up to me to talk about their child's "learning disorder," I ask them, "Oh, you mean his learning *opportunity?* What is your child good at? What does he like to do?" When I meet their kids, I tell them, "You are blessed." It is easy to forget that part of the equation in the face of a dire-sounding prognosis.

I didn't know it at the time I opened the first Kinko's, but there is a long history of innovators and achievers who owe their particular brilliance, at least in part, to their "deficits." This is a little appreciated fact, but those with learning opportunities, and even people with mood disorders, make up the ranks of some of the most successful and inventive members of our society. They have for millennia. Some speculate that Leonardo da Vinci, Winston Churchill, Albert Einstein, and Walt Disney were dyslexic, though there's no way to say for certain. A *Fortune* cover story, "The Dyslexic CEO," featured the startling number of successful businesspeople with dyslexia, from Virgin Record's founder Richard Branson and telecom pioneer Craig McCaw to Cisco CEO John Chambers and celebrated trial attorney David Boies to discount brokerage founder Charles Schwab. Add to that list IKEA founder Ingvar Kamprad, whose fortune *Forbes* estimates at $18.5 billion. I'm in good company. All of these innovators survived an educational system determined to make them feel like failures. We are the lucky ones. Some think our penal system is crammed with wayward visionaries who never found the support they needed to make the capitalist system work for them. Some of my closest friends in high school and college were social outcasts. Some of them did end up in jail. I could relate to them all.

Fortunately, my racing, jumping mind, my inability to sit still, my difficulty reading—all of these qualities led me to develop what other people call an unorthodox, people-centered, big-picture business model. To a peddler like me it's simply what came naturally. In this model, when all systems are go, businessmen and women value customers and each other, understand the importance of cash flow, liquidity, savings, and risk taking. They cut quickly through red tape (because there isn't any), grow rapidly without losing perspective, and surround themselves with the right people. To this day, Kinko's (now FedEx Kinko's) is one of only a very few competitors from that original field of mom-and-pop copy shops that has survived to become a multinational. FedEx Kinko's is now the dominant retail document management chain in the world. As we grew, we continued to insist on respecting every single one of our (at the time) 25,000 coworkers for their unique contributions. We created a unique company with a unique culture. The fact that *Fortune* repeatedly named it one of the best places to work is due, in no small part, to the fact that I understood that anybody else really *could* do it better.

With my lot in life, do you think I had any other choice of attitude? I was forced to trust the world and to trust other people. With my skill set, I certainly couldn't have built Kinko's alone. To my knowledge, none of the visionary thinkers mentioned above, some of whom were also labeled "learning disabled," have tried to explain the specific ways in which their "disabilities" contributed to their uncanny *abilities* to innovate and to create. That is my aim in writing this book. It is built around the set of concepts I used at first to survive when I was younger and, later, to build a multinational, store by store. Along the way, I relate the story of how Kinko's came to be.

Like my students in Santa Barbara, you don't have to have dyslexia to learn from my business experience. Nor do you have to be a businessperson to learn from my learning opportunity. In this book, you'll see that the line between the business and the personal is blurred because I don't think the two are really separable. My hope is that anyone who picks up this book (or listens to an audio version) will come away with new insights into how to better run their businesses, to cope with and capitalize on what others consider their flaws, to partner with others, to enjoy their families, and to live their lives.

In case I haven't already made it clear, I'm extremely human. I struggle with my temper, my "dark side." The dark side of the Kinko's story is that the company was built, at least in part, on emotional extremes, most of them my own. Both as an adult and when I was younger, my emotions and my creativity sometimes misfired. Once, when I was 12 years old, I tied myself up in ropes like Houdini, jumped in a pool, and sank to the bottom. Unlike Houdini, I failed to free myself. I nearly drowned before an alarmed cousin pulled me from the water. Chalk that one up to the perils of highly creative thinking.

Building an entirely new sort of business from a single Xerox copy machine was a more successful plunge. It gave me the life the world seemed determined to deny me when I was younger. I built personal and business relationships that endure to this day, both because of and despite my difficulties. I have my mother to thank for encouraging the development of my own view of the world. One day after I was expelled from school at the age of 13, the vice principal told my mother not to worry about her son's future. "Maybe some-day he can learn how to lay carpet," he said to console her. I remember my mom came home crying that day and said, "I just know Paul can do more than lay carpets." Mom dreamed her own dreams. She never relied upon the bleak assessments of others. Whenever I felt down, whenever I started wondering what homeless shelter I would die in, she used to buck me up by telling me:

"You know Paul, the A students work for the B students, the C students run the companies, and the D students dedicate the buildings."

Don't get me wrong. I'm not suggesting parents say this to a child who's getting A's and B's. But the child who *can't* play by the same rules needs to know there's so much more to life than what goes down on a report card. I had supportive parents and that made all the difference. I was a sensitive kid. I could have easily fallen through the cracks. My parents taught my brother, sister, and me to please ourselves first. They kept schoolwork in perspective. They never wanted us staying up late to study for tests because they knew we'd forget everything we'd memorized at the last minute. They schooled us in bigger concepts. Kids today need to spend more time learning to please themselves instead of pleasing others, instead of trying to conform to the one-size-fits-all measuring sticks of standardized tests and grading systems. My parents taught me to reject conventional wisdom and to rely on my own deepest instincts.

Whether you're reading this book or listening to it on tape, may it inspire you to do the same.

Chapter 1

Anybody Else

Can Do It Better

WHILE DRIVING ME TO SCHOOL ONE DAY IN 1957, my mother saw a dark-haired kid walking to class and, assuming he was Lebanese like the rest of our family, told me I should meet him. (I had curly blond hair at the time and never looked particularly Lebanese, but more on that subject later.) "Go talk to him," she said, letting me out of the car. I trailed after him. I needed help when I was young learning how to talk to people and I got it from my mother.

The kid turned out to be Danny Tevrizian, an Armenian, and he was everything I was not. While I floundered in class, he did well. While other kids teased or avoided me, they *liked* Danny. My family felt relieved when they saw us together because they saw that, through him, I'd found a toehold at school. What they didn't know was that I'd also found a terrific source for correct test answers. Danny never condoned cheating, but I began to cheat off his tests whenever I could get away with it since a certain amount of cheating in school is a matter of academic survival for someone who can barely read a sentence—not to mention write one. My teacher, Sister Sheila, had spent the two previous years paddling me because I cheated on my alphabet test.

So, at the outset of fourth grade, it was a relief to meet Danny. We played games like Risk, Stratego, and Monopoly together. We made bets as to who would become a millionaire first. When Danny decided to go to USC for college, I followed him and majored in loopholes. (I first picked up credits at Los Angeles Valley College, then talked my way into USC's regular degree program by starting with extension courses and taking classes with football players.)

I didn't know it at the time but, outside of the members of my family, Danny was my first partner. He was one of the first people who taught me that one plus one equals three, that people are always stronger together. You could say I partnered with his whole family. His mom helped rewrite my school papers. His sister Melanie reworked the essay I wrote on my college application about 20 times. His brother Dickran, now a federal judge, was a great mentor to me. Every major success I've had in my life has come about because I knew that somebody, often *anybody,* whether it was my wife, friend, or business partner, could do something better than I could.

The best students think they have to do it all themselves.

This is a difficult, if not impossible, concept for straight-A types to grasp. The best students think they have to do it all themselves. This isn't their fault. The educational system teaches kids they have to be good at *everything,* or else. They must excel at reading, writing, mathematics, history, geography, music, sports, and science. Out of the classroom, I've found this just isn't so. Adults have a much easier time than they did as kids. They get to specialize. They become musicians, doctors, teachers, and librarians. They pick one thing. It's a *whole lot easier.*

Danny and I are still best friends today, nearly 50 years later. He's watched me build my entire life through my relationships with other people. As he sees it, I go around looking for my "missing piece." I find that piece with one partner and then with another in an ever-widening circle of long-term collaborations. As Danny puts it, "I felt I was a piece that fit in there for a while, then other people take over that spot. Everybody gets to take a ride with Paul for a while. Paul enjoys this. It makes him whole." If it weren't for my learning opportunities, which make obvious my need for help, I might be deluded like others into thinking I could do everything on my own.

I got the idea for partnerships at home. My family, full of entrepreneurs, was built on them. First off, we are of Lebanese descent. Both of my parents, Al and Virginia Orfalea, were descended from immigrants. As a kid, I didn't know anyone who had a job. In my home, having a "job" and working for someone else was *not* a cool thing. When you're an employee, my mother used to say, "You're only as good as your last paycheck." Being part of a big family, my relatives worked with each other. It was only natural. As far as I was concerned, family and business were all mixed up together. My mother was one of seven, six of them girls. Four of her siblings lived within blocks of us. I spent my weekends walking, biking, and driving to and from our various cousins' homes. Our house was always full of cousins, aunts, and uncles. For many years, my father's mother lived with us. When I was born, my uncles took a look at my curly blond head and asked my mother, "Where'd you get the Swede?" I may have been one of the clan, but I didn't look like anybody else. If not being able to read made me feel like an outcast, the way I looked only deepened my alienation. I was always the oddball. Some things never change. I grew up accustomed to lots of shouting, pranks and huge family meals of fresh tabbouleh, hummus, and grape leaves. Over dinner, we talked and argued about the Vietnam War, the Commie threat, labor unions, and civil rights.

I watched partnerships at work everywhere within my family. All the adults were married. Most of their marriages were based on mutual respect and understanding—even if they included teasing and loud arguments. Family life was not particularly peaceful and, as it turned out decades later, neither was the family culture we built at Kinko's. Our motto at Kinko's in the eighties was "Keep the music playing." It inspired our coworkers to stay engaged, inspired, and talking with one another even when the lines were long and the demands bizarre at the front counter. It could have just as easily been the motto for my boisterous family.

At home, my father was the breadwinner and my mother oversaw the household. Dad ran his own women's clothing company in downtown Los Angeles called Charm of Hollywood. Even though she stayed at home, Mom was as skilled by nature at business as my father. Her mother, my grandmother, raised seven kids by herself in the Depression after her husband was killed in a trucking accident. Now, that's an achievement. Think about that for a moment—a single woman, raising seven kids in the Depression. I could never understand how the single mothers who worked at Kinko's did it. When my kids were little, I found them very difficult to manage. And I wasn't raising them alone. My grandmother ran a clothing store that was located right next to Canter's Delicatessen and Restaurant on Fairfax in Los Angeles. Maybe her store thrived because of all the free labor: my mother, her five sisters, and one brother grew up helping out there, interacting with customers and sweeping out the back room. Growing up, my aunts tell me that they rarely felt they lacked for anything, even without their father.

Your average street peddler has more business sense than the guy walking past in a suit.

My mother absorbed her mother's business smarts and shared them constantly with my father and with all of us kids. No one in business or in life has influenced me more. I have her and Father to thank for many of the principles that guided me while I helped build Kinko's. When I meet with businesspeople today, many of whom have fancy MBAs and lots of "book smarts," I can't shake the sense that we've gotten away from the immigrant values our grandparents brought to this country. In my family, we were all peddlers. I've found your average street peddler has more business sense than the guy walking past in a suit. They deal with customers in real time and get instant feedback from the market. In my experience, business smarts ultimately boil down to common sense and intuition. This is what my family, and especially my parents, passed down to me. My mother was a strong partner for my dad, giving him advice when he needed it about his clothing company.

My father and my Uncle Vic ran Charm of Hollywood together and shared the ownership 50–50. That was a *beautiful* partnership. I never saw either of them angry at each other. Uncle Vic was in charge of production while my Dad ran the business side and supervised the redesign of the clothing lines six times a year. As far as I know, they didn't compete, but thrived in each other's company. On my mother's side I particularly admired my Uncle Nick and my Uncle Aimel, who are married to two of mom's sisters. They are cool guys. They worked as bartenders after World War II. They learned the value of saving by living in an apartment my grandmother owned and storing up enough cash to open bars together. At one point, they owned and operated five bars and two liquor stores in downtown Los Angeles. After selling them, they went into real estate and built up a modest real estate empire for themselves. Work and family. Partnership and family. They went together. It made sense to me as a kid and it still does.

Unfortunately, though, there didn't seem to be a place for me in the workplace when I was young. One time when I was in high school, I was working at my father's clothing factory, as I did most afternoons. For the longest time my job had been buttoning up the dresses after they were steamed, but I really wanted to start assembling orders for customers, a job overseen by my Uncle Vic's wife, my Aunt Claudia. It paid more and the work was more interesting. My Aunt Claudia, however, was not a nice person at work. Once, she spotted me trying to pick orders and shouted at the man helping me out, "Don't let him do that! He can't even read." So much for nepotism. I walked out of the factory that day and sat in my car in the parking lot. It's possible that I cried for hours. It was the biggest cry of my life, and one of only a handful of times in my adult life that I have ever shed tears. I remember thinking, at that time, that it was no use trying to please anyone else. It simply wasn't possible, not with my skill set, so I might as well try to please myself.

It took me a lot longer before I actually succeeded in doing so. After my humiliation by Aunt Claudia, I returned many times to work at my dad's factory. But I was demoralized. Even though we had a great relationship, my dad eventually kicked me out. He just didn't know what to do with me. So I looked for work elsewhere. My neighbor Tim got me a job working at the local drugstore as a soda jerk serving up ice cream scoops and chocolate malts. A couple of days into my job I was fired after I spilled milk on the floor and a customer slipped and fell. Next, I tried a local gas station. My first day on the job, the station manager fired me because my handwriting was so poor no one could read what I wrote on the customers' charge slips. It probably didn't help that I wasn't eager to follow his—or anyone else's—direction. Most dyslexics have such bad early experiences with authority figures that they end up mistrusting authority in all forms for the rest of their lives. I'd say I got a healthy dose of that sort of experience. After getting fired from the gas station, I looked for other work. I tried painting sidewalk curbs with my cousins Denny and Steve Itule but spilled paint all over the upholstery of my cousin Brenda's car instead. (Denny, Steve, and Brenda all became partners of mine at Kinko's years later.) That was the end of that idea. I hated delivering newspapers. I loved talking with the customers when I sold Fuller brushes door to door. They let me in their homes and often made a purchase. But when I came back to collect payment later on, it seemed like no one was ever home. It didn't take long for me to conclude that I was basically unemployable.

> **It didn't take me long to conclude that I was basically unemployable.**

Clearly the only hope for me was to go into business for myself, to be my own boss. With so many entrepreneurs in the family, this wasn't a foreign concept. Even back when I was struggling through the second grade, I was making plans. I felt somewhere within me that I was going to own my own company one day and that I would have a secretary who would read and write for me. I had no idea how soon it would happen.

The spark came in the middle of my senior year at USC. I was taking a class with Danny. Our professor separated all of the students into groups. Danny and I ended up in the same one. We had to write a paper together for a shared grade on the Irvine Company, a huge real estate company in Orange County, California. Since I couldn't read well, I couldn't help much in the way of either research or writing. Instead, I became the gofer. I got the group coffee and pizza and generally entertained the other members. My one official job was to make copies of their paper and turn it in on time for the grade. This I could do.

I went to the university's copy center, paper in hand, on the day it was due. Right off, I saw something far more interesting: the copy center itself. This was the spring of 1970 and people were scurrying around making voluminous copies of legal paperwork for the trial of accused serial killer Charles Manson. I came running back to class, nearly out of breath. I had to talk to Danny. I was late with the paper and Danny was pretty angry that I'd jeopardized his grade.

"Gee, Paul," he said, "thanks a *lot.*"

As Danny remembers it, "Paul was shaking all over. He told me, 'Danny, I've got this great idea!'"

I realized I could start a copy shop myself, and I knew a place that needed one. My girlfriend at the time was a student two hours north of Los Angeles up the coast, at the University of California at Santa Barbara. There weren't any copy centers there for students or faculty. I didn't write out a business plan or study the market. But my gut told me I could make money selling what came out of those machines. It didn't matter that I had no idea how they worked.

Within a couple of months, in the fall of 1970, I found and rented out a small storefront near the university, only 100 square feet, attached to Carlos Hamburgers on Pardall Road in a part of Santa Barbara called Isla Vista. I was still a student down south, but I couldn't put off this brainstorm. The rent was $100 a month. The place was so small that by the time we needed a second machine we had to lug it out onto the sidewalk—yes, customers made their copies outdoors. The front of the store had a 6-foot-long flap of wood in the front secured with metal hooks that opened up like a garage door. When it was up, customers could stand under it out front and place their orders at a counter. A friend of mine who was an artist painted a series of mermaid-style women on the walls around the counter. They wore star-spangled bikini tops and their faces and hairdos looked like Marilyn Monroe's.

I rooted around for a name and found it on my own scalp. By the time I got to college, the curly blond locks of my youth had turned into a thick reddish afro. My friends called me Mohair, Carpethead, Pubehead, and Brillo Pad. I tried to straighten it a couple of times using some Afrosheen my mom gave me. I put the stuff in my hair and slept with a nylon stocking over my head. When I came to class the next day with my hair pancaked down over my skull, everyone stared. "Mr. Orfalea," my finance professor, James Stancill, asked in front of the whole class, "What happened to you?" For a short time that earned me the nickname Strato, a play on the word "straight." When I gave up on trying to tame my appearance, I became Kinkhead and then Kinko was coined by my friend Tim LaBrucherie, aka Zodo, whom you'll hear more about later. I never particularly liked being called Kinko, but it stuck. And I gave it to my new business.

It was no accident I chose it. Customers don't forget hard consonant names. That's another thing my mom used to tell me. Remember "goo-goo, ga-ga"? The first sounds that babies remember? That's why names like Xerox, Kodak, Costco, and Google lodge themselves in your mind. You never forget them, so I had a pretty good idea that Kinko's would catch on. By the time my artist friend was finished with his mural, the sign over the original store read, "The Grand Kinko's." The Marilyn Monroe mermaids, their arms raised high in the air as if they were dancing, set the tone. All I needed was a copier. My father cosigned on a $5,000 bank loan so that I could lease a copier from Xerox for $1,000 a month.

I called up Xerox. The company dispatched a technician named Harry Waaler from nearby Goleta to deliver a machine to us. Harry told me later that nothing about the description of our store made sense to him. "It just didn't compute," Harry said. "Why would anyone want a Xerox machine in Isla Vista, anyway?" The place was a densely populated college town. Hippie central. Somewhat rundown. Vietnam War protests were in full swing at the time. A local bank had been bombed. Another bomb at the faculty club, not far off, had killed a janitor. "The problem with our Xerox company cars is that they were black and looked like narc cars," Harry said. "I kind of hated to go down there and drive around."

When I finally stepped out to greet Harry on the sidewalk, he saw a kid with an afro, a walrus-style mustache, and bell-bottom pants. I was 22 years old. Harry told me later he figured he'd made a mistake. With my skills, how do you think I greeted people who came to help me out with my new company? I said, "I'm SO happy to meet you!" and I meant it. Harry didn't know it, but my future was in his hands—and in the hands of a bunch of other people I had yet to meet.

When we shook hands that day, another beautiful partnership was born. Or, as Harry puts it, "Paul became dependent on me." Xerox would become Kinko's' most important corporate partner for the next 30 years. It started with a handshake between two people. That's why I spend so much time teaching college students about how to present themselves and their ideas. I've found that most ventures in life begin this way.

Over the years, Harry and I did a lot of business with each other. We're still friends to this day. As Harry puts it, "I became a part of his family. Everybody does."

Before we opened, we put a sandwich board out front advertising copies at four cents a page. My father just couldn't comprehend how we could succeed by charging so little. He still cosigned on my loan, but it made no sense to him at all. "This company has as much chance of success as a fur company in Death Valley," he would say as we argued loudly about its chances.

We weren't so much selling copies as we were assuaging anxiety.

We were still setting up shop when a professor from the university came to us. Like each and every one of the subsequent millions of customers we would serve over the next three decades, he was stressed out and in a hurry. It was a state of mind all of us at Kinko's would come to be intimately familiar with. Later on, we would learn that we weren't so much selling copies as we were assuaging anxiety. He didn't know exactly what he wanted, but he wanted it done yesterday. He placed a $50 order with us and we hadn't even opened. It was a good omen.

Almost instantly it was apparent that we'd tapped into a strong demand, the central goal of any peddler or entrepreneur. We had found a means of helping people laboring with an unimaginable variety of desperate needs that the marketplace had yet to even identify. As a person who floundered for much of his childhood, who had so many unmet needs of my own, it was probably no accident.

Chapter 2

Are You "In" or "On" Your Business?

THE NIGHT BEFORE I OPENED THE ORIGINAL KINKO'S, I sat in my bedroom getting ready. I had bought plastic film dispensers (in addition to making copies, we sold and processed film). The work of filling each one with film rolls, one by one, was both lulling and boring. It had to be done. But it distracted me from thinking about more important issues. I reminded myself that *it's not the things you do, but the things you don't do that drive you crazy.* I didn't have any partners just yet, at this early stage, and that was my problem. I knew that, as soon as I could, I had to turn these tedious tasks over to others and pay them well for doing them. I could not let myself get swept under by all the monotonous busywork that comes along with starting a company. I was already vowing to stay "on" my business and not "in" it.

My dad worked in an inventory-based business and he knew what he was talking about. Managing inventory made it especially difficult for him to stay focused on the big picture. The stakes were too high. The apparel industry in downtown Los Angeles was and is a grind. I remember once a worker made an error while cutting a huge bolt of cloth. That single slipup cost my father's company $20,000. Dad could only grit his teeth, take the loss, and move on.

At Kinko's our errors cost us very little. We might waste some paper, but our botches were comparatively painless. This freed us to focus on the larger issues at work; it didn't cost us as much to leave daily tasks to others. This was one of the major advantages I saw to the retail copy business. At his apparel company, Dad was over-worked—even though there were 500 people working with him, he didn't delegate enough. He was simply too polite to raise a ruckus or complain. My father reminded me of the 1940s movie actor Ronald Colman—handsome, unflappable, debonair. He was a true states-man. I loved and admired my dad, but I didn't emulate him. (Ask anyone who knows me: I've never been accused of being unflappable *or* debonair.) Anybody could barge in on him. He got interrupted all the time, even on the weekends. Leo Finkenberg, one of his sales guys, called my father most Sundays. Dad would spend hours on the phone on a precious day off saying, "Yes, Leo. Yes, Leo."

Even though my father was the one who had told me, "The mundane is like a cancer," he knew his life was out of balance. But he didn't know how to fix it. Though he was a tremendous success in the clothing industry and received awards for his work, by the end of his life, he found he'd gotten too bogged down with details. From watching my dad, I learned the difference between "in" and "on." "Drive thy business," as Benjamin Franklin once said. "Let not thy business drive thee." Being "on" your business and your life means having enough detachment every day that you are constantly reassessing your direction, thinking creatively about your overall strategy, and scrutinizing your competitors' tactics. It means relying on others to attend to most of the details of the day-to-day opera-tions and employing a system of checks to verify that you are on the right track. Think of an airplane traveling from Los Angeles to New York. Most of the time while aloft, it is in fact *off course* while its navigational system continually makes adjustments so that it lands in the right place. Without constantly reassessing our direction to account for changes in the world around us, many companies (and lives) go way off track before anyone notices.

If this is happening to you, you may be "in" your life too much. If you are "in" your business, or your life, you aren't spending much time leading. You're putting out fires or attending to mindless tasks better left to your coworkers. Although I couldn't read well—maybe in part *because* I couldn't read well—I have a tremendous memory.

Or, so my friends say. I don't tend to forget details like coworkers' names, financial figures, or when to send a birthday card. When walking through stores, I always saw the tiniest items that needed fixing—from a tangled extension cord to a messy countertop. The key is that I did learn which details to focus on and which ones to ignore. I learned to turn a lot of busywork over to other people. That's an important skill. If you don't develop it, you'll be so busy, busy, busy that you can't get a free hour, not to mention a free week or month, to sit back and think creatively about where you want to be heading and how you are going to get there.

The Paul Orfalea In-or-On-Your-Business Quiz

1. Do you let people interrupt you whenever they want during the day?

2. Do your friends call you more often than you call them?

3. Do you work nights and weekends?

4. Do you take less than three weeks of vacation a year?

5. Do you lie awake at night feeling guilty?

6. Do you spend much of your time doing tasks someone else could do?

7. Do you often find yourself wondering what is happening at home or at one of your stores because you are rarely there?

My goal was always to answer "no" to each of these questions. For the most part I did, though in the years of our most furious growth at Kinko's, my wife, Natalie, says I was so preoccupied with work that, even when I was bodily at home, I was mentally elsewhere. I fought against that tendency in myself. When your mind can break free of all that worry and clutter, you will find yourself coming up with the most improbable and inspired ideas.

*   *   *

Staying "on" your business and not "in" it is a question of time-frame. Ask yourself where you are right now. Are you living in the past, the present, or the future? One of the most important things you carry with you is your frame of reference. Being constantly busy means you are too wedded to the past. When you're that busy, you can't see the present, and forget about the future. During my senior year at USC, if I had walked into that copy shop too preoccupied with the paper due that day (worrying about a grade!), I would never have seen the tremendous business opportunity staring me straight in the face. Pay attention to what is happening in your life. Do your homework, but don't let it distract you from what is really important in life. Sometimes you can't help getting stuck for a while in the past. Take accountants. *Accountants are in the past, managers are in the present, and leaders are in the future.* Know your job and you'll know what timeframe you live in from moment to moment. In the end, we are all the leaders of our own lives. Nobody else can do that job for us.

Guerrilla Retailing

A whole lot of ideas went into the first Kinko's. This is largely because I was so determined to stay "on" my business when I opened up that I did not allow myself the comfort of knowing what our business was going to be about! For all I knew in the beginning we might have ended up selling something else entirely. I knew that the students biking and walking past out front needed basics like pencils, pens, stationery, and notebooks. So we stocked up on those things. In addition to photocopying, we did a brisk business selling and process-ing film. Making passport photos, too, really helped us pay the bills. We constructed an extra storage area out back and used it to stock stacks and stacks of paper that we wholesaled to customers. Eventually we even brought a small printing press into that teeny 100-square-foot space. As far as I was concerned, any of those other lines of business might have proved strong enough to beat out copying. We might have grown into a stationery store, a wholesale paper venture, or a printing company. Our original store was a hothouse of experimentation.

For a time, it looked as though we might indeed go into printing. It didn't take long for the small printing business I had running in the back of our original store to outgrow the space. We moved it into another, bigger location and hung a huge, flying Superman out front with a big "K" on his chest. We were now getting a good stream of work: glossy menus from restaurants, full-color posters, orders from the university. I found my very first partner, Brad Krause, by turning up at a graphics arts and photography class at the local city college to look for someone who could run a printing press for me. Brad was one of the students and he took me up on the offer. We owned the printing business together and, later, all of Kinko's Northwest, one of our largest partnerships. Craig Redwine also came from the class with Brad to work at the printing business and, many years down the road, became a partner in Eureka and Arcata, California. They both did a great job, but I didn't like the printing business. There were too many variables to control. I knew we needed to get out of it the day I walked through the production room and found a check for $1,800 on the floor. I went ballistic. Our income was so precarious that we had no business misplacing $50, not to mention $1,800. Things were out of control. We sold the business to a nice guy named Tom Cole in 1976. Until 1995, when he closed it, he licensed the Kinko's name from us and that print shop was a lingering reminder of one of our roads not taken. But I'm getting ahead of my story.

To stay tuned into the market, as I've mentioned to you before, I didn't spend much time in the store. Now you may not believe that, but it's true. When I started the original Kinko's, I was still a student two hours south in Los Angeles at USC. I stayed in Santa Barbara for a full week when we opened the store. But, after that, I only worked there two days a week. The rest of the time I was down south, taking classes. I hired people to run Kinko's for me. And I left it in their care. As a result, there simply was no way to become too bogged down by lots of busywork.

On days I was there, I rarely made copies or worked behind the counter. To be honest, I was bored at the store. What I really enjoyed was getting out and meeting people —in a word, marketing. I went around campus handing out flyers. There's no better way to stay "on" your business than to think creatively and constantly about your marketing: how you are marketing, who you are marketing to, and, always, how you could be doing a better job at it. You'd be amazed what kind of business you can generate by a seemingly simple thing like handing out flyers. It's as true today as ever. My partners and I recently opened a bowling center in Santa Barbara called Zodo's and I spent an afternoon handing out flyers on campus just like I used to do 30 years ago. We had a great weekend as a result! During Kinko's' earliest days, I also sold pens and pencils out of a backpack or out in front of the store on the sidewalk by talking up passersby. I offered people specials and encouraged them to come and do business with us.

When this form of guerrilla marketing produced results, I expanded our use of it. I talked male students into selling pens, pencils, and notebooks out of backpacks by sending them to all the girls' dormitories. I gave them 20 percent of the sales. It was far easier to motivate people by tapping into Mother Nature. The guys wanted to meet the girls and the girls wanted the guys to come talk to them. In the process, I made a few bucks selling school supplies and spread the word about Kinko's. We didn't focus just on students, the poorest community in a university setting. We also targeted the faculty. By going into their departments and pretending we were supposed to be there, we stuffed flyers into the mailboxes of most of the professors on campus. University professors later drove some of our highest revenue business.

Now You See Me, Now You Don't

If it isn't completely obvious to you already, I think finding key partners is the most important ingredient in staying "on" your business. I didn't stuff each of those professors' boxes or visit all of those all-girls' dormitories myself. I got people to help me, to work with me. When you have the right people in your life or in your business, you can afford to contemplate the big picture. From the first day at Kinko's, I was doing my best to get out of "work." Some years later, when we had a few stores up and running, I made up my mind to truly be inaccessible. I happened to be sitting in my office that day when the phone rang. It was one of our store managers calling to ask me how to handle a bounced check. I held the receiver away from my face and looked at it, flabbergasted. If every store manager needed my help to deal with a bounced check, then we *really* had problems. I made up my mind then and there that I wouldn't be picking up my own phone every five minutes. Staying relatively inaccessible was the only way to stay "on" my business.

To that end, when I was in the office, I cultivated a closed-door policy. It's pretty popular among chief executives these days to brag about their open-door policies—how they get to the office at 7 A.M., eat lunch at their desks, and don't leave until well into the evening. That is crazy! When do they ever have time to sit back and think? Or wander or wonder? I made sure I had the time to think. This allowed me to scrutinize our competitors' tactics and concoct strategies for beating them. It gave me a chance to mull over the innovations coworkers in different stores had created. It gave me perspective. Part of the reason I could do this is because, as you already know, I didn't run Kinko's. I always left that to other very capable people. When we first opened, we had an ex-truck driver/office manager named Dottie Ault. As my longtime partner Tim Stancliffe puts it, "Tokyo had Godzilla. Kinko's had Dottie." Just like me, she used to yell and scream, and she really kept us all in line. She used to tell me, "You know, Paul, you're losing your effectiveness. You're calling your people too much. They don't take you seriously." So I let her do the calling for me. She was the master sergeant of Kinko's in the scattered seventies, during our earliest days of expansion.

> As my partner puts it, "Tokyo had Godzilla. Kinko's had Dottie."

Later, I extended my inaccessibility principle to board meetings. In fact, I wish I could have extended it even further. If I could live my life over at Kinko's, I would never have gone to a single board meeting.

I've found that next to nothing gets done in meetings anyway. I sat through *far* too many as it is. I was so unhappy while they were underway that I tended to be disruptive and that didn't help matters. I do much better with people one on one.

Chief Wanderer

Another way I stayed "on" my business in subsequent years was by getting out of the office. I worked in cycles, spending roughly three weeks on the road followed by three weeks back at the main office. On those trips I visited different parts of the country, different regions in the Kinko's network, and different stores. I also visited as many competitors as I could since the fact that they existed meant they were doing something right. I wanted to find out what those things were. These trips accomplished a couple of things. First off, they got me away from the main office so that I could leave people alone to do their work. Because the best way to show people you trust them is to leave them alone. I found that in the first week no one quite believed I was gone. By week two, they were getting used to my absence and by week three, they figured out everything on their own (sometimes I'd come back to the office and feel a bit adrift since everything was running so well without me). Equally important for me, I found that leaving headquarters got me away from the mundane, daily grind that left no space for insight, inspiration, or innovation. Here, as elsewhere, I was powerfully helped by my so-called disorders. I could never bear staying in one place for long. Thinking visually and not in words meant I needed three-dimensional, visual stimuli, the sort that can't be found in books. Instead of "chief executive," I preferred the title of "chief wanderer." While constant motion suited my constitution, it also fueled my creativity, which never seemed to flow in the office.

Getting out to the stores, and to the wide variety of coworkers who peopled them, fueled my imagination. I got out of the office so I could begin looking with my eyes. One time I got a Chinese fortune cookie that said, *"Your eyes believe what they see. Your ears believe others.*" I've never heard a truer statement. This has become a mantra for me ever since. Most people believe things others tell them, or things they read, as opposed to what they see—or experience—for themselves. I've always trusted my own sight. As a nonreader, this comes naturally to me. To mix a metaphor, I taught myself to smell opportunity with my eyes.

Out in the field, I passed the message of staying "on" the business to our partners. None of our stores had much equipment in the early seventies and Dennis Itule was spending all his time assembling large orders by hand. It wasn't the best use of his time. Denny recalls that I said, "If you want to open new stores, you've got to start trusting other people." Charlie Wright, a partner of Denny's and mine (and cousin by marriage) in Long Beach, remembers me accusing him of having a "lunch-pail mentality" because he liked to sweep out the back room rather than leave that work to others. It took many, many years for all of us to get better at getting out of work and trusting other people.

The day before I came back to headquarters, after one of my three-week trips or after a vacation, was a crucial time. I sorted through all the mail that had accumulated while I was away. No matter where I was, I always had it sent overnight to me before I came back to the office. One time, my wife, Natalie, remembers that, on a flight back from Australia, I didn't speak to her for the entire 14-hour journey. "I've got to do my Big List!" I told her. I spent the entire flight painstakingly sorting through all my mail and memos from the office. Then I composed my Big List of all my top priorities for the next week. Somebody once told me that people never do the big things in life. Well, I was determined to. Once my Big List was completed, I composed a Short List with my lesser items. I also wrote out Short Lists for my closest colleagues. I figured that on each trip back to the office, I would tackle one "Big" item like introducing color copiers or networking all the stores, something that would require monumental change. The first week back, I wandered around, spoke with people, collected ideas and impressions.

My wife has her own take on my "wandering." Here's Natalie: "When I wander, I tend to go mindless. Not Paul. When he wanders, he wanders with an eagle eye. Walking around the headquarters or one of the stores, he was being an observer in the most fine-tuned sense of the word. He would ask people why they were sending things by overnight delivery that could have gone by regular mail. He would remember that somebody's parent had died and offer condolences. He was constantly gauging the mood of the business. He was a master at attending to details."

That is, until the details got the better of me and inhibited my higher thinking. Then, I knew to turn them over to others. During week two back at the head office, I did just that. By week three, it was clearly getting time to leave. The longer I stayed, the more I became snowed under with the kinds of busywork you can't avoid at the office. I left so others could attend to it.

The Getaway Cure

In the early seventies, I had not yet established this rhythm. That's largely because in the first couple of years in the life of Kinko's, there was only one store. While the beginning was humble, it was a huge success when stacked up against my previous track record. We sold enough copies so quickly that it took only four months to pay off the bank loan my dad cosigned for me. We generated enough money to easily cover our $100 rent, our $1,000 Xerox machine rental, and other costs. Soon after, I had enough money to buy myself a 27-foot sailboat for $8,000. I lived on the water for a period of time in the early seventies. Staying "on" my business allowed me the free time to hang out on the boat, to socialize with other people. Even to get bored. No matter how busy I am, I still have the capacity to get bored. That's the ADHD in me.

After a time, having a single store got to be—well, a bore. Even worse, it started to scare me! I began to fear what would happen when, several decades down the road, the children of my current customers would show up at UCSB as freshmen themselves. Try this experiment yourself some time. One particularly effective way of staying "on" your life is to envision the kind of future you *do not want* for yourself. In my mind's eye, I saw this scene unfold: The parents of incoming freshmen take them on a tour of their old alma mater. "Look, Polly," one dad says, "There's Kinko. He runs Kinko's Copies." There I sit, my curly hair shot through with gray. I wave back at them. That was *not* where I wanted to be in my old age. But, try as I could to stay "on" my business, I couldn't figure out how to open another store.

This brings me to why I believe in vacations. It took a vacation in 1972 to help me get the right perspective on the company. Despite my best efforts to stay out of the mundane details of the store, I hadn't really mastered doing so. In truth, staying "on" my business was a never-ending fight from my first to my last day at Kinko's. Early on I learned that taking a good vacation was one way to win at it. Once, my mom and dad took a long vacation down in Mexico. I was conceived on that trip. Dad used to tell me that it was one of the few times he got a proper perspective on his life. He finally had time to think. So far as I remember, he never gave himself another trip like that again. Just short weekend jaunts here and there.

It wasn't enough. I saw the impact of this lack of reflection on my father. In the seventies, he toyed with the idea of going into designer jeans. Gloria Vanderbilt and Calvin Klein made fortunes with this strategy a few years later. But Dad never gave himself a chance to explore his half-conceptualized dream. Dad also used to own beautiful land in Malibu that would be worth millions of dollars today. He sold that land and sunk the proceeds into the business. Later in life, I remember him reflecting that he should have done exactly the reverse. When he closed his clothing company, all the value he'd once held in that land vanished with it. Not only would he have made more money in real estate than in his business, but managing property would have allowed him far more free time to think and dream. And he was a very creative person.

I don't know if I consciously went to Europe to get a new perspective on Kinko's, but frustration certainly propelled me to change my environment. In 1972, I left Kinko's in the care of my coworkers for a few months while I took off on my own. I backpacked and goofed around and stayed at cheap hotels. I watched vacationers strolling in and out of five-star hotels in Paris and Milan. I just could not *imagine* how they could afford those rooms. On that trip I got very bored and very poor. All young people should try the combination of boredom and poverty. It's highly motivating. I became ambitious again. That's what a little perspective can do for you. I started to envision how I might open a second store after all. I can't even tell you exactly what changed my mind. My thinking unstuck itself of its own accord and I felt better about the whole idea.

I came back full of energy. I took my sailboat down the coast and visited the University of California at Irvine. I found a storefront there even smaller than our first one in Santa Barbara. It was a converted garbage room attached to a restaurant and I paid $80 a month for it. After looking around for a while, I hired a woman to manage it. Tentative though it was, our expansion had begun. Don't let anyone tell you a well-placed vacation detracts from the bottom line.

By the time Kinko's was growing exponentially every year, I still managed to take three to five weeks vacation every summer. I needed that time to fully unplug. Any less time and your body doesn't trust it can relax. Have you ever heard the story about the tribal porters known for carrying things for others? Once, a passerby came upon a group of them, sitting by the side of the road, clearly in no hurry to go anywhere. "What are you doing?" he asked them, confused. Weren't they supposed to be rushing about? They replied, "We're letting our souls catch up with our bodies." Do what you need to do to get some time off. Let your soul catch up with your body. It could change your life.

Chapter 3

Manage

the Environment,

Not the People

T HE COWORKERS WHO WORKED BEHIND THE COUNTER were the true heroes of Kinko's. They performed heroic acts every day, taking on tasks that were exacting, tedious, and important all at once. Without them, we had nothing. I wasn't the boss; they were. The care of coworkers was crucial because the most perfect relationship at Kinko's was the one between the customer and the coworker. The customer walks into a store stressed out and confused. She doesn't know what she wants and she wants it done yesterday. She sees the "manufacturing process" at work. The coworker humanizes all this technology for her and solves her problem. At the end, the coworker sees the customer's smile. What could I add to that relationship? Nothing. I could only screw it up. I knew I needed to get out of the way. My wife gave me the best definition of management I've ever heard. She said, "The goal of management is to remove obstacles."

Here's a secret: We all think we're the boss, but it's a bunch of baloney. If you are confused about who really runs your business, consider this: a coworker with a bad attitude can (a) steal your money or products, (b) fudge on their hours, (c) undermine your relationship with customers, and (d) poison the morale of everyone else. So, if you think you're the head honcho at the office, think again. Your coworkers really run the business. The same goes with your family. I may be the father, but do you think I'm going to be content if my kids or my wife aren't? I don't think so. Someone once said to me, "Happy wife, happy life." It's true. At work, a different motto applies, "Happy fingers, happy registers." If somebody was ringing a register that had my name on the deposit slip, do you think I wanted to slap that hand—or kiss it? The choice was mine. At Kinko's, I had basically one advantage over our competitors. I could make Kinko's a great place to work. The way I saw it, we had to. What else did we have beyond our culture? All we had going for us at Kinko's was the sparkle in our coworkers' eyes. Instead of dwelling on peoples' personality problems, I focused on what they could do. Beyond that sparkle, there was nothing preventing any of our coworkers from walking across the street and going to work for somebody else or setting up their own businesses. Remember, at the time, the growth of retail copy centers was just starting. There were no barriers to entry. Any mom-and-pop copy shop could open up directly across the street from us. Many did. Instilling loyalty in our coworkers and partners was priority number one.

I couldn't accomplish this by berating everybody or trying to force them to work long hours. As it happens, we did work long hours, but I didn't want to work with a bunch of exhausted automatons. I didn't want "employees." One of the definitions of the word "employ" is "to make use of." I didn't want to use people. I wanted coworkers who would be "empowered entrepreneurs"; we tried to instill a sense of entrepreneurship in all our workers. One very important way we accomplished this was by giving everyone—partners, managers, and the guys behind the counter—a share of the profits from their stores (more about this in a minute). I never wanted to work with people I made money *on;* I wanted to work with people I made money *with.* "Coworker" became the official term to designate all of the people who worked with us at Kinko's.

Do you know what the key word is in that last sentence? It's *with.* I don't believe anybody really works *for* anybody else. We all work with each other. It's a fundamental distinction. I am forever correcting people who describe themselves as working *for* me—or for anybody else.

We work together because we choose to. It's up to the leader to make sure that people actually want to work with him or her. Nobody wants to follow a leader who is tired, haggard, and miserable. I heard once that 80 percent of the people in America think they're smarter than their boss. I've always believed that to be true. The first Kinko's coworkers ran our Xerox machines in flip-flops and cut-offs. They brought their pets to work. While pulling late shifts, we cracked open beers and laughed and talked late into the night. We had paper airplane contests in the street outside the front door of our original store in Isla Vista. In a way, it wasn't so different from the chaos in my parents' home.

At Kinko's, we were building a family together at the same time we were building a business.

"Do You Want to Do a Boogie with Me?"

The day Tim Stancliffe first walked into the original Kinko's, he was just stopping in to visit a friend who worked there. He found four people running the machines, all in sandals and shorts. "It seemed like the inmates were running the asylum," Tim said. "You didn't have the sense of anyone being in charge. Their copiers were so slow. Every time classes would let out a whole stream of people would come through the door. It lead to this kind of frenetic boom or bust thing. I'm something of an anarchist myself. I didn't have a problem with the chaos. It was progressive and young."

Eventually Tim came to work at Kinko's. In fact, I ended up meeting three of my largest and most important partners—Jimmy Warren, Brad Krause, and Tim Stancliffe—in the earliest days of the company. My cousin Dennis Itule and I go even farther back. He's a member of the 100-plus club, too. Each of these four men eventually came to own and manage partnership stakes in more than 100 stores apiece, becoming huge entrepreneurs in their own right. It wasn't the task of copy making that attracted them to Kinko's, obviously. It was the culture, the feel of the place.

It took me several years to convince people to become my partners. I worked on my cousin Denny from 1970 to 1973. "Paul wasn't the most credible guy back then," Denny recalls. "He'd call and say, '*You've* got a lot of credibility. I've got to get you on my team.'" I finally persuaded Denny to open a location in downtown Los Angeles in the summer of 1973.

That same year, I met Jim Warren for the first time at a party not long after he came to work at the original Kinko's location. Jim had no particular interest in going into the copy business or any business at all. He wanted to be a high school track coach. When I tried to convince him to manage the original store, he at first refused because he could make more money painting houses. But eventually, three long years later, he did come to work with us as a partner and found it hard to leave.

I was walking down the street in Isla Vista one day in 1976 when I bumped into him. As Jimmy remembers it, "Paul didn't exactly ask if I wanted to start a new store with him. What he actually said was, 'Do you want to do a boogie with me?'" What can I say? It was the seventies.

The way my partnership with Tim Stancliffe started wasn't all that different. One day, Tim stopped by the original store, again, to see a friend. I bumped into him as he was walking in the back door and I was walking out. As Tim recalls, I said, "'Hey man, how are you doing? Come talk to me in my office.' He's like the Pied Piper and I followed him. I'm pretty sure he thought I was someone else."

That could be true. I do remember that when I sat down with Tim that day, we talked about a lot of things completely unrelated to business. Tim told me he was planning to spend a year skiing. We started talking about whether he could open a Kinko's near a ski slope somewhere. (Another partner of mine, Craig Redwine, calls the process by which I selected my earliest partners "deification." I had a need and if somebody could fill it, I nabbed him or her. My belief was total. In this case, that person was Tim.) My coworkers trained Tim for a couple of weeks. We sent him to one of Denny's first stores, a crappy little location we had near Loyola Marymount University, just south of Los Angeles, to try running a store by himself. Tim learned just enough to set out on his own. From there, we flew him to Boulder to open our first out-of-state location. It was December of 1975. Tim says, "I thought Boulder was in the middle of the mountains. I saw myself working in the mornings and skiing in the afternoons." As it turned out, the nearest ski lift was a three-hour drive away. Tim never did spend his year as a ski bum, but he became a business owner.

Tim picked up a lot of ideas from our original store. Beyond that he was on his own. He liked the fact that he was in charge. I had already signed a lease on a location near the University of Colorado at Boulder. When I flew out to join Tim and saw it again, we both realized it was in a terrible spot, much too far away from the sort of foot traffic we needed from the university. The landlord was nice enough to let us out of the lease and we found a new spot in an area of town known as "The Hill." It measured only 240 square feet.

Tim: "It was a little stall with some wooden doors on the front. We did $5.89 our first day in business and $1,000 our first month. We were guerrilla marketers. We put out flyers, advertising copies for two-and-a-half cents. As in Santa Barbara, we put them in the professors' boxes. We got the word out."

Jim didn't follow a master plan because we didn't have one.

By the time Tim got Colorado humming, a handful of partners had opened, or were in the process of opening, a total of about 15 locations elsewhere. In the summer of 1975 alone, we'd doubled the number of our stores. Things were starting to move. In addition to the original store and Tim's store in Boulder, there was the Irvine store and another one in downtown Los Angeles, opened by Denny two years earlier. We also had stores in Fullerton, Van Nuys, San Luis Obispo, and Westminster. Eventually Jim decided to drive down to open a store near the campus of San Diego State University, where he grew up. Like most of our earliest partners, he opened that store in whatever way he saw fit. Jim remembers that I didn't give him too many instructions. "I bought saws," Jim recalls. "I got all my friends together and we built cabinets." The first San Diego store represented a real enlargement on earlier locations. It was about 800 square feet, eight times larger than the store in Isla Vista. The store cost about $10,000 to open and, by the mid-seventies, the Xerox rentals were up to about $2,000 a month. Jim didn't follow a master plan because we didn't have one. And we wouldn't for another decade or so.

Scout It Out

Jim stayed with the San Diego location for only about six months. Then he found someone to manage it and took off across the country in his Volkswagen van in 1976. He became our head scout, looking for new locations across the country. Our plan for expansion was a pretty simple one. To be honest, I got the idea for how to grow by playing the board game Risk when I was a kid. In Risk, the object of the game is world domination, with 42 territories on six continents that must be conquered. Playing the game taught me there was no reason to expand in a neat geographic progression. In fact, we didn't need to respect geographic boundaries at all. We knew there was not just a strong, but an overwhelming demand for retail copy centers on college campuses. Our first couple of stores taught us that.

So we decided to open up on or near colleges or universities where we were assured both a hungry customer base and a ready source of smart coworkers. We pinned a map of the country on the wall. I told my first partners, "Pick your territory. This thing is going to really *grow.*" My largest partners and I divvied up much of the country. Being sports fans (actually, I'm less interested in sports than I am in betting on them), we targeted big schools with big football teams. We also targeted other large state universities—"the public Ivies"—and colleges and universities with great reputations. Berkeley was the only place that already boasted a bunch of copy shops, probably because it is such a creative town. We stuck red pins into the campuses we figured would be the best ones. Blue pins marked second-tier locations and green pins the third tier. We soon discovered that the smarter and larger the student population, the more copies we were going to be selling.

Jimmy's first Volkswagen van tour lead him right up the West Coast, through Oregon and up all the way to Vancouver, B.C. For Jim it was a lark. He wasn't fully committed to the company yet, but he was willing to be our eyes and ears for a time. Here's Jimmy: "For me, it was an adventure. I got to travel around and see the country and get paid for it. Paul joined me now and then. We were really frugal. I remember nights where we'd sleep in our cars at airports. Pretty often, to save on hotel rooms, I drove my car and stayed at different Campgrounds of America all over the country. Occasionally, I also slept in stores. We'd change our clothes anywhere."

Twice Jim got fed up with the work. Once he went and painted houses for a while. Another time, he went back to school for two quarters. When he came back again, in 1978, he met his future wife, Barbara Warren, in Baton Rouge, Louisiana. Meeting Barbara—and seeing the success of partners elsewhere in the country—sealed Jim's commitment to Kinko's. He came on as a partner, started his own corporation, and opened his first store as a partner in Athens, Georgia, a short while later.

A lot of people benefited from Jim's good scouting. Dave Gibson, a childhood family friend of mine, became a partner in Eugene, Oregon, and another family friend, Steve McLaughlin, became a partner in Corvallis, Oregon. Jim found both locations. When Jim saw a choice strip mall or building, he'd find out who owned the property and then mail out a formal-looking letter on nice stationery requesting the chance to lease property the minute anything became available. Never having met us, the landlords assumed we were an established organization, not a bunch of recent college grads with crazy hair driving around in a Volkswagen bus. We got a lot of prime pieces of real estate that way.

It didn't take long for Jim to figure out—in no small part because I kept hammering the idea home to him—that the people were the key to the success of any new store. We were becoming adults in the era when the concept of freedom of expression was exerting a huge countercultural pressure on society. We embraced it. We knew what it was like growing up in the stifling atmosphere of the fifties. We wanted our partners to be themselves, not to conform to us. "In our early days," Jim recalls, "the look of the store was determined by whatever the partner or the manager was into. In those days we wanted local flavor, not a uniform look. One store at the University of Kansas had clouds painted all over it. At one of my stores, I had my brother's surf photography on the walls. Another store had a counter made of wavy, polished driftwood. I was always surprised that people wanted to hang around our stores, but they did. Right from the start, we had all kinds of characters."

The Power of Picking the Right People

People were likely to hang out at our stores if they liked the people who worked there. We quickly found out that the most important key to a store's success was the manager. If we found people who could do a good job and stood a good chance of being happy working with us, not only would we make more money, we would build a better work environment overall. This is a prime ingredient, I've found, for keeping any enterprise, personal or business, thriving. I've always believed in *managing the environment and not the people.* Our work environment wasn't highly structured, but we made sure we had the right incentives in place. I've found that when people are properly motivated, they will essentially manage themselves.

To find people, I employ what I like to call the "likeability test." I was open-minded about everybody who came to work at Kinko's. As long as someone could ring a register, he or she could work with us. But I did have to like the person. One of my first criteria for a potential partnership is pretty straightforward: Do I want to hang out with you? Do you pass the likeability test? Lots of people don't know how to present themselves to others, how to have a pleasant conversation. This isn't a peripheral issue. I always figured that, once we started working together, we were family. We're going to be spending a lot of time with one another, so we ought to like each other.

> **When people are properly motivated, they will essentially manage themselves.**

At Kinko's, we hired people we wanted to spend time with. This goes back in part to my restlessness. I can't stand business meetings. I never could. I prefer going out for a meal or having a drink together. It's far more effective. People from Japan and the Middle

East understand this concept of doing business. They've perfected it. To this day, much of my business is conducted over a nice meal and a good bottle of wine.

I've never been shy about asking questions, so I tend to get a beam on people quickly. In my family, while I was growing up, everybody liked to talk. People didn't listen to me much. No one knew what to make of me, so I learned to listen to others. I learned empathy because I had to. Studies have shown this is true for most kids with dyslexia—they tend to be highly empathetic. The unanswered question is whether dyslexics are empathetic inherently or develop empathy because their struggles give them compassion for others. Whatever the reason, I fit the model. I learned to ask lots of questions. You could say I built my life on asking questions, even when I didn't get the responses I was seeking. From Mel Levine, an expert on learning differences and a best-selling author of books on the subject, I learned not to ask my kids, "How was school today?" but instead to ask them, "What questions did you ask today?" You'll instill much better instincts into your kids and get a better answer to your own question. (Instead of warning my kids against substance abuse, for example, I like to hit them with off-handed questions like "What would you rather die of: cirrhosis of the liver or coughing to death from emphysema?" That gets them thinking.)

I have a couple informal rules of thumb I follow when selecting the people I work with, especially our partners. First off, they had to have the ability to save money. Most partners made an initial investment of as little as $2,000. It wasn't a lot, but it was something. As with a good poker game, everybody had to buy his or her way in. In this way, I could tell right at the start whether they were a saver or a spender. I never want to do business with people who can't save. Spenders won't be cautious with their stores' profits. Those are my profits, too! I made sure to choose partners who were on time. I can't stand it if people are late. By policy, I don't keep people waiting and I expect the same in return. I make a real effort to return phone calls promptly and to arrive on time everywhere I go. I always asked a potential partner—or anybody I worked with—to do some small thing at the end of our first meeting: to make a call or send a letter. I want to see what their follow-through is like. I've found these are reliable screeners of potential business partners, coworkers, and vendors.

I also took time over drinks to find out about my potential partners' family backgrounds. Were they married? Did they have kids? Did they want to have kids? Where did their parents live and what did they do? We didn't talk about work; we talked about everything else. I wanted to know if they had passion. Without passion, we could never work together. I always asked them a question that I pretty well knew they couldn't answer, something along the lines of "Do you think the Cultural Revolution in China achieved its ends?" That way I could tell if I was dealing with a bullshitter. I didn't hire people who complained about tortured relationships with their mothers or fathers. I figured if they didn't get along with their parents that probably meant they had trouble with authority. In all likelihood, they wouldn't get along with me either.

The Paul Orfalea Personality Test

1. Do I like them?

2. Do they have passion?

3. Do they get along with their family and parents?

4. Are they bullshitters?

5. Have they saved money?

6. Are they honest?

7. Are they kind to people whether it's a waiter, a janitor, or a competitor?

8. Do they arrive on time?

9. Do they speak clearly?

10. Do they have good follow-through?

11. What are they like over a drink?

*   *   *

Taking Care of People

A nother great way to manage the environment of a business is to offer people real incentives to work there. I don't understand why more companies don't take better care of their coworkers by offering them more perks and benefits. They cost so little and pay themselves back many times over in the loyalty and goodwill they inspire. As we grew, in the eighties, we offered 401(k) retirement plans to all our coworkers. Sometimes we had quite a job trying to convince our coworkers, most of whom were in their twenties, to divert money into their retirement accounts, but with some persuading many of them did. Our finance arm, Kinko's Financial Services, which Jimmy, Dan Frederickson, our second president, and I started in the late eighties as an in-house financing arm to loan money to our partners, lent $15,000 to longtime coworkers to buy their first homes.

In 1986, personal loss inspired my wife, Natalie, and me to build a daycare center for our coworkers at our head office in Ventura. That year, our first-born son, Ryan, died of a congenital heart defect. Some things you never really "get over"; you just try to come to terms with them. Ryan was seven months old and had been doing well when he died unexpectedly. We were with him long enough to know he was a special boy, with mystical qualities. He could look at you and see straight into your soul. He had a shock of blond-red hair just as I did when I was a kid. We still keep photos of him in our house. Two years after we lost him, we opened a state-of-the-art daycare facility next to our head office in Ventura. The center enabled our coworkers to leave their kids there at a subsidized rate while they worked. After a couple of years we persuaded most Kinko's vendors to make contributions to keep the center running at an affordable rate for workers who were parents.

When I proposed building the center, all I got was stalling and debate. I'll tell you more later about the kind of frustration I experienced as Kinko's grew and there was more and more bureaucracy to contend with. Eventually, I went ahead and circumvented our own top officers, bringing in my cousin Jeannie Smith, from Arizona, to manage it. We spent $800,000 on it and the effect the center had on our coworkers was worth every penny. It was electric.

Around the same time, we formed the Ryan Orfalea Scholarship program. Thereafter we held an annual auction at our partners meeting at which our first company president, Ken Hightower, often acted as auctioneer. We sold all kinds of crazy things (I washed the car of one highest bidder). Coworkers with school-age kids applied for and received college scholarship money from the auction proceeds. I'm very proud of the fact that over the years we sent hundreds of kids to college.

We also held an annual picnic and, at the head office, served free lunches for everybody on Fridays and kept free sodas flowing seven days a week. All this made for a great work environment. The extras did not cost us much but, again, the return on investments of this nature are extraordinary. One of our former coworkers used to refer to the Kinko's of old as Camelot. That's certainly what we were trying to build.

A Fraction of the Action

The most tangible way we took care of our managers and all our coworkers, however, was by giving them "a fraction of the action." Initially, we gave each manager 25 percent of his or her store's profits. Later, we expanded the system of profit sharing when we started giving each manager 15 percent of the store's profits and earmarking the remaining 10 percent to be split among that store's coworkers. As I've explained before, my philosophy on this is twofold. Giving your coworkers a piece of the action is the best way to ensure their personal investment in your venture. There's simply no better way to motivate the people you work with and to inspire their loyalty. In more general terms, *I always figured I wanted a smaller piece of a bigger pie.* I knew if I gave away ownership my partners would be highly motivated to grow their companies because they were owners. My share of the companies they built would be incrementally larger than if I had hung onto the businesses and kept them as employees, who are never as motivated as owners.

I'm always happiest when I know I'm making money and I like it when everyone associated with me is making money, too. My mom used to say, "Laugh and the world laughs with you. Cry and you cry alone." When I was little, I noticed that there was always a lot of laughter at all my aunts' and uncles' homes. They made good money and had enough to provide for their families. Like my relatives, I tried to create an environment where people could laugh a lot.

Profit sharing also lured our earliest coworkers away from the careers for which they had initially decided to attend college. For the most part, our first partners and our first coworkers weren't business majors. They weren't even particularly interested in business. This was fine by me. We had biologists, philosophers, psychologists, English majors, and lawyers. We had more degrees at Kinko's than a thermometer. My partner Tim was in the process of completing a degree in environmental studies when he came to work at Kinko's. Tim was like me in that he wasn't particularly mechanically inclined and not particularly interested in the tedious details of the business.

> **Like my relatives, I tried to create an environment where people could laugh a lot.**

Tim: "But I hadn't done very well in school, gradewise. Working with Paul and being unleashed by him was the right thing for me. I'd liken my career at Kinko's to flunking up. I had the desire to keep opening stores and the ability to hire the right people. It was kind of a crusade. When people saw and understood the dream, they became enchanted with the opportunity at Kinko's. We found we got people who were very well educated, but not necessarily happy with where their lives were heading."

When Tim opened his store in Boulder, he was making $500 a month in salary. He felt a huge sense of accomplishment watching his store's revenues climb to a couple of thousand dollars a month. A few months later, I asked him to become a partner. We split the ownership of the company 50–50. He didn't have the $2,000 for his share, so his parents cosigned on a bank loan for that sum and he paid it off within a year's time.

With Tim, Jim, Brad, and Denny, as with all our partners, we formed Subchapter S corporations to set up the company. We developed a system for opening a lot of stores in other locations by taking on new partners. To do so, my older partner—let's say it was Denny—and I would each typically keep 30 percent of the new store. Then, we'd give 40 percent of the store to the newer partner. That way, all of us continued to make money while we slept and the newer partner took the largest single chunk in the store. At the same time, Denny and I retained ultimate control over that location. If a partner didn't work out, we bought him or her out. Through partnerships of this sort, Denny and his networks of partners managed to open more than 100 stores all around California. Other partners and I used variants of this model all over the country.

Dave Bolton can give you a sense of how we treated our first coworkers, the people who took care of customers from behind the counter. Dave started working with Kinko's in the mid-eighties at the store near the campus of San Diego State University. Dave, who was 21 or 22 at the time and studying business finance, "thought this Kinko's was a small, little mom-and-pop shop." He was planning on going into a career in money management, but the stock market took a dive. All of a sudden he wasn't in a hurry to leave his job at the copy shop. One weekend, he was working at Kinko's with another coworker, wearing a T-shirt and shorts, with the music blaring, when I happened to drive up out front. There were no managers around and neither Dave nor his coworker knew me.

As Dave recalls, "I remember seeing this old, beat-up car out front. This guy came in. He introduced himself. He checked out what we were doing. He asked us questions. I remember looking at him and thinking, 'Who *is* this guy?' He looked maybe not like a bum off the street, but pretty close to that. But he seemed to know what he was doing. He went into the office, shut the door for about ten minutes and then left. On Monday, I was coming into work and my manager called us in. I thought we were in trouble, but he commended us."

As I often did in other stores, I let Dave's manager know what a great job these two coworkers were doing for us. A short while after that, Dave moved up north and took a job managing a store in Cupertino. He was then 23 and his monthly profit-sharing checks, on top of his salary, ranged from $500 to $1,000. Says Dave, "It seems small now, but it was exciting." Dave went on to work closely with the manager of the Palo Alto store, which by the nineties was grossing several million dollars a year and making $1 million in profits. This meant the manager was taking home $150,000 a year on top of his regular salary. In 1994, Dave became a regional manager of stores in one section of the Bay Area. In his peak earning years with Kinko's he was making upwards of $300,000 a year as he shared in the profits of the dozen or so stores he managed.

Cutting Loose

Money wasn't the only way we kept our coworkers happy. We also relied on silliness. Our annual picnic, which I'll tell you more about later, gave us a chance to cut loose together at least once a year. In the early days, we ran advertisements in the local student newspapers that you wouldn't exactly describe as brilliant. "If you can fart, you can copy," read one. And another: "Even ax murderers make copies." Stupid? Sure! But they drew in the college crowd. We abandoned all those sorts of ads in the early eighties, but their irreverence still makes me laugh.

Humor is a diversionary tool many kids with learning opportunities employ to subvert authority. Many dyslexics grow up with a strong distaste for authority. Our earliest experiences with teachers and parents as authority figures are usually pretty negative. That certainly was the case with me, as it was with several of my cousins and business partners who are also dyslexic.

I like the way my younger nephew, and former Kinko's partner, Harry Johansing puts it: "All I know is my Mom was constantly making me sit down to do stuff I couldn't do. And, then, being asked to read out loud in class? Talk about stress. There were lots of times I felt inferior to my peers. I've never been trusting of authority because of my early childhood experiences. It wasn't until I was older that I realized I could go head-to-head with anyone."

Like Harry, my siblings and cousins and I also developed a taste for challenging authority through humor. When I was a senior at USC—not far from achieving the long-sought-after goal of earning a business degree—I happened to walk past a patch of newly poured cement on the campus, right near the center of the school in front of Doheny Library. Here was my thinking at the time: If you see wet cement, you're going to write something, aren't you? I inscribed a bunch of names: Sirhan Sirhan, Lee Harvey Oswald (as you can see, I didn't identify with the Establishment), Paul Orfalea, and Danny Tevrizian (my best friend). It was broad daylight—not the best time to deface public property and get away with it. Before I'd finished, a police officer collared me and sent me to talk to a dean. He wanted to know what, exactly, I thought I was doing. I told him I was a business major and that he had to give me credit for grasping at least one of the principles of effective marketing. I pointed to Doheny Library. "See that guy Doheny?" I asked. "He paid a lot of money to get his name on the library. I got it done for free." Everyone cracked up and they let me go. (What goes around comes around; a couple decades later, my family and I gave the university $10 million dollars to construct a new building on campus.)

I like the way learning differences expert Mel Levine characterizes this impulse in people like me. Mel says, "Great minds communicate through unconventional channels. You don't hurt anyone, but you break a taboo. You go out on a limb and you push the limits of expression."

At Kinko's, we managed to have fun wherever and however we could, even when we faced serious problems. In 1973, for instance, we ran into a conflict with Xerox over the way the machines were counting copies at our first site. With the tacit approval of Xerox salespeople, we would spread some of the copies from our high-volume months over our lower-volume months. It was standard practice in the industry to volume-average over time on a specific machine. Xerox had been extending the same benefit quietly to accountants to help them cope with tax season. But it didn't square with the U.S. Federal Trade Commission. The FTC sued Xerox and, in an effort to change its ways, Xerox threatened to sue Kinko's. Instead, we made an end run around them. We copied the lawsuit filed by the federal government and sued Xerox before Xerox sued us.

The suit was settled eventually and we mended fences. But we went through a tense period for a spell. One day we heard Xerox was driving over to reclaim its machines. I was determined they wouldn't get them until we'd installed the replacements from IBM. We posted a sentry at the corner by the gas station and anytime a moving van came by, he'd run back to the shop like a horseless Paul Revere telling us: "The suits are coming! The suits are coming!" We'd scramble to hang a "Closed" sign and hide in the back. It was like a fire drill. We laughed ourselves silly, but we never knew if we were really going to be able to weather these bumps and stay in business. IBM came to our rescue that time. Eventually Xerox did get its machines back, but we enjoyed faking them out in the meanwhile. Even during stressful times, we had fun together.

The Meaning of Meaning

Of course there was a serious side to everything we did at Kinko's, too. Whenever we could, we tried to connect our coworkers to the sense of meaning behind the work they did. Remember that Michelin ad, with the baby sitting inside a tire? That ad wasn't just for the people who bought and used those tires. It also gave the people at Michelin a real sense of why they went to work every day. People want to know they are contributing to society. If they made good tires, they knew they were keeping lots of babies, and their families, safe.

Even more than money and levity, perhaps, this sense of mission kept our workers both happy and motivated. It was an easy task to show Kinko's workers how important their jobs were. I often recall the time in 1989 in Spokane, Washington, when two parents launched a desperate hunt for their missing child. The second place they visited, after the police station, was our store. This scenario is repeated at stores around the country every week. These stories create powerful ties to planet Earth. We knew we were making a direct and positive impact on peoples' lives. We weren't just selling sugar water in a can. According to psychiatrist Abraham Maslow's hierarchy of human needs, we were the caretakers of our customers' highest creative and intellectual pursuits. We helped people through important life transitions. We helped them get new jobs, start new businesses, change careers, plan their weddings, announce births and deaths, overcome layoffs, develop their artistic visions, find their kids and their pets. Our partners and I made a regular habit of reminding all our coworkers of this fact.

Todd Ordal, a partner of ours based in the Midwest who made only $9,300 a year when he started with Kinko's in 1980, put it this way: "People would say, for God's sake, you're just making copies, but we felt like we were saving the world."

Chapter 4

The Business of
Business is Emotion

THE NIGHT BEFORE WE OPENED THE ORIGINAL KINKO'S, our very first customer gave us a $50 order. He was like future customers who would be drawn to Kinko's over the next several decades—so anxiety-ridden he couldn't wait for our doors to open. He wanted us to print flyers supporting the Kurds. I've loved the Kurds and Kurdistan ever since. Later, when there was a war between India and Pakistan, people from both sides of that conflict descended upon the first Kinko's. They argued so much you would have thought that war was being fought over our first copier (you gotta love college campuses). They were killing each other with flyers. The passion of all our customers—the Kurds, the Pakistanis, the Indians, the stressed-out professors and students—was good for our business. In return, we gave them all an immediate channel for that pent-up passion.

For three full decades, I waged a constant battle to get our coworkers to understand what our business was about. The biggest challenge we had at Kinko's was going from a culture of *things* to a culture of *people*. Our business was much more about emotion than copy machines, toner cartridges, paper quality, and advanced communications technologies. I've never had much interest in technology. I could care less about bits and bytes. I don't send or receive e-mail. I couldn't run any of our copy machines myself except the first one, and I ran it badly. All I knew was I could sell what came out onto the exit tray. Our customers didn't particularly care *how* the work got done either. But they cared passionately about obtaining relief, symbolized by the finished product. For a while, our second president, Dan Frederickson, used to call us "the soup kitchen for the technologically homeless." It was our customers' passion, their stress, and their anguish that interested me.

Retail Is Detail

How would you feel if you entered a doctor's office and found yourself walking on blood-stained carpets? I constantly asked my partners this question. You'd probably turn around and run back to your car. At times, it seemed as if 90 percent of what I did while traveling store to store was "cleaning up the blood." I looked at each and every Kinko's location from the customer's perspective. If they didn't walk in to find a soothing environment, not only would they be disagreeable to serve, they probably wouldn't come back again. When entering a store, I never walked in the back door used by coworkers. I walked in the front door so I could see things from the customer's perspective. I was maniacal about the layout and appearance of each store. If the managers in a particular store got their business right at the front door, then I was convinced that they got everything else right, too. Retail is detail, I told them all.

This is something most people simply don't understand. So, take this trip with me. Walk with me into the fancy lobby of the Waldorf Astoria in New York City. In the lobby, we push open the glass doors of an elegant jewelry store. "What do you see?" I ask. "What is your eye drawn to?" Under bright lights, jewels glisten in every display case. Everything dazzles. But wait another minute and your eye locks onto a door to the back room. It is slightly ajar. You can just spy an aging computer sitting next to stacks of papers. Doesn't that completely mar the effect? Maybe you were tempted to try on a bracelet, but instead you find yourself walking out the door.

We had this problem in spades at Kinko's. Nests of wires sprouted behind the copiers and computers, creating a feeling of havoc and uncleanliness. In a word, clutter. Some locations had dirty carpets or bad paint jobs. Others were so poorly laid out that customers walked through the door to find a jarring arrangement of countertops, display racks, and machines. What a customer wants is to walk into a store and have a feeling of symmetry. Without realizing it, many store managers instinctively laid out their floor plans to please the eye of the coworker *behind* the counter, not the customer in front of it; it was only from the coworker's point of view behind the register that you saw the order and symmetry.

This made me nuts. I threw fits trying to persuade our partners to rearrange their stores. For a guy who wasn't always neat in his personal life, I couldn't stand a slovenly or disorderly work environment. I was into symmetry. I asked our partners, "Are we looking *as* our customers or *at* our customers?" I'm acutely aware of how the difference can affect a paying customer. My doctor's office example may sound extreme, but at Kinko's we were attempting a surgery of our own—on our customers' frazzled psyches. When I walked through the front door and into a store that was badly designed, I insisted on changes. We wanted the stores to attract people and draw them in immediately. We wanted them to see more than a copy shop. We wanted them to see a sanctuary where they could come to solve their problems, whether it would take ten minutes or ten hours.

At Kinko's, we were attempting a surgery of our own.

My uncle Nick, who used to own and run bars, helped me with this. He walked into one of our stores and pointed at the glue table, the central production area in between all of the copiers. "That's the most important place in your store," he told me. The glue tables are where our customers got down to business and labored over their projects.

Mazen Safadi, my partner in Western Pennsylvania: "Paul was really big about the comfort level. He said, 'Make the coworkers and the customers comfortable and they'll give you their lives.' In the stores, we put in seating areas. We put in plants. We played soft music. Paul didn't want any rock 'n' roll. We even had play areas for children in some stores."

As the look of our stores gradually evolved, we argued constantly about every single detail. Lighting, for example, could make or break a location. Some managers blocked out the windows, not realizing the stores should be flooded with natural sunlight. Even the smallest items in the store—like the stapler, the paper cutter, or the hole punch— became sources of contention. We were never satisfied with our lay-outs. I studied other retail companies to see how they maintained order behind the counter. Once Jim and I convinced the manager of our local McDonald's, Herb Peterson (who invented the Egg McMuffin), to let us come behind the counter to learn, firsthand, how McDonald's does it. I often told our coworkers, "Everything has a place and everything in its place." McDonald's really taught us how this principle looked in action. People have no idea how important this is. Alhough layout and placement are hailed today as a science among retailers, many of them still don't get it. All you have to do is walk in their stores.

The Real Deal Is to Feel

Of course, you can't very well relieve another person's pain if you can't feel it. And, boy, did I have an advantage there. Our customers' frenetic quality? I recognized it in myself. Half the customers who walked into a Kinko's were so worked up they acted as if they were having their own bouts with ADHD. Being dyslexic and having ADHD myself, I felt other people's pain, even when I didn't want to. Take rejection. When you experience rejection in love, say, or from an unhappy customer, you can take it two ways: you can get angry or you can see it from the other person's point of view. Try subordinating yourself to another person for a time. Walk in their shoes. We tried to build a company at Kinko's in which we subordinated ourselves to the needs and demands of our customers. From a management standpoint, we also tried to subordinate ourselves to the needs of our coworkers. By and large, when our customers walked out the door, they were relieved. They started to trust us and we started establishing bonds with them.

That's a necessary skill for someone in business. Whether your business is selling sodas, dry cleaning, or financial advice, it wouldn't hurt to pair a psychology minor with your business degree. Coca-

Cola has been one of my favorite stocks for years because the leaders of that company understand emotion so well. Coke wouldn't be the global phenomenon it is today if the owners of the trademark didn't whip people into a frenzy of excitement over every can of pop. I also love the equities for Tootsie Roll and Wrigley gum, both impulse buys that we've been trained to respond to emotionally at every checkout aisle since we were kids. Starbucks understands emotion particularly well and is a favorite investment of mine. Its business is not so much about coffee as it is about taking a break and letting your soul catch up with your body. Understanding and attending to our customers' and workers' emotional needs, I think, set us far ahead of the field of competing copy shops such as Postal Instant Press (PIP), Sir Speedy, and countless small, independent outfits.

I don't have to explain much about empathy to any dyslexics out there who may be working their way through this book or listening to it on tape or CD. Dyslexia researchers report anecdotally that most dyslexics are extraordinarily empathetic. Sometimes I'm so empathetic that I drive myself and others crazy. Even after yelling at a partner, I usually called back and apologized, often minutes later. I not only feel other people's pain—I even feel the pain I cause.

My partner Charlie Wright: "Paul's an awfully sensitive guy. He could be screaming at you one minute, but worrying about your welfare the next."

Perhaps dyslexics are so empathetic because, as kids, so many of us became accustomed to *not* being listened to. They suffer and pick up on the suffering of others. That was the case with me. I became a good listener to cope. I also learned empathy from my parents—my mother, especially. She constantly talked and worried about the people who worked with my dad at the clothing factory. My mother and father spent a lot of time trying to see the world through the eyes of the people around them.

Some of our partners created an inhospitable climate for customers and coworkers alike. Some posted negative signs. At one store in Riverside, California, a manager hung a sign in red warning customers that they would be charged a steep fee if they bounced a check. It said, "The bank doesn't make copies and we don't cash checks." That really got me boiling. I jumped up on the counter and ripped it down as customers and coworkers looked on, amazed. That may sound extreme, but I needed to make the point in a memorable way. I didn't want signs like that staring our customers in the face. I told our coworkers that the occasional hit we took for a bounced check cost far less than what we lost—and couldn't quantify—by creating a subtly hostile atmosphere. Customers didn't need to be reminded not to write bad checks, especially when, as we knew, they were stressed-out and anxiety-ridden to start with. At our Riverside location and lots of other stores, I noticed that managers had stopped putting out the little freebies customers love so much: the paper clips, the liquid paper, and the pens.

"But the customers steal them," our partners complained.

"Of course they do!" I said.

Some of them did, but the large majority did not and we needed to do right by our upstanding customers. I reminded our partners about the law of karma. When you put good out into

> **Our customers didn't need to be reminded not to write bad checks.**

the universe it will come back to you. Our managers needed to understand how comforting it was to our anxious customers to come in and find that they could still complete a project, even if they'd forgotten to bring some of their own supplies. Plus, we were charging the highest prices around and our customers expected and deserved the extras. Those managers couldn't see that by taking away the freebies, we would lose more than we would gain.

A couple of years back, a magazine called *Radar* published a story about Kinko's that took an emotional snapshot of customers of the typical store. It ran under the headline "Anxiety. Hope. Ambition. Desperation. Rage. Relief. And copies. There's one place where you can find them all." At our stores, the story reported:

> . . . displaced office workers attempt to carry on business as usual in a simulacrum of a corporate workplace. They shuffle

and collate and talk on their phones. They massage their foreheads, they grow impatient, they check their watches incessantly. They do everything real office workers do except quit. And maybe that's what makes being at Kinko's both scary and exhilarating. You can't quit, because you've already quit or been fired. From Kinko's, there's nowhere to go but up. Despite the displays of frenzy, exhaustion, and, in many cases, unadulterated bitterness, Kinko's is nothing if not a modern striver's row.

Kinko's has always been a repository for our customers' restless ambition and striving. I don't think it's any surprise that the feel of the company we started mimics the mix of both anxiety and ambition that our partners and I brought to the job ourselves.

The Blue Period

We knew we needed to create a unique experience for our customers in much the same way that we tried to create a unique experience for our coworkers. This was a driving factor behind our move to stay open 24 hours. What could be more comforting than knowing that the source of your comfort was always available to you? We also used décor to comfort. Back in the seventies, it made sense that each store had its own look. Kinko's was still a new company then. We had only about 80 stores by 1980, ten years after we were founded. Each was located on a campus. Our partner in Columbus, Ohio, Todd Johnson, remembers that "the decor in each store was based on what was on sale that day: in Columbus, we had orange carpet. The walls were all covered with cedar planks. The signage was mustard yellow with dark brown letters." Back then, we had virtually no commercial business. Our traffic came almost entirely from academic orders. None of our customers expected to complete a project at a Kinko's in Boise and walk into an all but identical store later in the week in Atlanta.

By the middle of the eighties, this had changed. We were attracting more business customers. We had several hundred Kinko's locations and it was time to develop a uniform look. We hired designers to offer suggestions. They said, "Blue. Paint all your stores blue." It made immediate sense to me. The blue of the sky, the blue of the ocean. Banks use blue to convey serenity. It took a long time to get all our partners to adopt the change, but eventually they did. My wife, Natalie, came up with the idea for the red dot on the "i" in Kinko's.

We also worked on our attire. The hippie look was out by the middle of the eighties, the so-called Me Decade. We didn't demand that our coworkers groom themselves in any particular way. We still had artsy coworkers with tattoos and long hair, but flip-flops and shorts went by the wayside. Whom would you rather hand your dissertation or PowerPoint presentation over to, a guy in flip-flops or a guy in a pair of crisp slacks? As I got older, I discovered that to succeed in business you've got to dress like a Republican. So our coworkers began wearing professional-looking slacks and shirts in order to inspire confidence. I made a stink about everyone wearing aprons to emphasize the service nature of our business. Once coworkers noticed that customers treated their well-dressed colleagues better, they changed their clothes, too.

Dead Bird, Naked Man, and Other Originals

No matter how we dressed, we could never predict what sorts of projects we might be asked to take on for our customers. None of it was standard. Although we were a retail company serving the general public, every single order we took was customizable. This made for some very strange moments. Every store had its share of crackpots and eccentrics. One customer in New Orleans, an artist, liked to bring in dead birds to photocopy. Then there were the folks who liked to hang out and photocopy nude parts of their bodies. They'd drop their pants and jump on the copiers so fast we couldn't stop them. Our partner in North Carolina, Dana Jennings, remembers how one customer liked to photograph himself in this manner after hours. "Then he would want me to stand there and critique the work," she recalls. "I was always tempted to say, 'Do you want this enlarged or reduced?'"

Brenda Helfert, my cousin in Arizona, had the misfortune of owning a store next to a bar. One night a man tottered in, brandishing a large, live snake, and announced, "I'm here to make copies." He told the coworkers to take all the signs off the wall and duplicate them for him. Another regular back at Dana's store was an Elvis impersonator. He wore his full regalia while spending hours making "missing" posters for the late singer as if he were a stray dog.

Mixed right in with this crowd were serious artists, celebrities, adventurers, and scientists. One laboratory sent Brenda such a volume of complex and top-secret jobs that she set up a back room in one of her stores so that workers could complete them without interruption. One customer, conservationist Mike Fay, stayed up until 4 A.M. at his local Kinko's plasticizing maps of the African rainforest. The next day he flew to Africa and spent 456 days trekking through the forest on foot—navigating with those maps. Sometimes seemingly simple jobs really could be a matter of life or death. You never knew what the person at the next copier was embroiled in. When the band R.E.M. was getting its start, its members used to come into the Athens, Georgia, Kinko's and make funky cassette tape covers. Coworkers at that same store copied posters for The Police during the band's 1978 tour.

With jobs of this wide a variety, it helped tremendously that our coworkers were "people" people. They understood that everyone has quirks. So did we. Brenda was a stay-at-home mom and former grade school teacher when Denny and I persuaded her to open the first Kinko's in Arizona by showing up on her doorstep with a key to a newly leased property. "Oh, what the heck," she thought. She ended up owning and running 15 stores in the state. Her experience dealing with grade schoolers helped with ungovernable customers, like the woman who insisted that Brenda copy a whole box of stock certificates. Not wanting to commit a criminal forgery, Brenda called all her other stores to make sure the order was not processed. She could only shake her head when the woman insisted on doing it herself on the public machines, incurring her own bad karma.

Most orders were far more enjoyable and engrossing, especially when our coworkers focused on the emotional end of the transaction.

Brad Krause, my first partner, says, "When you were close to a customer and you could help them with a project and make them successful, then the business was truly rewarding."

Midwifing Brainstorms

That certainly was the case with two of our customers, Richard Tait and Whit Alexander. In the late nineties, Richard and Whit decided to quit prestigious jobs at Microsoft to start a board game company. Whit had two kids at the time and Richard had twins on the way. Both men were fed up with the kinds of violent entertainment they saw on television and wanted to create a better form of play for their kids. Suddenly, they were on their own. Freelancers. They no longer had the backing of a huge name and institution like Microsoft. They no longer had a steady income.

Richard: "It was a dark time. It was very hard to admit to people that we'd left our jobs at Microsoft to start this company. We were so vulnerable. We were trying to create our dream. We were trying to create something that would change the world. If you're an entrepreneur, Kinko's gives you such a sense of companionship. We were doing play tests in early 1998 at two Kinko's stores, one on Pike Street and the other on Third Street in Seattle. We would go into people's homes and hide behind their couches while they played. Based on their input, we would go to Kinko's and change our prototypes three or four times in an evening. Kinko's printed our game cards and laminated our boards.

"There are two aspects to the experience at Kinko's. There is the physical machinery capability; Kinko's had all the foam boards and machines and printing equipment we needed. Then there's the people. The people are key. I can still remember the faces of the coworkers who helped us. They know they are handling people's dreams. They were the custodians of our dreams. And they never let us down."

I bet you want to know what happened with the game they developed. Do you recognize the name Cranium? It went on to become the fastest-selling independent game in history. Richard and Whit started a company by the same name. Their games beat out Nintendo and even the Cranium founders' alma mater Microsoft's famous Xbox for the title of the best game in the industry three years in a row. More than 30 million "Craniacs" play the game! Our coworkers in Seattle were some of the first.

Recently, Richard and Whit were in Los Angeles pitching an idea for a new business venture. They printed and bound their proposal for this newest project at a nearby FedEx Kinko's. Richard says, "For every new business venture that we have, Kinko's plays a role."

By taking care of our customers' emotions, we gave them a chance to fly to the moon and change the world on the way.

Face Outward

I REALLY LOVE THE CONSTITUTION. I MAY NOT HAVE GOTTEN good grades, but that doesn't mean I didn't learn. I paid attention in class, especially when we were studying the U.S. government. It was one of my favorite subjects. I learned that the Founding Fathers mistrusted authority almost as much as dyslexics do. Did you know that James Madison, one of the framers of our Constitution, said that through selfishness, people would form a collective order? Through debate and the art of compromise, selfishness would become the first step toward the common good. It fascinated me to learn that uniqueness and nonconformity are protected by the Constitution. I wish that were true in grade school. I also love the First Amendment. It's all about the squeaky wheel. The Constitution provided inspiration for me when I was groping around for the right model for our company structure at Kinko's. I believe that democracy is the best means available to get people to buy in. That's what we needed, more than anything else, from everybody at Kinko's, partners, coworkers, and customers. To get it, I was forever protecting the small from the big.

You could say that a similar spirit drove the opening of the first Kinko's back in 1970. Kinko's is an inherently democratic business, a democratizing business. When you think of it, what was at the heart of the business of Kinko's? It was all about taking technological power that once resided only within the walls of large institutions and corporations—the IBMs, the Xeroxes, and the other large businesses of the world—and making it available to the guy on the street. It was about taking intellectual property and spreading it to whomever our customers felt needed it. As Thomas Jefferson said, "The lost cannot be recovered; but let us save what remains: not by vaults and locks which fence them from the public eye and use, in consigning them to the waste of time, but by such multiplication of copies, as shall place them beyond the reach of accident." I traveled to the Soviet Union several years before the fall of Communism and discovered that people there considered the copy machine a great instrument of liberation. You could say it was the natural extension of an earlier revolution that began in the mid-fifteenth century when the printing press was invented. The nature of our business was subversive, at least initially, and empowering. We encouraged the outlaw spirit of our customers and their wildly varied projects. We encouraged the uniqueness of our own coworkers as much as humanly possible. We created a partnership with our coworkers, then extended the concept of partnership to our customers as well. In the nineties, when huge waves of people were laid off in the economic downturn, our customers needed their personal projects and documents to look as professional as possible. We helped them look corporate even if they were working in their pajamas all day.

We, Not Me

Our earliest partners and I devised a flat organization for Kinko's. Or, I should say, the organization of the company evolved that way organically, guided by our own deeply held values. We were not into hierarchy. We did not want all the power concentrated in our hands, even if we knew some of it had to be. As we grew, we designed a structure for our company that would be as democratic as the services we were providing. For me, this was the true brilliance of the Kinko's we created. Whether we were top executives, partners, regional managers, store managers, or coworkers, we all faced outward—outward toward the customer. The central office that handled logistics for the stores eventually came to be called the Kinko's Service Corporation, with the emphasis on *service*. The presidents of Kinko's were all really presidents of this service corporation. We were there to serve the stores. The coworkers in the field commanded the greatest respect. In the mid-eighties we instituted an "80/20" policy in our stores. This encouraged our managers to spend 80 percent of their time out on the floor of the stores with coworkers and customers and only 20 percent of their time behind doors in their offices. If one of our top partners or I telephoned a manager in a store, we asked, "Can you talk? Are you busy right now?" If a manager sounded swamped, we said, "Why don't you call me back when you're free?" At least that is how we operated on our best days. There was constant tension between Kinko's management team and the field, and whenever I saw managers from the head office disrespecting coworkers from the field, I defended the field.

The energy in most other companies runs in exactly the opposite direction; no one thinks twice when the headquarters rules with an iron fist. This attitude is most succinctly reflected in the language of presidents like George W. Bush and Bill Clinton, who both regularly repeated the phrase "*my* administration." Where do they get off saying that? It isn't *their* administration. It's *our* administration! Or, at least it should be. Where is "Of the people, by the people, and for the people"? Most large companies operate as if they had Bush or Clinton at the helm. Picture a traditional hub-and-spokes organizational system. In a hierarchical, corporate environment, everyone out along those spokes faces inward toward headquarters, from which all knowledge and guidance is expected to flow. When an executive makes a call out to the field to speak with a manager, that manager drops everything in front of him or her—including the customer—to talk to the boss. When everyone faces inward, guess who's left staring at a bunch of backs?

When everyone faces inward, guess who's left staring at a bunch of backs?

The customer, that's who.

Our president Dan Frederickson likened this structure to a flower that blooms when it faces the sun (the customer, not the CEO) and withers when deprived of light. Facing outward enabled us to put the customer first, to constantly dream up new ideas, to innovate, and to experiment. This was a central concern because ideas were the lifeblood of the company. By the time we had 450 stores in 1990, we had hundreds of entrepreneurs out there running them all, working not only for themselves, but for the greater good. We also tried to get not just the partners, but the coworkers to think and act like independent entrepreneurs. We didn't want our coworkers behind the counter to have to ask for permission when they had a new idea for taking care of customers. We empowered them to think for themselves. Having so many autonomous thinkers in one company meant we never had a research and development department. What for? We didn't need one. We could experiment with new ideas constantly in the field without waiting to test them in a laboratory somewhere. We looked to the field—and to our competitors—relentlessly for inspiration and innovation instead of trying to legislate creativity from out of our central office where, because we were all stuck in cubicles, no one was getting much good thinking done anyway.

In Ideas We Trust

To tease out the best ideas from the field, we held an annual company-wide "Best Ideas" contest. A committee chose some of the best ideas and a single winner was voted on by store managers and announced at the picnic. This contest gave rise to products like the personalized calendars for which customers could select a photograph for each month of the year. Instantly, this became a top seller for us. It remains so today. They cost $3 and we sold them for $30. Our partner in La Jolla, California, Chip Stanczak, Jimmy Warren's brother-in-law, came up with the idea. Jimmy says "Chip made one of them for my mom and recognized by her reaction that there was a market for it." In another year, a coworker proposed pulling the color copy machines around the front counter and making them available for customers in the stores' public areas. That became standard. Another year, a coworker suggested a new tabulator key system by which customers could keep accurate count of the copies they made. We adopted that idea, too.

As a reward, we would send all the workers from the store with the winning idea to either Disneyland or Disney World for the weekend. While they were gone, we supposed bigwigs of Kinko's would fly out from the head office in California and descend upon the store for several days. We would sweep out the back room, run the copiers, and ring up all the orders. We worked around the clock. It was like an Outward Bound program for executives and board directors—a crash course on what it was like to work in the field. It was exhausting, but a lot of fun. And it made the point that as management we were subordinate to both our workers and to our customers.

We didn't just depend on the picnic for new ideas, by any means. Starting in the eighties, Dan Frederickson and a group of people in the Kinko's Service Corporation set up a voice mail system internally, known as KVMX, which facilitated broad idea-sharing between stores nationwide throughout the year, day in, day out. We turned to voice mail, in large part because, as a leader with learning opportunities like dyslexia, I didn't—I couldn't—rely on emails or mass mailings to communicate with our coworkers. Tim Stancliffe thinks that voice mail became an extension both of my personality and of our shared culture. As Tim puts it, "It fit in with everyone's short attention spans. We were all very entrepreneurial." For many years, voice mail was Kinko's main form of communication. Wherever I traveled around the country, I found great ideas. Let's say a coworker in Pocatello, Idaho, had devised a particularly brilliant inventory system. When I met this coworker, I dialed into our voice mail system and then handed him the phone. "Go ahead," I'd say, "introduce yourself and explain it." The coworker was often startled, but he got a chance to explain his idea in his own voice. By the end of the week, thousands of other people would have heard about it, too.

I sent out voice mail messages to everyone at Kinko's all the time. Tim and Dan used to plow through upwards of 50 on Fridays when many of our voice mails would be delivered system wide. I could configure my voice mail messages so they went out only to partners, only to managers, or to coworkers throughout the company. Many of our front-counter coworkers had voice mail boxes they dialed into. If a coworker had a message she wanted to deliver to me personally, she could call my voice mail directly. If I thought it was a good idea, I sent it out over the company-wide system. So, even though I was generally inaccessible at any given moment, it was still possible to reach me. Talking and listening to each other was the way we got things done. Tim Stancliffe remembers that he had dozens of voice mails each morning. There were so many ideas to be shared that the voice mails were a blessing and a curse. He learned to triage and forward them on to other people in his organization. "Paul had so many ideas," Tim recalls, "that you really had to claw your way through them." But there were jewels hidden among them. I encouraged all our managers and partners to call those stores with the best ideas and get firsthand advice on how to implement them. Voice mail is still my preferred mode of communication with my colleagues and many business partners. It's a great tool.

I relayed as many great ideas as I could to our coworkers in person while traveling store to store. Louisiana-based Annie Odell, one of my all-time favorite partners, says lots of people couldn't deal with this barrage of input. Annie: "Paul is a walking brainstorm. I found his visits exhausting and stimulating at the same time. Some partners got defensive when Paul offered ideas. If you got defensive, you got attacked. I found if you listened and took notes and implemented even a fraction of his new ideas, you'd do really well. You had to remember he'd been picking up the best ideas from all around the country." It drove me crazy when I ran into coworkers or partners who were resistant to innovating; I lost patience with them and let them know it. Believe me, this happened a lot.

We also relied on the prosaic suggestion box for input from our customers. Dean Zatkowsky, a former marketing manager for Kinko's Northwest, remembers that he, along with Mike Fasth, president of Kinko's Northwest, read every single customer suggestion from their region for nine years. Same with Mazen Safadi, a partner in western Pennsylvania. He began a coworker-of-the-month program in his stores after a customer suggested it. "I was surprised at how many customers would walk in and say, 'Hey, congratulations!' to the coworker. It gave the coworker a lot of pride," Mazen says.

These strategies reduced the constant encroachment of bureaucracy and hierarchy. As long as the field could talk directly to and directly affect the powers that be, I knew we were doing OK.

In Trust We Trust

The only way such an outward-facing structure could function, of course, was if it were founded on trust. In any relationship, trust is the magic ingredient. Trusting people is very emancipating. If you don't, you ought to give it a try. You'll find your life will work better and be much more fun if you do. Without trust, you'll be forever miserable in marriage or friendship. And, in business, nothing you plan will work well if you don't extend trust to the people you do business with. As a leader, all you do is manage trust. I learned about trust at first from my family. My sense of the importance of trust deepened when I studied our system of government. (Other kids studied hard for their A's and forgot everything they memorized for the test. I took the D, but I came away with the concept.) I still love learning about the U.S. Constitution and the U.S. government. This is because the democratic system, no matter what you think about it, and despite all its flaws, is based almost entirely on trust. We trust that cars will stop when the light turns red, that water will flow out of the tap, and that we get to elect our public officials ourselves. The government trusts that most citizens pay their taxes, that the legal system fundamentally works, and that most people aren't particularly interested in crime. I've traveled a lot around the world and ours is a system that works.

When people asked Tim how he could trust his coworkers, this is how he responded: "I'd say, you just do. Of course, there will be a percentage of the population who will take advantage of you. But the rest will flourish. Paul would say that the coworkers at the counter need to make decisions on their own. They're the heroes of the company. I bought into that hook, line, and sinker."

States' Rights

A cornerstone of a democratic government is achieving the right balance between federal and states' rights, or protecting the minority from the tyranny of the majority. We built our own version of this system in which the different partnerships around the country enjoyed "states' rights." No matter how many stores he or she owned, each partner was given one vote per store to cast at company-wide meetings. Most broad policy decisions required a three-quarters majority to pass, similar to amending the Constitution. Major votes on financial matters could be passed only with a vote of two thirds of the partners. Although I was the largest shareholder, with 100 percent ownership in many stores and lesser stakes in all the others, I didn't give myself a vote. I reserved for myself the role of the nag, albeit an influential one.

I also insisted we keep one store manager on the board of the company. Like so many issues at Kinko's, this prompted heated debate among the partners. But on this one eventually I prevailed, even though partners like Tim fought me tooth and nail. The store manager kept us grounded in the day-to-day reality of operations.

I reserved for myself the role of the nag.

As our partners got better and better at staying "on" their businesses, we ran the risk of coming up with ideas that were just too exotic or expensive to really work. I fell prey to this tendency myself. As we grew, more and more of our competitors dropped so far behind us that we no longer felt as threatened as we did in the early years. We needed someone to take us down a peg. Our store manager board member provided regular reality checks.

To this end, Jim Warren and our first president, Ken Hightower, designed a structure for the board, which they decided would be composed of seven members. One board member for partners with 5 or fewer stores, one for partners with 5 to 15 stores, and one for partners with 15 or more stores. So, you can see how the smaller operators were given equal, if not preferential, board representation relative to their size. Some of our partners eventually had more than 100 stores under management, but their say at the board level was no greater than that of the small operator. We also kept an outside director on the board. John Davis, now a professor at Harvard Business School, held this slot for more than a decade. Our company president, one store manager, and I also had seats.

Relying on that store manager director, and on the managers in the field, saved us from making any number of cockeyed decisions. For a time, in the early nineties, several other board members and I became enamored of a large format fax machine. It could transmit huge documents such as an architect's blueprints, so the customer didn't need to send them overnight by FedEx or Express Mail. We advocated the machine energetically to our partners. But our store manager board member was not impressed. Different store managers around the country also resisted it. Smaller stores didn't have the space for these big machines. Using one required the recipient to have access to a large format fax, too, reducing the size of its potential market. And it was expensive. Although we couldn't see it at the time, it was a bad idea. The 300 machines we leased to test at different stores never caught on. They were used mainly by coworkers who liked to fax supersized insults to their friends at other stores. Because of the opposition, both on the board and in the field, large format fax machines lasted only a short while.

My partners liked to tease me that when a vote didn't go my way, we simply voted again and again until it did. As my friend John Davis puts it: "Paul was always the biggest gorilla in the room." I'll admit I often prevailed in important debates. I had a lot of heavy-handed influence at Kinko's, but I really gave away a lot of the formal power.

Within the Kinko's network there were several large companies owned by the large partners. (See illustration next page.) I had one of my own, Kinko's Graphics Corporation (KGC), which managed a network of more than 100 stores that I owned outright. I let the president of KGC cast the votes that, by all rights, should have been mine. In the early years, Jimmy Warren was the first KGC president, followed by Mark Madden, and, finally, Dan Frederickson. I trusted the judgment of all of these men. One time in the late eighties, we were in the middle of a debate about a large proposed advertising expenditure. I was lobbying all our partners to pay for it. As the meeting was about to end, Jimmy Warren pulled up outside. He had been away on a business trip. Bad luck

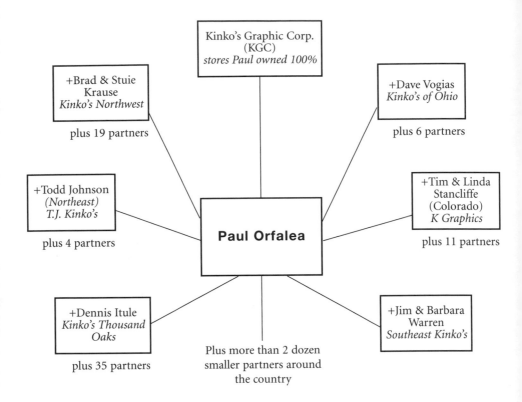

Kinko's Graphic Corp.
(KGC)
stores Paul owned 100%

+Brad & Stuie
Krause
Kinko's Northwest

plus 19 partners

+Dave Vogias
Kinko's of Ohio

plus 6 partners

+Todd Johnson
(Northeast)
T.J. Kinko's

plus 4 partners

Paul Orfalea

+Tim & Linda
Stancliffe
(Colorado)
K Graphics

plus 11 partners

+Dennis Itule
*Kinko's Thousand
Oaks*

plus 35 partners

Plus more than 2 dozen
smaller partners around
the country

+Jim & Barbara
Warren
Southeast Kinko's

All stores serviced by KSC, Kinko's Service Corporation
and their partnership office. President, Dan Frederickson.

THE BASIC STRUCTURE OF KINKO'S BEFORE 1997

for me. Just when I thought I was about to win the day, Jimmy protested that the advertising plan was a bad one. He argued that it would cost us too much money. The president of my own company shot me down! The vote went against me. I gnashed my teeth, but accepted it as cast. When I did weigh in on an issue, no matter how strongly I felt about it, there was always a forum for debate and dissension. I also knew it was important, symbolically, to show that I could lose.

"What Is He—Nuts?"

For years, from 1984 to about 1987, I proselytized about the wisdom of staying open for 24 hours. I became possessed, absolutely possessed, with the idea that this was a change we had to make. I'd met a convenience store owner who found his overall sales jumped 50 percent when he decided to stay open for 24 hours. At first, the increase seemed like a mystery. His foot traffic wasn't great during the overnight hours. But his customers liked knowing they could patronize his stores any time day or night. They never had to worry when he was open or closed. At that time, I remembered a discussion I overheard between my parents. As we were driving past the Hollywood Ranch Market in Los Angeles, Mom looked up and noticed that it was open 24 hours a day. "That's smart," she said, "Look at how they're spreading their overhead." I never forgot that remark. At Kinko's, many of our customers were students who tended to pull all-nighters and, increasingly, we served small business owners who often needed to do more work in the off-hours. By keeping our doors open all night we could attend to those customers and, at the same time, the assets for which we were paying substantial property and equipment leases became far more productive.

> It was open 24 hours a day. "That's smart," Mom said.

If I were the founder of a typical corporation, I would have simply issued an edict about going 24 hours and that would have been that. But I knew better than to kill the spirit of our partners. I was determined that we retain our flat structure, in which we worked together like an office of independent architects, each retaining his autonomy. It takes longer (much longer) to manage this way, but the payoff is greater because, in the end, everyone buys in.

It doesn't always look pretty. Our partner Todd Ordal sums up the general reaction to my 24-hour campaign: "People thought, 'What Is He—Nuts?'" When Charlie Wright, our partner in stores in and near Long Beach, heard about the 24-hour idea, he thought, "Oh, no. Who's going to work that shift?" Other partners, too, like Mazen

Safadi, worried about the security in keeping stores open overnight in high crime areas. I didn't dwell on these concerns. I knew they were distractions from the main issue. Once we got a few stores open for 24 hours, the rest of our partners would see the light, despite legitimate, serious concerns over challenges like security.

After what felt like an eon, our partner in Chicago, Theresa Thompson, went 24 hours and it was a huge success. The truth is, our partners weren't terribly interested in hearing from me about going 24 hours. They were far more impressed when one of their own took a chance and succeeded. As we'd hoped, our store revenues jumped anywhere from 10 percent to as much as 50 percent after the switch. For many stores, staying open overnight wasn't a huge stretch anyway. They were so busy that coworkers tended to work late into the night completing back orders that were placed earlier in the day. Often it was only a matter of hiring one extra person (and sometimes even that wasn't necessary) in order to keep the doors open all night long. Mostly, the overnight foot traffic was low and the coworkers could get those overflow orders done while still attending to the front counter.

After a large partner meeting in which Theresa extolled the virtue of making the switch, more partners decided to experiment. I was watching democracy at work. Both Mazen and Charlie were among the earliest partners who followed suit. They were shocked at how much more income their stores produced. Partners like them became my greatest advocates. At a large meeting once, Charlie stood up and told everyone, "If you like money, then do it."

Keeping power out in the field at Kinko's was a big part of keeping our coworkers and customers happy. It was yet another, and a particularly profound, way to manage the environment so you didn't have to spend so much time managing people. When I picture all the workers at Enron who conspired to keep their company's fraud from the public light—going so far as to simulate an entirely bogus trading room with dead telephone lines they pretended were live—I think these are people who did *not* think for themselves. I didn't want our store managers or partners too dependent on the head office any more than I want our kids saddled with too much dependence on their mother or me. In both cases, I wanted them to think for themselves. That way not only would the stores run by themselves, but our coworkers could constantly surprise us with ideas that would benefit the entire network of Kinko's stores.

To me, this is a far more practical and exciting structure than the franchise model used by most retail organizations. In my view, franchising sets up an adversarial relationship. The franchisee has an expectation that the franchiser will make him successful. In a franchise relationship, the store manager is not a full partner and I didn't want that. I wanted our coworkers to know their success depended on them and not on the head office.

"*You* are going to make yourself successful," I'd tell them. "Not me." That's what I told our first partners decades ago and it's what I tell my newest partners today.

Facing Far East

The issue of franchising played a role in the story of how Kinko's Japan got its start. In 1988, Hiro Izutsu was a young MBA candidate at the University of Michigan. His employer, Sumitomo Metal Mining Co., Ltd., had sent him to the United States and was footing the bill for his education. For one of his classes, Hiro wrote a paper proposing that Sumitomo and Kinko's form a joint venture to bring Kinko's to Japan. His professor gave him a B$^+$ on the paper. Hiro's story shows yet again that there's little guarantee that straight A's lead to success in life. (In fact, legend has it that when Fred Smith, the founder of FedEx, wrote a paper on an overnight delivery service for his professors at Yale, they gave him a C!) Hiro sent it to me and to his bosses in a very Japanese act of appreciation. He was grateful to Sumitomo for giving him the opportunity to complete the MBA in the United States and he was grateful to Kinko's coworkers for so attentively helping him to prepare the paper for his class. (He was also particularly impressed that the stores stayed open for 24 hours.)

I got back to Hiro right away. I liked the idea. Hiro called the vice president of development at Sumitomo and the feeling was mutual.

An executive from Sumitomo named Saburo Shigeno flew to our head office in Ventura, California, for our first meeting. I was also there along with Hiro and Mark Madden.

As Mark remembers it, "Mr. Shigeno didn't speak much English. When he asked Paul why Kinko's didn't use a franchise model, Paul looked directly at him and started speaking really passionately. He said, 'Do you know what a franchise relationship is?' He said, 'This is the franchisee and this is the franchiser,' and he flipped the bird with both hands to show two sides of a conflict at war with each other. Mr. Shigeno had no idea what Paul was saying. He thought Paul was flipping him off. All hell broke loose in Japanese. To this day, I don't think Paul understood what the upset was about."

I certainly didn't mean to insult the guy, but I wanted him to understand that we do things differently at Kinko's. The Japanese are known for their hierarchical businesses and we couldn't partner with Sumitomo if they had that expectation of us. Eventually, Sumitomo agreed to use the partnership structure we'd pioneered. Convincing our joint venture partner that each and every coworker in Japan needed to share in the profits from each store took longer. I asked and asked and *asked* our Japanese partners to agree to offer profit sharing to our stores in Japan. I never got an answer one way or another. They just smiled and changed the subject. It may be because profit sharing introduced an uncomfortable "imbalance." If profits were to be shared, then store managers stood to make more money than the suits who supervised them! This was often the case in the U.S. market. Finally, I realized I had to do something. At a meeting we had with all our coworkers in Japan, I simply went ahead and publicly announced that we would have profit sharing. No one at Sumitomo ever complained and "a fraction of the action" took effect. Kinko's Japan was officially formed in 1991. We were exporting a new way of using democratic principles in the international marketplace. What could be more exciting!

We hired Hiro to work with us for three months in Ventura and then he went back to work with Sumitomo in Japan. Mark, who was in his early thirties, became the president of Kinko's Japan while he continued to manage my stores.

At other companies, it might have seemed strange to seize on an idea offered by an observant college kid, but at Kinko's it was par for the course. We started the company as college students ourselves. College kids were our first customers and our first coworkers. We were accustomed to going to them for ideas when they worked with us. While I was still with Kinko's, I taught college kids economics at the University of California at Santa Barbara. For years, I told them to visit Kinko's stores to critique what they observed. Then, as part of their final, we set up meetings where Kinko's partners listened to their feedback and criticism. It benefited the students and it benefited Kinko's. We didn't shield ourselves from input. We sought it out.

I like the way our board director John Davis put it: "A lot of what Paul did was to really attack arrogance at its root. You constantly have to ask yourself, 'What business are we in?' This is actually a complicated question because you're trying to serve different markets at different times. At Kinko's, we were always trying to figure out what business we were in. What's often the case is even top management isn't clear on what business they're in and that confusion gets filtered down through the organization."

That's what happens when you're "in" your business and not "on" it.

Back to School

If you're going to have an effective democracy, it needs to be an educated one. At a partner meeting sometime in the eighties, John, our resident academic, asked all the partners with business degrees to raise their hands. All hands remained in their owners' laps; there simply weren't any (except for me; I did end up getting a business degree from USC). So many of our partners started at Kinko's as young kids in college and worked their ways up that, by the time they were a few years older and the organization had grown to a substantial size, we all needed to learn better ways of managing our growth, our relationships, and ourselves. To this end, we asked

John to set up a series of regular classes for our partners and our store managers. We called it Kinko's University. For ten years, from 1987 to 1997, Kinko's University convened once a year for a week in various parts of the country.

John assembled an impressive roster of professors from top business schools to come and instruct the leaders within the company. We didn't award grades, but everyone learned together while running true-to-life experiments. As Charlie Wright recalls, "I never went to college so I benefited tremendously from the executive classes." During the sessions, our partners sometimes stayed up half the night devising business plans or case scenarios. They made competing presentations to each other the next day. Not only did Kinko's University enrich their understanding of their business, it also provided a good break. It gave partners a chance to get away from the grind of their day-to-day lives for a spell so they could think creatively about their goals and aspirations.

Not only did we encourage education and debate from within our ranks, we paid attention to our critics on the outside. In 1992, for instance, members of the environmental activist group Greenpeace began trying to persuade some of our stores in California to stop selling paper made by a process using chlorine bleach. When news of the dispute reached the head office, someone had the brilliant idea of calling in a crisis management expert. This so-called expert advised us not to talk to Greenpeace directly. I thought this was a bad idea. I pulled out the Kinko's Philosophy, which you'll read more about in the next chapter, and read aloud the part about open communication and admitting our mistakes. We took a different tack. Instead of stonewalling, we invited people from Greenpeace to fly out to our offices in Ventura.

Mark Floegel, who at the time was a toxics campaigner with Greenpeace, and one of his associates, took us up on the offer. They met with two of our vice presidents. Floegel was startled because he was accustomed to dealing with people at other companies who had titles like "environmental director" but who, in reality, were experts in public relations.

Mark remembers, "They took us seriously. They wanted to hear our point of view. They wanted to hear what we could offer in the way of solutions."

We reached a compromise in which Kinko's stores began offering chlorine-free paper to customers who requested it. We also began offering more recycled paper as well. From a long-term perspective, this was a qualified success because paper made with chlorine is still standard in the United States. However, at the time, it felt like real progress. Later, Mark came to one of our partners meetings in Houston. He presented us with an oversized card of acknowledgment signed by 2,000 Greenpeace people. That was a great day for everybody at Kinko's.

Our experience with Greenpeace was invigorating. It inspired us to introduce a new annual award for the store that runs the most environmentally-conscious business. This award is still being given today. Later, we added a statement to the Philosophy expressing our concern for our environment. We relied on the same principle that underlies the First Amendment, and trusted that open communication would give us the right solution. In the process, we made a friend where we might have had an enemy.

Bright White

In one aspect of democracy building, we did not live up to our ideals, at least before the eighties and perhaps until the early nineties. While our in-store staffs around the country were diverse, the racial makeup of our head office wasn't. A nationwide partner meeting we held in Toronto some years back pointed out our weakness in this area.

Karen Madden remembers that we were all hanging out together in a hotel lobby. "As we were talking," Karen says, "this older, dapper black man comes up to us. He asked us who we were. We were feeling bright and happy and we said we were from Kinko's. This man comes right up to Paul and he lays into him. He says, 'Look at your group! Look at how lily white you are!' He really read us the riot act. It was true. We had only two people who were black in the whole partnership group. After he left, Paul turned to us and said, 'This guy's right. We're too white.'"

"One of the things I always loved about Paul is that he would talk and listen to anybody," Karen says. "I never felt like we were at all prejudiced. It's just that people kept hiring their friends."

That was our problem. We would have liked to have diversified our partnership group, but we'd already locked most of our partners in place. And these were long-term relationships. Ironically, the one time we did face the specter of a lawsuit charging us with discrimination, it was threatened by workers at one of our most racially diverse locations in New Haven, Connecticut. After a dispute with management in the early nineties, a group of those workers began picketing outside of the store and local newspapers covered the conflict. The New Haven chapter of the National Association for the Advancement of Colored People supported their efforts. Because the targeted store was part of Kinko's Graphics Corp., my partnership, the president, Mark Madden, flew out to see what he could do. "They were threatening us with a class action lawsuit," Mark says. "I was worried about the situation exploding."

He says, "Look at your group! Look at how lily white you are!"

I was too. We hired crisis management consultants who somehow put us in touch with Willie Brown, who was at the time the powerful speaker of the Assembly in California. Brown steered us to a friend of his, a lawyer in Connecticut, by the name of John C. Brittain, then a law professor at the University of Connecticut. John said he would represent us, but he also disclosed that he had close ties to the NAACP in Connecticut. Both sides agreed to let him mediate. As Mark remembers it, "John was the wise sage who held the middle ground." John helped us negotiate a settlement in which each of the coworkers' various grievances was investigated. Then, we reported back to the NAACP about what we'd found in each case. For our part, we did what we always did in a crisis. We talked a lot about the philosophy and that inspired us to treat everybody involved with respect and to keep an open mind.

What started out as a fearful prospect turned into an opportunity for us to build new bridges. After the threat of the suit was dropped, Mark flew out to Connecticut again to attend the NAACP's annual Freedom Fund Banquet in New Haven. At the banquet, Mark announced our intention to make ten $1,000 donations to charities of the NAACP's choice. We also set up an intern program to train a worker chosen by the NAACP. Mark received a standing ovation that evening when he announced these programs. "As a white male in the United States, you just don't get a chance to experience something like that," Mark said. "It was just one of the coolest nights of my life."

As Kinko's continued to grow, the ranks of our coworkers became more and more diverse. I always said that it didn't matter to me if your skin was green or if you were a zebra, if you could ring a register you could work with us. If we weren't as racially integrated as we wanted to be, we were diverse in other ways. In some parts of the country, we had a strong representation of women among the ranks of both partners and managers. Jimmy says, "For a long time, my feeling was that we had more good women managers than men." This may be simply because women tended to score higher on empathy. Jim's sister Liz Warren (later Stanczak) started at Kinko's when she was 19 in the mid-seventies. She helped open and became a partner in a dozen stores in the San Diego area. Jim's first three managers in the Southwest were women: Dana Jennings, Carolyn Gehl, and Annie Odell. They all went on to become partners. Jimmy also worked with two of the most profitable partners at Kinko's. Both of them, Faye Matthews and Annie Odell, happened to be women.

A high percentage of gay men and women also came to work with us at Kinko's. (I fought strenuously for same-sex benefits and we got them.) And the intellectual backgrounds of our coworkers were extremely varied. The clash of so many styles proved to be a real catalyst for inspiration within the company. We never suffered from "Groupthink."

When Charlie Wright came to work with us in the late seventies, he had never seen so many guys with long hair. Some of our oldest partners at the time, Jimmy, Brad, and Craig Redwine had hair, as Craig put it, "down to our asses." (Jimmy says, "I had moderately long hair. They had pony tails.") Charlie: "It was pretty much the hippie crowd. But the guys with the longest hair were the most successful. After a while, I realized they were the guys I wanted to be like. They knew how to enjoy life and they knew how to not take things too seriously, other than delivering the product. We all became friendly competitors."

The Limits of Laid-Back Lifestyle

You can't beat an environment of friendly competition for motivating people. Still, from day one at Kinko's there was constant, constant pressure to homogenize the culture, to add layers of bureaucracy, to fall prey to the temptation to become more hierarchical. Some of it couldn't be avoided. We needed a head office, a central body that would do our partners' books, lend money, negotiate contracts, and handle company-wide design and legal matters. When we first started charging stores for services provided by the head office, the monthly per-store fee was $300 per store; later it jumped to around $4,000. There was a great hue and cry from the field about the increases, but they couldn't be avoided. In all other respects, I tried to avoid centralization and homogenization as much as I could.

Charlie remembers the time he accompanied me on a trip to one of our stores in South Bend, Indiana. The computers for rent there were arrayed in spacious diagonal rows that allowed room for more computers and more customers. The furniture was of an elegant steel case design. The signs directing customers were easy to find and to read. As I walked around marveling at the fantastic layout, Charlie asked me a question: "Paul," he said. "If this is so great, why don't you just make it a mandate and tell the other partners, 'If you want to do business with me, this is the way you're going to set up your computers?'"

It seemed like such an obvious choice, but I couldn't do it. I wouldn't do it. I turned to him and replied, "If that's what I do, then this is the best it will *ever* be."

I like the way my partner Tim Stancliffe describes his view of the evolution we all went through as people and entrepreneurs in trying to build a democracy at Kinko's:

"We were kind of antibusiness in a way in the beginning. We were all really children and adolescents. We were struggling with becoming adults. We felt like we were going to do it our own way. We are going to have good values and we are going to make money. All of the stuff that Jack Welch stands for, we are against. We didn't buy into severe command and control, or that the bottom 10 percent performers should be taken out to dig their graves before they were shot. I was 21 in 1969. It was the civil rights movement. The Vietnam War was raging and I was antiwar. It was the beginning of the women's movement and the beginning of the environmental movement. I thought, 'Change the world!' I never thought business was a good place to do that. But I discovered we can change people's lives. We can give them benefits. We can extend decision-making to them. It was maybe naive. All my business friends said we were naive the way we at Kinko's were trusting people so much. But today I say to kids, 'Don't turn your back on business. Business needs caring people. It *can* be an agent for social change.'"

Chapter 6

Find Your

Philosophy

B Y 1983, WE WERE DOING ABOUT $70 MILLION IN SALES a year with slightly more than 120 stores. We also had about 30 independent-minded partners running various corners of Kinko's. We were 30 partners—with an average age of about 28—motivated by our own value systems, ideals, and ambitions. With scant input from the head office, each person made his or her own decisions, whether they ran a single store or a string of them. The growth, even at that early point, was getting out of hand.

At the time, our head office was located on the second floor of the El Mercado shopping center in Santa Barbara. We were experiencing growing pains. The first half of the eighties was a time of furious growth and none of us had bothered to put certain fundamentals into place. I remember Dorothy Sandow, who used to do the books in our office, wondering out loud, "How will we stay the same as we grow?" Good question. I didn't have the answer. We'd grown so fast that we hadn't even bothered to secure trademark protections for ourselves nationwide. We hardly had any written agreements with anybody; most of our business was conducted on a handshake. Aside from our status as independent Subchapter S corporations, we lacked any structure to speak of.

To get some perspective on things, I enrolled in the Owner/ President Management Program at Harvard Business School, which I attended three weeks a year for three years. While sitting through classes there (and never taking a note, though I did read my case studies), I realized we needed somebody—an outsider definitely and maybe an academic—to help us continue to grow while still retaining our unique culture and not killing each other in the process. My hunt lead me to John Davis, who got his doctorate at Harvard Business School and was an assistant professor at USC at the time. I called up John to ask him to meet and talk things over with me. John agreed to, even though at the end of our first conversation I abruptly hung up on him—"I gotta go," John remembers me saying, leaving him listening to a dead phone line. I guess he understood I was busy. Somehow, he was intrigued enough to follow through.

John's association with Kinko's would last for nearly two decades. He drove up to meet me and got a look at how our head office functioned. My partnership, Kinko's Graphics Corp., was still handling all the books for the partners for a low monthly fee. It wasn't the greatest structure. We were getting by, but we could do better. Later, John turned up at one of our partner meetings. He sat in the back, scribbling enigmatically into a small red notebook. Here's John:

> **Things just happened as they needed to happen, or maybe a little later.**

"In my field we learn about organic organizations, but I think it's fair to say that I'd never seen, at that point and subsequent to that time, an organization that was quite so organic. Things just happened as they needed to happen, or maybe a little later than they needed to happen, but they happened. There didn't seem to be a plan. There didn't seem to be a structure. There didn't seem to be much of anything, but a lot of things were getting done at the right time. It was fascinating to me. I felt like an anthropologist trekking through the jungle and kind of stumbling on this tribe that I had never seen an example of before. I had never seen organic Republicans. They were really interesting creatures. They were capitalist hippies, really. It was bordering on strange. You can only be so organic without defying the public health laws, right? The growth of this company and the growth of the people was clearly managing to outstrip any reasonable attempts to provide logical, sane infrastructure to the company. There were costs to it, but it was part of the magic of the company."

At the end of that first partners meeting that he attended, everyone was curious to know who this scholar in our midst was, taking notes and saying nothing while the rest of us argued, pontificated, and generally exercised our democratic rights. Eventually, John took the microphone and shared some of his observations about what he saw in us and in Kinko's. He told us he saw us moving toward a more formal organization, but he saw us doing it in our own "organic" way. He made us laugh. We liked him. We liked what he had to say.

Over the years, he came to play a variety of roles at the company. He started as an outside consultant and eventually became a full board member, a position he held for ten years. He also served as, variously, educator-in-chief, peacemaker, resident shrink, and company philosopher. As my partner Tim remembers it, "We had to start growing up once John Davis became involved. He realized we were struggling with late adolescence. We didn't yet realize that commitment and hard work could go a long way. He had a fabulous influence on us." A lot of our partners were somewhat like me. We got things done, but we couldn't talk about what we were doing with the sort of context and eloquence that John brought to bear in any discussion. He became our spokesman. He helped us to communicate better with each other and with the outside world.

John noticed our tendency to philosophize right off the bat. "At that first partner meeting," John says, "they were all just sitting around talking about their business not just in financial terms and marketing terms, but in philosophical terms as well. It was like being on the set of *The Big Chill*. These people didn't go to college together, but it was almost like they did. And even though Paul played the role of paterfamilias he was basically just the big brother. He encouraged very collegial relationships, buddy relationships."

Two years later, in 1985, John decided he would put our proclivity for debate and discussion to work for us. He made a suggestion. John felt strongly that we needed to write down a set of guiding principles to unite our far-flung factions, giving us a flag to rally around. We took John up on it. We decided we would go ahead and try to put something on paper about who we were and who we wanted to be. John drew up the first draft and derived the content from what he'd observed in us for two years. The result came to be called the "Kinko's Philosophy." Like so many of our best ideas at Kinko's, this one originated not with me, but with someone from the outside who, by virtue of being undistracted by being in the business, was able to offer some valuable insight. We spent six months hashing out the Philosophy, and then continued to revise it over the years. The final version read as follows:

Kinko's Philosophy

Our primary objective is to take care of our customers. We are proud of our ability to serve him or her in a timely and helpful manner, and to provide high quality at a reasonable price. We develop long-term relationships that promote mutual growth and prosperity. We value creativity, productivity, and loyalty, and we encourage independent thinking and teamwork.

Our co-workers are the foundation of our success. We consider ourselves part of the Kinko's family. We trust and care for each other, and treat everyone with respect. We openly communicate our accomplishments and mistakes so we can learn from each other. We strive to live balanced lives in work, love, and play. We are confident of our future and point with pride to the way we run our business, and treat each other.

We plastered the Philosophy everywhere. We printed it up on small, laminated wallet-sized cards so that people could carry it around in their pockets. Some partners hung the Philosophy on the walls of their stores. Eventually, and even though it seemed hokey at first, we started reciting it at our partner meetings and picnics as if it were the Pledge of Allegiance. But we didn't view it as fixed in stone. The tenets of the Philosophy were inherently contradictory: even though we valued "independent thinking," we also encouraged "teamwork." The

Philosophy became a tool for managing ambiguity, one of the most difficult challenges in any business. It provided a ready forum for discussions about how we would continue to grow and work together as individuals who were also members of a collective. As we changed, we constantly floated ideas for how to further hone, expand, or otherwise alter it. I was forever asking people, "Do you think we should change the Philosophy? How would *you* rewrite the Philosophy?" It became a mechanism by which everyone became invested in the direction of the company.

In the Judeo-Christian tradition, there are the Ten Commandments. We may not abide by all of them all of the time, but they are there to guide us. Every company should take the time to write a philosophy statement. One of my favorite companies, Johnson & Johnson (also one of my longtime favorite investments), has a great one. I bought the stock after I watched a *60 Minutes* piece on the infamous crisis during which eight people died from poisoned Tylenol pills back in the eighties. J&J decided that any response it made to the crisis would be true to its credo, which has guided the company through the past 60 years. The first sentence of that credo reads, "We believe our first responsibility is to the doctors, nurses, patients, to mothers and fathers and all others who use our products and services." In other words, covering their own butts is explicitly not priority number one of J&J's leadership. The company leaned on its own stated belief system in a time of need. J&J responded to the crisis quickly, with compassion and, in the process, won new loyalty from its customers.

Having a high-minded vision that we all embraced for Kinko's was immeasurably helpful. At least we knew if we failed to meet its ideals, we could get back on track and point ourselves in the right direction. As John puts it, "The Philosophy was the expression of the ideal culture. But it was our goal. It was what we wanted." The only limit to your growth as a person or a company is your imagination. When you think about it, there are only two things in life: matter (cars, sidewalks, bodies, etc.) and ideas. These are the only two things on Earth. (In fact, scientists now believe that, at the subatomic level, there is really no significant difference between matter and thought;

in other words, our thoughts truly create our reality. Isn't that cool?) The way I see it, you're only as good as your dreams. If all of us at Kinko's could imagine an ideal place where we could all work together, we had a shot at achieving it and much of the time we did.

Envision Your Vision

Having a vision is beneficial in the private, not just the corporate, realm. Early in my time at Kinko's, I took a class on goal setting at the University of Virginia, but goal setting has always been in my blood. Picturing myself owning my own business one day helped me to navigate through my difficulties in the second grade. Even as Sister Sheila paddled me, I told myself that someday I would own my own business and have secretaries who would read for me. By the time Kinko's was up and running, I made a habit of setting new goals every six weeks or so. Wherever I went when I was with Kinko's, I carried a four-subject notebook. I didn't write long letters or reports, of course, but I did make lists. The notebook was full of them. I was an inveterate list maker. I set personal goals. I set play goals (every January 1, I scheduled my blocks of vacation for the year). I set business goals. I set financial goals. I worked out the cash flow for Kinko's in one section of the notebook. I always say that if you don't know your business well enough to calculate your cash flow on the back of an envelope, you've got problems. My coworkers were constantly criticizing me for having too many top-priority items to attend to. It was tough for me to stay "on" my business while addressing so many priority issues. So I classed them as Big, and then Big-Big, and, finally, Big-Big-Big. It sounds corny, but it worked for me.

At the end of our family vacations, or any business trips, I became maniacal about getting my lists in order. Before I headed back to work, I got to work on these lists. Completing them could take me the better part of the day.

I quickly learned not to be too specific in putting my goals onto paper. I remember one time in 1975 I set an arbitrary goal for myself to open three new stores between September and December. In order to open store number three, I pushed too hard. The store, in Westchester, California, turned out to be one of our worst locations ever. We constantly clashed with the landlord at that site. Eventually, we closed it. I've since learned that goal setting should be more like an impressionistic painting. As opposed to "Open three new stores by the end of the year," my goal became simply "Expand the business." Keep your goals as anchors and then wander around among them, giving yourself plenty of room for error and experimentation. I used to sketch the following illustration for my partners back in my twenties. You start with some clear goals. Here they are represented by two straight lines:

Then you allow for a little spontaneity. You wander around among them. Like this:

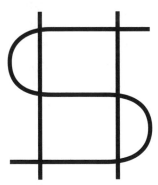

Ta-da! See what you end up with? Know where you're going, but don't be too wedded to the result. My friend John Davis used to say,

"The best part about goal setting is going through the process. First make your plan, and then throw it out!" Remember that line from the old musical *South Pacific*, "If you don't have a dream, how you gonna make a dream come true?" Good question. I love to sing that line to my partners from time to time. As far as I was concerned, the Philosophy was our strategic plan. It was the expression of our collective dreaming at Kinko's. We each need to do our individual dreaming as well.

Living It

The more we recited the Philosophy and embraced it as something real, the more it became, over time, something we held very close to our hearts. Some of our former coworkers have imported modified versions of it into the new companies they started after leaving Kinko's. I carry a copy of the Philosophy around with me on one of those laminated cards and still find myself having reason to pull it out and refer to it.

At every picnic and partner meeting, someone was chosen to go to the front of the room and recite the Philosophy at the microphone for the rest of us. It could be someone who had made a pioneering change or someone who had survived hardship. One year it was our partner in Chicago, Theresa Thompson, the first of us to take her stores to a 24-hour schedule, who led us at the mike. Other times, Karen chose a partner who had recently struggled through a trying time. My partner Todd Johnson was only 30 and had been working with us for eight years when his young wife died suddenly in 1984 from an aneurysm. She was 28 years old and pregnant with their fourth child. Doctors managed to save the infant but couldn't save her. She died a month before Natalie and I were married. I'd gotten to know Todd and his family well over the years so I flew out to them after it happened. He was planning on coming out to Santa Barbara from Utah for our wedding anyhow. I told him to bring his kids and stay at our place while Natalie and I went on our honeymoon. At a partners meeting about a year later, Todd read the Philosophy out loud to everybody. In the midst of all the general zaniness and uproar that accompanied most of our company meetings, moments like these were powerful.

Todd: "Reading the Philosophy made it more than a written philosophy. It became a living philosophy. I've never been great verbally, but the first time somebody laid out the Philosophy, I thought, 'That's *exactly* how I feel.' You heard it all the time. When Paul picks up on something, he's relentless. It became a way of life in the stores. At first, when we recited it, I kept thinking that I felt like I was working for Amway, but I knew that Paul believed in it. When someone practices a belief system in his life, you can see it. It was Paul's own philosophy and he promoted it to the point where it became everyone else's philosophy."

If you flipped over the small laminated card that was printed with the Philosophy on one side, you would find a list of guiding principles. These are the "Kinko's Commitments to Communication." There were 14 points, with a final add-on at the end:

1. I will recognize your value to Kinko's.

2. I will share my goals with you, and together we will develop an action plan.

3. I will respect and utilize the chain of command to resolve problems.

4. I will solicit immediate feedback to assure we understand each other.

5. I will talk with you, not at you.

6. I will listen with an open mind.

7. I will try to see the situation from all points of view.

8. I will tell you when I don't know the answer, and together we will seek the answer.

9. I will give you honest and sincere feedback.

10. I will not usurp your authority.

11. I will not confront you when I am angry.

12. I will not gossip.

13. I will not publicly embarrass you.

14. I will admit when I am wrong.

   . . . and in every case, I am worthy of the same from you.

I wish I could tell you I abided by each of these tenets all the time myself, but I'm a human being and we were a company of human beings. I always figured when we hired someone, we got the whole enchilada. That applied to all of us. I plead guilty to personally violating many of these tenets. But, just because I fell short myself from time to time doesn't mean I underestimate their importance. Our partner David Vogias, who owned and ran stores in Ohio, Pennsylvania, New Jersey, and New York, was the driving force behind the Commitments to Communication. Dave felt we needed the commitments to further define how the Philosophy should be implemented—to make sure it was being implemented. The truth is, Dave and I argued so much that he proposed the commitments as an effort to lay down the rules of engagement between him and me. The commitments weren't passed by all the partners. They were passed in a committee of which Dave was a member. As Dave remembers it, "I forced the Commitments to Communication."

Looking back I should have argued more to change some of these commitments. Number 12, for example: "I will not gossip." What does that mean, really? I never understood that one. How can we function as a community and a family if we don't talk about each other? Talking and learning about each other is one of the great pleasures in life. I think that commitment should have read, "I will not engage in *malicious* gossip." You can see how much debate these value statements can inspire. In retrospect, I would have also instituted a values statement covering all meetings. It would have stipulated that, when it comes to meetings, everyone in attendance would

(a) arrive on time, (b) understand what the purpose of the meeting is, and (c) seek together to find a conclusion so that the meeting could end—and end quickly.

Nitpicking aside, the Commitments to Communication further refined some of the practical ways we sought to live by the Philosophy.

As we grew, we came to rely on the Philosophy in more concrete ways. By the late eighties, we began circulating anonymous coworker surveys to determine whether the Philosophy was being applied in all our stores. We used the Philosophy to devise a set of criteria that we used to evaluate coworkers. As we matured as a company, our president, Dan Frederickson, instituted a program of management effectiveness surveys and, later, 360-degree reviews wherein coworkers at the head office, Kinko's Service Corp., were evaluated by their colleagues, by the people who reported to them, and by those they reported to. From all directions, coworkers evaluated each other against the principles we'd voted on and laid out together in the Philosophy.

> **Our partner Gerry Alesia hadn't come across anything like the Philosophy.**

Before coming to Kinko's, our partner Gerry Alesia had worked at Ralph's Grocery Co., General Foods, Bally's, and Ramada and he hadn't come across anything like the Philosophy. "It was very unusual," Gerry says. "It took several meetings for us to write and there was a lot of fighting about the individual words. We pretty much lived and believed what the Philosophy said. We believed that the coworkers were the foundation of our success. It wasn't just lip service."

The fact that we shared a belief in a set of fundamental principles and tenets made it, paradoxically, easier for us to tolerate conflict. I've always loved controversy and debate. I believe it's necessary for a healthy company, indeed, every healthy relationship.

Here's my partner Mark Madden, "Paul and I once met with a real estate guy in Santa Barbara. He asked us what the perfect size was for a Kinko's store. Paul said about 8,000 to 10,000 square feet and I said about 4,000 square feet. Obviously, quite a difference. We debated with each other a few minutes and then looked up, a bit embarrassed that we couldn't even agree on the size of a store. The guy got a huge kick out of seeing us debate basic business principles. He was used to seeing a boss and a bunch of yes-men and -women who would never disagree with the leader. He loved that Paul was the one pushing for a bigger, longer-term opportunity, while I was the one pushing for moderation and improved short-term profitability."

We all did business differently. Take my partners David Vogias and Tim Stancliffe. Dave, who ended up with 50 stores, admired and sought to emulate big blue-chip companies like General Electric. He ran his company with many more levels of bureaucracy than I would have. And yet, the policy manual that his company wrote up for one of our core businesses, Professor Publishing, ended up being adopted by most of the other partners. I hate policy manuals myself. Obviously, I'm never going to spend free time reading them. But, if our other partners could make use of one, I'm glad Dave got it written. He loved concocting five-year strategic plans—an activity I find pointless and unbearable. In contrast, he thought my stores were loosely and poorly run. I repeatedly told him that he could have expanded his business ten times faster were he not so wrapped up in tending to all that bureaucratic mumbo jumbo. Then there was Tim, who owned stakes in about 170 stores in Colorado and surrounding states. Tim was so frugal with his money that, in my view, he never invested enough of his profits in testing new ideas. Tim didn't protest this view of his management strategy because he liked to put new products through a lot of testing and careful consideration before using them. Tim: "No-new-products-Tim was one of my nicknames. I reveled in that kind of attention." As a result, he was never on the cutting edge of adopting our newest innovations. This meant that all the Kinko's locations in one entire corner of the country lagged behind other regions. We constantly argued about our different views of the world and of business.

Simply put, we didn't treat each other with kid gloves. We knew we didn't have to. We could stand a little controversy and trust we'd emerge the better for it. Having a shared philosophy gave us resilience.

As John Davis observed, "The Philosophy became a fundamental aspect of the Kinko's religion. When somebody stood up and recited the Philosophy at the end of each meeting, it was like a recitation of the Nicene Creed [a doctrine of Christian faith adopted in A.D. 325]. It was 'This is who we are.' People really understood that the strength of the group came from the ability to speak openly about things and to challenge each other. It was a culture of being open and honest. You could go through really turbulent meetings where there was yelling and arguing and some harsh things said, and at the end of the meeting, we would recite the Philosophy together. And it was OK."

Chapter 7

Life Is a Picnic

THE DIFFERENCE BETWEEN THE CULTURE AT KINKO'S and those of other companies was most obvious in our respect for—in our *insistence* on—abandoning all sense of propriety on a regular basis and having fun together. If you think that a "lack of decorum" isn't healthy for people or for a company, remember that *no one wants to follow a leader who is tired, haggard, and miserable.* We needed breaks, as people and as a company, both because they kept us happy and alert and productive and because we needed to know there was more to life than just working. I've always valued thinking hard over working hard. The best thinking reduces the hours you have to work. But without enough rest and recreation, we lose the ability to get any good thinking done at all.

Who doesn't want to go through life and giggle and laugh a lot? I know I do. Some would disagree, but I think mischievous kids are the most stable. They feel secure enough to horse around and challenge authority. I've always found that half the fun of doing stuff is getting caught. Today, the best thing about being an adult is that I've got the freedom to act my true age, which at any given moment, ranges from 12 to 57. I always get a kick when somebody tells me to grow up. Even when I was invited to the White House during the Clinton years, I got in trouble. It was just like being back in school! I got so bored waiting for Vice President Gore to turn up for a talk that I took myself on a little tour, which the security guards didn't much appreciate. They threw me out!

Here is a secret not widely known in corporate America: The best human relationships are forged when people can be stupid together and still respect one another the next day. When they can play with each other. In most workplaces, people are so busy trying to impress each other they never really get to know their coworkers who sit a cubicle away. We never had that problem at Kinko's. Traveling between different locations around the country, sometimes my partners and I used to dash into a convenience store, buy the largest iced teas we could, drink them, and see who could hold out the longest before going to the bathroom. One time, when I was traveling with my partner Brad and my coworker Mike Fasth, they faked me out and dashed into a bathroom at one of our stores to relieve themselves when I wasn't looking. Later, I had to go so badly that I made them pull the car over to the side of the road. (I used to hold it so often that, later in life, I ended up having surgery on my bladder.) My longtime coworker Dean Zatkowsky, a marketing director for Kinko's Northwest, figured all the game playing enabled me to master a central principle of good leadership: managing attention. I never thought of it that way. As far as I was concerned, it was just fun.

Power to the Picnic

We institutionalized fun by throwing a huge party every year—our annual picnic. Human organizations of every scale—cultures, countries, cities, and clubs—have annual celebrations. Our first was held at Skofield Park in Santa Barbara in 1971. As with most great things at Kinko's, this wasn't my idea. Our partners Brad and Stuie Krause threw it and I came as a guest. I was so excited that I brought a bunch of my cousins and friends from Los Angeles with me. When we arrived, we felt overdressed. Everybody else was wearing, well, practically nothing. Just shorts or bathing suits to swim in the creek. Brad and Stuie grilled hot dogs and beans. We played Frisbee and relaxed.

The picnics were such a success that, as the years went on, I became pretty insistent that everyone attend. It was a means of uniting our far-flung tribe. I quickly learned I could use it as a tool. Looking back, it seems highly improbable that our four largest partners and I would have gone on to build Kinko's together. Those guys—Jimmy, Denny, Brad, and Tim—could not have been more different from one another, in almost every way. Jimmy was the jock and aspiring track coach. Tim was an intellectual with his degree in environmental studies. Brad was a hippie with long hair and a beard. Denny was a Republican; we used to call him "designer Denny" because he was such a sharp dresser.

And I had to get them all to like one another! This was no simple task. The picnic did it. In later years, whenever I had two coworkers who either didn't like each other or who tended to disagree, I threw them together in social situations, just as I did our very first partners. If they got to know each other better, they would in all likelihood work their differences out on their own. I counted on it. There was something about getting together and letting loose that both attracted people to Kinko's and each other and inspired everyone involved.

David Vogias wasn't too sure about Kinko's when he first came to work with us. Dave's wife worked at our first location in Isla Vista and she told Dave that we were expanding pretty quickly. Dave became a partner after he and I went sailing to negotiate our partnership arrangement (and nearly crashed into a breakwater). Not long after, he came to one of our first picnics, sporting long hair and beard.

Dave: "I walked into the park and I could smell the meat cooking. I saw a lot of dogs and Frisbees. I had never had tri-tip steak before. Tri-tip [part of the sirloin] at the picnic is the food that bonded Kinko's together for years. There was a bluegrass band playing. I thought, 'I can do this.'" Not long after, Dave headed east to open our first location in Ohio, his home state.

"I loaded my things into a U-Haul. Paul gave me four sets of pricing signs. He said, 'On your way home, you should drop these off at some other stores and see what they look like.' Paul had already negotiated a lease for our new location. We each put in $2,500. My $2,500 was a loan from a local bank, backed by the same amount of money in my savings account. I started with the one store in Kent." Dave would go on to open more than 50 stores in Ohio, Florida, New

Jersey, New York, and Pennsylvania. It's amazing what a little blue-grass and tri-tip can get started.

I believed so deeply in the power of the picnic that I insisted people come even if they had to go to great trouble to do so. In 1979, I called up one of our managers, Jay Richardson, who had just opened a store in Provo, Utah. As Jay remembers it, I told him, "You are required to come to this picnic." Jay had a company truck at the time and he drove it for 14 hours—without air conditioning, cruise control, or even a bottle of water—across the Mojave Desert. He hung his head out the window in a vain attempt to cool himself down. When he got to California, baked as the beans we were serv-ing, he pulled up to a house where a bunch of us were gathered. Our office manager, Dottie Ault, ran out to greet him like his long-lost grandmother. Jay recalls, "It was like being in a family reunion where you don't know anybody and you're supposed to know everybody, so you sit there with a big smile on your face. I thought this was just a summer job, but I became a member of Paul's family right then."

As a member of the Church of Jesus Christ of Latter-day Saints (the Mormons), he was one of the few sober coworkers that week-end. It didn't stop him from jumping off the motel balcony and into the swimming pool—repeatedly. "It was a peer pressure thing," Jay recalls, laughing. "I would not do that now, ever." Jay drove back across the Mojave Desert—again without air conditioning—vowing to never come to another picnic. Over the next two decades, he became a partner and didn't miss one. Nor did his wife or four chil-dren. "I decided that this is the kind of culture I would like to be involved in for the long run," Jay says.

The Bathing Suit Factor

In its later years, the picnic stretched over four days, included meet-ings, trainings, and annual planning exercises, and was held in places like Florida, North Carolina, or Hawaii. By then, thousands of newer coworkers were being drawn under the picnic's crazy spell. The picnic broke the ice for new people while giving the old guard a chance to reconnect with one another and meet the newcomers. Blaise Simqu was one. He came from the publishing industry to work with us at Kinko's in 1991. His first day at work was a Monday and when he got to the office, someone handed him a plane ticket to fly out to Lake of the Ozarks in Missouri that weekend. When he arrived, Blaise had a flash of insecurity.

"One night," he says, "I go down to the lake. I was drinking a beer and sitting on a rock. I'm watching all these people out on the shore laughing and pushing each other in the water. It turned out to be Brad and Stuie Krause, Karen and Mark Madden, and Craig Redwine. All the old guard at Kinko's. They were like a rock band that had never broken up. I looked at that and thought, oh my God, what have I done? I can never break into this group. These guys are a bunch of ex-hippies and I was a suit. I was not a guy who would have worked at a copy shop and moved up. But what was amazing was how they really took me in. I ended up breaking into that group *easily*."

> **His first day at work someone handed him a plane ticket to Lake of the Ozarks.**

No one was too senior or too new to jump in together. At one point during most picnics every year, somebody started chucking water balloons at everybody else. I didn't hold back. Wham! I'd deliver a zinger into the backside of one of my coworkers. Splat! Splat! Wham! Coworkers would get me back and good. Dave Bolton, then our regional manager in the Bay Area, said, "Watching the owner of the company out there throwing water at people, and getting hit, it was just fun to see."

Mark Madden and I first met at the picnic. At the time, Mark was a store manager in DeKalb, Illinois. I don't precisely remember the moment we met since I was talking to a dozen people at once. But Mark remembers jumping on board a bus filled with a bunch of people about to drive to another event at the picnic. "Paul was standing there shaking hands with everybody," Mark says. "I remember having a beer in my hand and he looked down and went, '*Beer*.' And I thought, 'Oh no, I've blown it. I shouldn't be bringing beer on the bus.' But Paul looked at me and said, 'That's a great idea. Why don't you guys get a case, so that everybody has enough beer.' And that was pretty much my introduction to him."

Probably each of our former coworkers has a theory about what made the culture at Kinko's unique. I like the one that Blaise came up with. In 1996, when we began what would be a long process of selling Kinko's (much more on this later), many of our coworkers left the company. Blaise returned to a more traditional work environment, to a place where people go home after work without knowing much about one another. They live in their separate worlds. There isn't much conflict but, then, there isn't as much passion either.

"Looking back," Blaise said, "I have wondered over the years why it was so possible at Kinko's to communicate so much with each other, to fight and argue and still work together. I have concluded that it comes down to the Bathing Suit Factor. This means that, at one time or another, everybody at Kinko's had seen each other in a bathing suit, no matter what you looked like or if you were comfortable about it. Paul made all of us part of his family and forced us to spend so much time with each other. There was this tremendous barrier-breaking undercurrent in the culture."

Good Gossip

One of the best things about Kinko's is that we created an open society. This stems from the fact that I'm genuinely interested in all the details of our coworkers' lives. I find people, in general, endlessly fascinating and I've never believed there are really any secrets in life, anyway. In other sectors of the economy, like government defense work, this may not be so, but in retail there really are very few secrets. Ninety percent of what we were and what we did at Kinko's was obvious to customers, coworkers, and competitors alike the minute they walked in the front door. This fact further encouraged the sort of openness demanded by a democratic organizational structure. Socializing and celebrating together helped, too.

I talked to coworkers wherever I went, whenever I could, whether I was traveling store to store or meeting them at the annual picnic.

At the picnic, I spent hours greeting every single person—thousands of them—in person and handing out Kinko's baseball caps or T-shirts (some years we printed the Kinko's logo or a slogan on improbable items like rolls of toilet paper or pillow cases). I got this habit from my parents. Lebanese people are nutty about hospitality and greeting people.

"Paul wanted every possible need anticipated for his guests," says Karen Madden. "He wanted this multiday extravaganza and he spared no expense. I remember once we had an accountant who looked at the bill for the picnic and said, 'What *is* this and why does it cost so much?' If somebody suggested starting breakfast at 7 A.M. instead of 6 A.M., Paul would read him the riot act and say, 'Don't you have any feeling for people on the East Coast? They will be hungry!' And woe to the partner who did not personally turn up to greet his or her coworkers."

I did expect all the leaders at Kinko's to put themselves out during the picnic. After each one, I was so exhausted myself that I could scarcely open my mouth. I spent a couple days zoning out in front of the TV afterward. But talking to that many people gave me a chance to ask them about their lives, their experiences with their managers and customers. I'd start by walking around and asking people, "What can we do to make your life easier." The answers might incorporate love, work, or health care. I remember one time a coworker told me he couldn't find any doctors who were part of our health plan, so I asked our HR department to make up a list of approved doctors.

This was exactly the kind of information I was after. I wanted to hear the complaints. Often a coworker would stop himself in midsentence and say, "I might get in trouble if I tell you about this." That drove me crazy! I never let a coworker get away with that excuse. Not only did I want to know, I needed to know. Getting people to talk, to me and to one another, was a big part of my job.

I needed to know what they had to say because, ultimately, *my* money was on the line. I was an owner or part owner in each of these stores and I wanted to know what was happening inside of them. The laid-back environment of the picnic helped. Our coworkers were so distracted they might not have realized I wasn't just talking with them, I was watching them, too. I paid attention to the way managers or partners spoke about their coworkers. After they'd had a couple of drinks, I could pick out the ones who were domineering or mean or arbitrary. You really had no choice but to reveal your true nature in an environment like the picnic. Once a year, I got a chance to pick out the bad apples.

I've observed that corporate executives—those who take a salary but don't have a stake in their enterprises—like to be lied to. It makes them feel comfortable. Country club types like to be deluded into thinking that everything runs as smoothly as the table service at their favorite restaurant. They don't want to know about the problems. It might upset them. They are more interested in managing their careers than their companies. But if it's your own money on the line, you have a completely different attitude—you want to find out all the dirt. You don't want to be spared the gory details.

> **You really had no choice but to reveal your true nature at the picnic.**

My father knew that if salespeople weren't constantly aggravating him—about keeping the inventory stocks high or advertising—they weren't doing their jobs. Dad used to say that "a good salesperson will sell you broke." He meant that if your salespeople aren't complaining and pushing, you've got problems. They are the eyes and ears of the company. Ask yourself: How much do you really know about what is happening at the farthest reaches of your company or even your family? It was my job not only to praise people at Kinko's but to challenge them and get upset as often as was necessary.

Our partners picked up on this ethos and encouraged communication throughout their companies as well. In Las Vegas, every time Gerry Alesia's store trained a new crop of coworkers, he made the point of spending an hour with the new hires and urging them to come and talk with him about any of their difficulties or complaints. At first, he could tell they didn't believe a word he was saying. It wasn't the sort of thing they were accustomed to hearing in a corporate training environment. Later, after they got to know Gerry and Kinko's, they began to see they really could come and talk with him about issues arising in the workplace. "Then we'd have the opposite problem," Gerry recalls. "Lots of people would come and bring in problems that could have been solved better elsewhere." But all that communication generated a surfeit of trust and loyalty.

Picnicking the Partnerships

The zaniness of the picnic rubbed off elsewhere. Mark Madden once hosted a party for everyone who worked for Kinko's Graphics. Somebody decided to tape together 10 or 15 Twister games and everybody played mega-Twister together until three in the morning. At every partner meeting, we always threw a dance on at least one of the nights. Dana Jennings, our partner in North Carolina: "We'd take over the dance floor and just get crazy."

For the longest time, in many stores, coworkers brought their dogs to work. When we opened Kinko's stores in Manhattan, each of them had its own "house cat." Gerry in Las Vegas held a Fourth of July party every year for all of his coworkers as well as a Christmas party. "People brought their kids. I think it helped in the long run in terms of turnover." Because we attracted so many students as coworkers, average turnover at many stores was six months to a year. Anything we could do to raise that average helped. In the Bay Area, our coworkers played softball in local leagues together. From partnership to partnership, we acknowledged not only our coworkers but their families because spouses, kids, and other family members made sacrifices that contributed to each breadwinner's success. In North Carolina, Dana hosted large holiday meals and toasted the coworkers' spouses. At the head office, people played volleyball and softball together. It was an athletic culture. There were runners. There were volleyball players. We held annual 5-K runs.

Karen, who helped organize many of the picnics, doesn't think we had so much balanced our lives between work, love, and play—

our stated goal in the Philosophy— as we had completely blurred the lines between those three areas. "Most of us were in our twenties or younger when we started working together, so we really grew up together," Karen says. It was easier working long hours, knowing your work and your social life were one and the same.

Dan Frederickson, our company president from 1986 until 1998, was not exempt from this rule. Dan sang in a rock group called the Super Session Band (a confederation of former members of bands Dan played with in the sixties and seventies). Even though Dan came to work with us from the more straight-laced culture at Xerox, where he was a financial executive for the western United States, he cut loose at Kinko's. He fronted his band and sang at many of the picnics. Everyone loved watching the company president up there on the stage. Throughout some of the later picnics, a group of coworkers filmed all the festivities. They pulled an all-nighter the last night, putting together a video that was shown to everybody the final evening of the event. It was like a movie premiere. Coworkers arrived as much as two hours before the screening to get the best seats.

We always held a costume party at the picnic. My mosquito costume was my personal favorite. My gorilla costume was a close second. There was the Tacky Tourist dance, the Hollywood dance where everyone came dressed as a star (Natalie and I turned up as Scarlett O'Hara and Rhett Butler), and the Adult Prom. Karen met her husband, Mark, at that dance. They're married now and have two children.

Like a lot of people at Kinko's, Karen dated people she worked with. Before meeting Mark, she dated one of our regional managers, Charley Williams. Later, she dated our philosopher-in-chief John Davis. Her whole love life was at Kinko's. We all went to Karen and Mark's wedding. So many people from so many parts of the state and the country slept at their place afterwards that Karen ended up sleeping on the floor. It may not have been the most romantic of wedding nights for a bride, but it was a memorable one.

Chief Executive Mascot

A t the picnic and elsewhere, being the company founder didn't spare me from becoming the butt of jokes. I was the company mascot, as well. One time on a ski trip with a bunch of my partners and their spouses, Brad Krause's wife, Stuie, snuck into my bedroom and sewed all the flaps on my underwear closed. The next day we were all having a drink together.

Tim Stancliffe: "Paul goes off to the restroom and he comes out and he looks like he's seen a ghost. He turns to Stuie and says, 'Boy, I've got to stop drinking. I put my underwear on backwards for the first time in 35 years.' Everyone went ballistic. We were just cracking up. Paul goes to the fireplace and drops his drawers and says, 'Hey, somebody sewed them shut!' We were all laughing so hard that the group in the condo next to us knocked on our door and invited us to a party because they thought we were having more fun than they were."

Our earliest partner meetings were not formal affairs by any stretch of the imagination. Did you know that 80 percent of what people learn at conferences they pick up during the breaks? Knowing this, we built in a lot of playtime. In the late seventies and early eighties, I still had only a handful of partners. When I felt we needed to get together to talk things over, I sometimes called them up and we all flew to Colorado or Utah to ski together. These meetings were never particularly organized. We sat around in the evenings and talked about business and how we could grow the company. We usually had an agenda to get through.

Dave: Vogias "We would go into a room. We would throw on the floor of the condo all these 8½ by 11 sheets of our potential ads. Someone would say, 'I can't deal with that one,' and another would say, 'I really like this one.' We would party and go out to dinner. After a full day of skiing and work, Paul would burn out. He'd go out to his car to sleep. It was winter and freezing and he'd be in his parka. He was like a firecracker. Boom, his energy would crash and he'd be out."

Todd: "This was only the first or second time I'd been skiing. One time, we were all waiting at the bottom of the slope and, all of a sudden, I see this guy skiing down the hill toward us. It was Paul. He had a beat-up gray jumpsuit on, with duct tape over a couple of rips. You know how when you ski, you're supposed to crouch down? Paul skied almost straight-legged. He didn't turn back and forth at all. He didn't look coordinated at all, either. He just came straight down the hill. When, he got to the bottom, he ground to a halt and said, 'Whoa! That was exhilarating.'"

In later years, we formalized our partners meetings and the ski trips were replaced by more conventional gatherings. But even when we weren't out in parks for picnics or on ski slopes, we tried to bring that spirit of fun—mixed in with plenty of debate—into the meeting rooms. Without a little fun or debate, I could never bear sitting through them.

Embrace the Defect

If you're going to enjoy the picnic that life really is, you'd better learn to like yourself, not despite your flaws and so-called deficits, but because of them. As a dyslexic, I've truly embraced this concept. The picnic was a place where all of us at Kinko's got to be ourselves, to show our goofy, flawed, human sides, and to learn we could like and work with one another despite—or even because—of them.

My college friend Tim LaBrucherie—who first called me Kinko—helped teach me this lesson. If you drive out to the somewhat remote town of El Centro, California, near the Mexican border, and swing by Tim's office, you'll meet the one person on the planet who still insists on calling me Kinko. Here, he runs a farming company that grows lettuce and carrots in the Imperial Valley. Tim had his own nickname: Zodo. Back in the seventies, there was a serial murderer known as the Zodiac Killer because of the enigmatic astrological clues he left for police. Tim's dark sense of humor earned him the name.

In college, Zodo surrounded himself with a group of friends who were even more oddball than he was. There was Treadface. He had survived a car wreck and looked it. One of Pixiehand's hands was slightly smaller than the other. Noodlearm had a shriveled arm from a polio vaccine gone bad and a metal plate in one side of his head from an accident. Craterface had acne. Brute looked like the comic strip character of the same name.

One time, Zodo and Noodlearm were out drinking together when Noodlearm started complaining that no girl at USC would date him. Soon enough, he started sounding positively suicidal.

"But, Noodlearm," Zodo said. "You've got the noodle arm on the left side and a steel plate on the right." Zodo crossed an imaginary gun in his right hand over to point it awkwardly at his left temple. "To shoot yourself, you'd have to go like this."

The two of them cracked up. So, those were my friends. The truth is we bonded over our so-called defects. Instead of hiding them, we flaunted them. These guys took their obvious imperfections and made humor out of them. Humor may be a mask for pain, but it is also a means of transcending it. They taught me that embracing your so-called defects is a constructive thing. It can be a source of strength.

> **We all want to get back to when we were little kids.**

At Kinko's we underwent the same sort of bonding by partying together and watching each other behave like goof-offs, by wearing bathing suits together no matter how we looked, and by generally letting down our guards with each other. The only things we took seriously were taking care of our coworkers, paying our bills, and the work we performed for customers. We did not build a culture based on the pursuit of perfection or trying to one-up each other. We tried to make work fun. Lately I've been inspired watching Pete Carroll, the football coach at USC. He's a top coach, the best. And he's constantly pulling funny pranks on his players. He makes football fun. No wonder his team wins so much.

You see, you've got to have balance in your life—or try to—or what's the point? Even if people act as though they don't want to giggle and laugh a lot in life, even if they act like they want to be serious all of the time, somewhere down inside of them, it's just not true. We all want to get back to the way we used to be when we were little kids. A lot of people don't believe me when they hear me say that I'm just not interested in power. But, in the deepest sense, I'm really not. Power to me means having to do a lot of work. I believe in getting out of as much work as I possibly can. When you're not stuck working 12 hours a day, you've got time left over to goof around, to think creatively, to get to know the people next to you and, eventually, you'll be back "on" your business instead of "in" it.

My parents, Virginia and Al Orfalea, cared far more about my savings than about my grades.

My brother, Dick, and sister, Marlene, teased me mercilessly.

Bucking convention, as usual, at Knott's Berry Farm in 1954.

Here I am in full kinkitude, during my USC years.

Exterior shot of first Kinko's in Isla Vista, California, 1970.

Me, with early Kinkoids in front of bus. Future head of Kinko's Northwest, Brad Krause, top left; bottom right, Craig Redwine, future partner in Arcada and Eureka, California.

Early ads.

Me and Dan Tevrizian at my wedding, 1984.

To Paul Orfalea
With best wishes, *Gy Bush*

Receiving an award from President George H. Bush for outstanding accomplishment for "a learning-challenged citizen."

Here I am with Dan Frederickson, handing out hats at one of our annual picnics.

*Xerox sand sculpture
at the picnic in 1995.*

Me, Natalie, Mason, and Keenan at a family wedding.

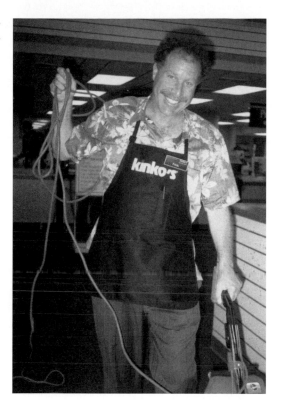

Filling in for the winners of the annual Best Ideas contest.

With original Kinko's partners, Brad Krause, Dennis Itule, Jimmy Warren, and Tim Stancliffe at the 25th anniversary picnic, with a reproduction of the original Kinko's behind us.

Here I am, "repurposing" with kids at the Cuesta Community College Day Care Center in San Luis Obispo, California.

My wife and soulmate, Natalie.

Chapter 8

Deal with

Your Dark Side

B Y NOW, YOU'D HAVE TO BE AS BAD A READER AS I AM not to figure out that I have a dark side. You rarely hear people talk about their dark sides, especially business leaders, which is a shame because successful businesses aren't usually started by laid-back personalities. I don't hide the fact that I have a problem with anger. Aside from happiness, anger was the chief feeling we expressed at home when I was a kid. (My wife thinks the only emotion I ever knew was anger.) The teasing in our house often got out of hand, and since I was the baby of the family I took the brunt of it. I don't ever remember receiving any nurturing from either of my siblings. As my brother, Dickie, put it recently, "We didn't give Paul a very good sense of himself." He and Marlene teased me relentlessly.

For years, they told me mom and dad's real son had died and that they went to a zoo and got a monkey to replace him, and the monkey was me. To the tune of the theme song of *The Mickey Mouse Club,* they serenaded me with "M–O–N–K–E–Y—Why? Because he's a monkey! C–H–I–L–D—monkey-child, monkey-child. . . ." We laugh about it today, but there was a time when I believed them.

To make things much, much worse, I was kidnapped for a day and sexually molested by a neighbor a few years older than me when I was 14. He was jailed for the crime and I made the conscious choice to forgive him, but it's possible that I have suppressed a good deal of anger over this experience. For many of our coworkers and partners who've had to deal with my occasional outbursts of wrath, it's been the chief price they've paid for all the good that came with helping to build Kinko's. I'm not proud of these outbursts. I apologize to all my coworkers and partners who had to deal with the worst of my anger.

You can manage people with the velvet glove or the iron fist, and occasionally you need both. I think I overdid the iron fist. John Davis once observed that I was under such pressure at Kinko's, especially in the later years, that I never got the credit I deserved for keeping myself in check as much as I did. It was a daily struggle. I fought my emotions. Someone once told me that the only true victories in life are victories over ourselves. I think that's true. My suggestion is: Fight your emotions. Don't let them rule you. I let my anger rule me too often at Kinko's and at home.

The only true victories in life are victories over ourselves.

In my family, anger wasn't simply a sign of dysfunction, but part and parcel of all the love. I'm not trying to romanticize dysfunction. I just wasn't raised to keep my feelings to myself. We understood, in my family, that you could express yourself to your offspring, siblings, cousins, or parents and know that doing so didn't mean anyone was going to up and leave. We were stuck with each other. If we weren't exactly gentle with one another, we also didn't leave anyone guessing as to our true feelings. I felt I owed nothing less to our partners at Kinko's. They never had to wonder what I thought about them. And they knew that, when I did lose my cool, it was almost always in defense of one of the cornerstone principles on which our business was built or in defense of our frontline coworkers. Like the time I caught two of our senior partners flying first-class to a picnic while all their coworkers flew behind them in coach. That hit a 10 on the Richter scale of my anger, and I let them have it.

On a regular basis, my mother would blow the roof off the house. My brother, Dickie, tells a story about once when we kids aggravated her so much that, like a provoked Greek goddess, she bellowed at us from the top of the stairs and tore her own dress in a rage! Mom suffered from a nervous breakdown when we were young. She recovered, but her temper, of course, did too. Mom could say such funny things when she was angry that Dickie, Marlene, and I used to provoke her just to get a reaction. If she was angry about something, all I had to do to wind her up was to say, "Mom, how do you *really* feel?" She would explode until something in her tirade struck us as funny and we'd laugh. Eventually, she'd laugh, too. The flip side of Mom's personality is that she was widely acknowledged to be among the most caring of people, a tireless hostess, and a great friend. The same description might be applied to me, too. I have my mother's nervous system. She couldn't handle stress well, and neither could I.

It's clear that I carried into adulthood a potent mix of strong emotion: a huge capacity for rage blended with a strong sense of compassion for everyone from people I met on the street to the neighbor who molested me. Though he didn't know all of my history, Mark Madden knew about my problem with anger when he came to work with me directly. At my request, Mark moved to California from Missouri in 1988 to become our vice president of operations at Kinko's Graphics Corp. Six months later, Jimmy Warren and I set out to convince Mark to become president of KGC. For a long time, Jimmy had been pulling double duty, trying to run KGC and his own company in the South. It was too much for one person. The three of us went out to breakfast at a hotel in Santa Barbara.

As Mark remembers it, "Paul was saying, 'You tell him, Jimmy.' And Jim would say, 'No, you tell him, Paul.' And back and forth. Finally Paul said, 'Jimmy's going to run his own company and I want you to run mine.' Paul's company was probably a $50 or a $60 million company at the time. I was 31. I said OK.

"Then I started thinking, 'This is just bizarre,'" Mark recalls. "I looked at Paul and said, 'Hey, man, aren't you going to ask me any *questions?*' It felt weird that he was saying, 'You're the man.' And he said, 'Yeah, yeah buddy, I should ask you a question.' He said, 'Can you make a quick decision?' I said, 'Yes, I can. I just want you to know they're not always going to be right.' He said, 'Yeah, do you learn from your mistakes?' I said, 'I don't make the same mistake twice.'

Then he asked if I was a 'budget guy.' I said, 'Hell, no. I hate budgets.' Then I asked Paul to explain his management style. He really had to think about that one a lot. Finally he said, 'I tell you what, if I yell at you for an hour a day, it means I love you the other 23.' And there were days when he did yell at me for an hour a day."

Mark put up with it because the other 23 hours were pretty good. Warts and all, Mark and I worked so well together that he soon took on another job title. "The next thing you know," he says, "I'm 32 and in Tokyo and I've got all these older guys bowing to me because I'm the president of Kinko's Japan."

> **If I yell at you for an hour a day, it means I love you the other 23.**

The truth is that Kinko's grew as rapidly as it did in good part because I did blow my top regularly, especially during our years of exponential growth. I worked with a lot of great people, a lot of nice people. The downside to this was that some of my largest partners, in my opinion, were too busy trying to make sure everyone liked them. I often felt I was the only leader at Kinko's who was willing to be the bad cop when we needed to make changes.

I never felt people were candid enough at Kinko's. Looking back I wish I had emphasized candor more. For all the debate in our culture, I still felt our partners and coworkers avoided confrontation. There's a great quote from *In Search of Excellence,* the business management classic my professors at Harvard Business School constantly referred me to. (I didn't read it all the way through, but my coauthor did!) It gets to the heart of my paranoia on this subject:

> Chronic use of the military metaphor leads people repeatedly to overlook a different kind of organization, one that values improvisation rather than forecasting, dwells on opportunities rather than restraints, discovers new actions rather than defends past actions, *values arguments more highly than serenity and encourages doubt and contradiction rather than belief.* (emphasis mine)

In the early years, you could say I even "outsourced" some of my temper to our first office manager, Dottie Ault. Each of my partners in the seventies and eighties was expected to file a "daily" back to the head office so we could have an accounting of each day's revenue. Dottie looked them over. She'd call up all our partners and holler at them for small accounting errors or other foul-ups. She yelled at me, too, when the mood seized her. She kept all of us in line.

As David Vogias recalls, "Dottie was a very abrupt, rude person but I liked her a lot. She'd call me and say, 'What are you, *stupid?*' That kind of gruffness doesn't bother me a lot, but it's not always the best way to get your point across." Our partner Todd Johnson used to set the phone down on the counter and take care of customers so Dottie could scream at him to her heart's content. He'd pick the receiver back up when she was through. The truth is I may have kept Dottie at Kinko's longer than I should have, even though my own volatility, I admit, set the tone. But for many years, we needed her full-throttle temper on our side. After she retired, we brought in one of our partners, Ken Hightower, as our first president. I unloaded on our partners to keep them moving and innovating. After 1982, I never unloaded on my frontline coworkers. One time that year, Ken and Jim Warren watched me explode in a store in Washington, D.C., where the carpet was so filthy I could smell it. They told me to never, ever lose my cool in front of our coworkers in a store again. They also convinced me to curb the overwhelming urges I had to rearrange stores myself, on the spot, seconds after I walked in the front door. I managed to tone down my behavior in the stores, though it's always been difficult for me to be calculating about my rage. When I was angry, I couldn't easily contain myself. One of our partners used to call me "Hurricane Paul." The dark side of our partners—their own fears and preoccupation with minutiae—inclined some of them to slack off from time to time. I understood this. We all needed a fire lit under us.

Preaching But Not Practicing

Because of the structure of Kinko's, a fire constantly, constantly burned beneath me. It drove me crazy that it was increasingly difficult for me to really stay "on" the business. Of all people, I understood the importance of doing so, but increasingly I was getting dragged down into the sort of repetitive busywork for which I was especially unsuited. I also no longer had the time to debate everything with everybody. This no doubt only contributed to my struggle with anger. By the time the nineties rolled around, we had well over 100 partnerships (when we sold the company, there were 127 in all, including my own). Everything in each of our businesses was guaranteed with personal signatures. I personally was on the hook, as were many of our partners like Jim Warren, for every Xerox machine and lease guarantee in the entire business. If Kinko's took a dive —as it nearly did at several junctures in its rapid, stepladder-like growth—I stood to lose everything. By 1990, when we had about 450 stores, I remember running the numbers and discovering that my liability was many times greater than my net worth. So, for many years there, despite the motivational pep talks I delivered at company meetings, I was literally running scared.

I wasn't only scared that my family could lose the roof over its head. I was also scared for the people who worked with us. By the mid-nineties, we had more than 20,000 coworkers around the world. That's a huge number of souls to look after. I've never understood why the president of IBM or some other big company takes time to sit on the board of a charity like Easter Seals. Doesn't he understand there's plenty of charitable work to be done back in his own office? I didn't give much to charity when I was at Kinko's. I figured I had more pressing charitable work to attend to. This is why I got so worked up over profit sharing and benefits like daycare, scholarships, orthodontia coverage, contributions to first-time home purchases, and pensions. I fought for them. I didn't only pressure our coworkers to institute them, I pushed our suppliers, too, to contribute to causes like our subsidized daycare center.

For the longest time I didn't drive a new car. I couldn't; I didn't feel secure enough. I used to visit our partners and goggle over the fancy cars they bought themselves. I visited one partner who took me for a ride in her new Jaguar. As she was explaining to me that she needed it to visit all her different stores, she suddenly lost her way to a location. Clearly she wasn't making the rounds as much as she claimed. It was all a bunch of B.S. to justify her excess. This drove me crazy! Weren't my partners concerned about their futures? Weren't they saving money for their retirements? I've always believed in savings. It was one of the first lessons I learned from my family. All of a sudden, I felt responsible for an uncomfortably large number of lives.

After a time, these fears wore me down. In my mid- to late-forties, I struggled increasingly to manage my own emotional nature. Sometimes I felt I'd created a monster. The monster wasn't Kinko's, it was me. After I retired, I started taking Prozac and, believe me, it's a much more pleasant experience living in my own skin. It's much more pleasant for the people around me, too. I sometimes wonder what it would have been like if I had started taking Prozac while I was still with Kinko's. Back then (I refer to this era as "P.P." [pre-Prozac]), I didn't take the time to find out. In the P.P. days, when I got a partner on the line who just wasn't innovating, expanding, or

> **I didn't have the time to ask nicely for changes.**

performing as quickly as I believed he or she should, I didn't have the time to ask nicely for changes. I got personal. One time I called my cousin Rose Orfalea, who's like an aunt to me. She and my cousin Aref, her husband, were partners in several Kinko's locations in California's San Fernando Valley. When she resisted one of my suggestions, I told her, "Listen, Rose, God hates a coward."

Rose: "That got my dander up. I was on the verge of tears. I said, 'Don't you ever call me a coward again.' That night Paul called me back and said, 'I want to apologize for what I said to you. I didn't mean that. I have no right to say that to you.'"

Rose stood up for herself, which is something I've always admired. I sent her a bouquet of flowers.

Dave Vogias, my partner based in Ohio, recalls that I used to give him a hard time about one of his coworkers. His books were completely out of line. Dave says, "Paul would call up and say, 'He's stealing from us.' I was like, 'Dude, what are you talking about?' He would call me up and rip me a new one. I couldn't deal with it. I finally realized that, with Paul, you couldn't listen to or respond to everything he said. I used to say, 'You know what, Paul, I'm going to have to get back to you.' I used my 24-hour rule before returning that call."

I'll let Dave tell you an ugly story:

"In the prime of my Kinko's life, in 1992, in September, I was in the hospital. I'd been diagnosed with leukemia. I'd already written out all my read-upon-my-death letters to my kids and gone through massive doses of chemotherapy to wipe out my bone marrow. I had no bone marrow left in my body. I was left totally without an immune system and any sort of infection would have killed me. I get this phone call from Paul and he says, 'What about these P&Ls? What's the problem with them?' He just gets on me. He's the god-father of my daughter. He's the lead trustee on my living trust. I just knew Paul didn't know what to say. He's a rhinoceros. I just said, 'Paul, I'm going to have to get back to you on that.'"

I regret that conversation, but I also think Dave was much far-ther along in his recovery than he recalls. (Dave: "Not true. That was the precise moment when I was going to live or die. But the cool thing was he did call and I knew that he cared.") For all our arguments, Dave was a contender for the title of Most Outspoken Partner. He ran his business his own way, no matter what I thought or said to him or how much I threatened. Though I still don't agree with him on every aspect of running a business, I have great respect for Dave. As with all my relationships, ours is a complex one.

As Dave says, "The most difficult thing about being in a relation-ship with Paul is Paul. Given the fact that he was the glue that held us all together, that he was the common partner to all of us, it was some-times hard for Paul not to be self-absorbed or single-minded. He had so many responsibilities."

Our philosopher-in-chief, John Davis, puts it this way, "Paul was a lot like Lyndon Johnson. He argued principles, but he also made deals. He was good at using coercion when he needed to. He knew how to twist arms. He was tough on people when he wanted them to cooperate."

Charlie Wright: "The flip side to all the trust that Paul invests in you is that if you don't follow through, the shit's going to hit the fan."

War and Peace

If there was one person, and one relationship at Kinko's that I struggled with the most, it was with Dan Frederickson, who succeeded Ken Hightower as president after Ken returned to his previous job as a partner. Dan went on to lead Kinko's during its period of most furious growth. Dan and I escalated from conflict to a deep-seated bitterness before we worked things out. Not incidentally, over the course of that time, we sold Kinko's to outsiders. My wife, Natalie, had known Dan when she worked with him at Xerox. She knew I was looking for a new president in the mid-eighties and suggested him. Dan had been at Xerox for 14 years. When he made the switch, he was in a senior financial position in their West Coast operation, overseeing Xerox's relationship with Kinko's. Eventually, Dan came to run Kinko's Service Corporation, Kinko's Financial Services, our in-house bank, as well as Kinko's Graphic Corporation. He also helped develop our international division and managed 13 of his own stores in Missouri. It was a lot for one person. Long before he took on all those responsibilities, when Dan became president in 1986, he thought Kinko's was "a friggin' mess." We had about 140 stores at the time and had formed a board only two years earlier. My company, KGC, was still handling many financial duties for the partners. Dan had his work cut out for him.

> "Paul was an ex-hippie and I was an ex-marine."

As Dan puts it, "Paul was an ex-hippie and I was an ex-marine, Vietnam vet. That should give you some sense of the tension between us. At the same time, we were a little bit alike. Paul grew up dyslexic and I was a fat kid. We'd both had to overcome challenges. We were both used to trying harder than most people. There was this kinship between us. He and I were always more comfortable with the working class than with the New York elites."

Talk about passion. Working together—fighting, mending fences, and fighting some more—Dan and I forged a partnership that grew Kinko's from a couple of hundred locations to more than 800 in just over a decade. As Dan puts it, "When we got going, we were a machine. We were a damn machine."

At the same time, we were like a bitter married couple who managed to raise a huge number of kids, but at the expense of their mutual sanity. Kinko's was just getting to the point where the individualistic look and structure of our different stores wasn't serving us well anymore. We needed a uniform look. We had very little in the way of standardization from store to store. When it comes to managing ambiguity, this presented a big challenge. On the one hand, I cherished the democracy we'd built; I did not like dictating anything to our coworkers. On the other hand, I was absolutely convinced we needed to come together and start acting and looking like one company. Dan felt the same way.

His challenge as president was to logistically bring all our disparate partners together. It was like herding cats. With my tendency to cause disruption, he didn't always feel I helped the cause. While he knew what he had to do, the very structure of the company made his task extraordinarily difficult. I was constantly trolling in the field and managing from the fringes. Dan felt this hampered him. Kinko's had two parents, two kings, in the era of its fastest growth. Dan saw the company structure in his own way.

As he puts it, "It was like a feudal dukedom. Paul was king. The four largest partners—Brad, Jim, Denny, and Tim—were the dukes. And I was the tax collector."

I needed Dan to take on the day-to-day details of running the company. I couldn't do that myself. To help the company grow faster, for example, Dan brought in two of his former colleagues from Xerox, JoAnne Robin and Edd Hoyes, to help run the financial side of the business. That was a great success; they were *great* people. Otherwise, Dan and I struggled to mesh our different styles and practices. Dan was a professional manager and a real diplomat. He has the ability to convey respect even when he disagrees entirely with another person's point of view. He could barely tolerate my outbursts and the rapid-fire way in which I tended to change my mind.

As Dan recalls, "I would take him out of a meeting and sit him down like a kid and say, 'Paul, you're a bully.' Then he would get apologetic. I would tell him it would have been helpful if he had ever had a job working for somebody else."

That made an impact on me. For the first time in my life I started to see that perhaps I'd missed out by not being able to work for anybody else. It isn't pretty, but I'll let Dan tell you his side of the story.

Dan: "Paul could be abusive. He's immature. He could be hostile. But he could flip that and be phenomenally gracious. He would create chaos. There was constant turmoil in the organization. You never knew what was expected of you. Paul's extremely difficult to work with because everything is so personal. It was very hard on me, especially in the long run. Some of the partners thought the most important thing in the world was to manage him. You look at the stress I put myself through personally. I definitely would have taken the job, but I would have gotten out earlier. As for the company, it was a very in-your-face culture. The partners were very independent. They felt they owned the business and no one could tell them what to do."

We weren't Xerox, that's for sure.

We weren't Xerox, that's for sure.

By the mid-nineties, by the time we'd begun taking steps to sell Kinko's, relations between Dan and me had disintegrated badly. For many years, John Davis had done his best to help us work together and manage our relationship. But he finally called up a psychiatrist named Pierre Mornell who was known for working with, as Pierre puts it, "difficult personalities."

When Pierre came to Santa Barbara, we had an initial meeting, which quickly disintegrated into a fight. Dan says, "Paul was attacking me like he'd never attacked me before. I remember being horrified. I was blindsided. It was like being in a marriage and finding out that somebody you'd lived with for five years didn't like you. Afterwards Pierre and I went for a walk. I said, 'I feel like I'm in an insane asylum.'"

Pierre liked us both, but pegged us an "odd couple." For more than two years he worked with us. Typically, we met separately and took advantage of the time to vent.

As Pierre remembers it, "They were very full sponges. They needed to get angry. They'd just unload."

Pierre urged me to be less capricious and urged Dan to speak up for himself more. We had only modest success with this strategy. After we sold Kinko's, the feelings were so strained that Dan and I didn't talk for nearly two years. It took the efforts of Dan's wife, CiCie Frederickson, to talk him into reconciling with me. CiCie is my closest long-time colleague and confidant. She runs my personal finances, but has the more difficult task of generally managing *me.* Talk about shuttle diplomacy. CiCie was in a very difficult position there for a number of years. She probably did more to hold Kinko's together at that time than anyone else, Dan and myself included.

Dan remembers that "Paul was phenomenally apologetic." The funny thing about Dan and me is that, after all these years, and after so much strife, we're very close to each other again today. Dan is a Christian and he made the choice to forgive me. We still work with each other. We share an office in Ventura, California, so we see each other regularly. We do business together. We share something else as well. I introduced CiCie to Dan years ago and, like a lot of people who worked together at Kinko's, they got married. That's the thing about family. We really are stuck with each other.

I do have to give Dan credit for dealing with one important challenge I struggled with at Kinko's: managing the growth and development of our headquarters. The other side to my devotion to the field was the contempt I felt for the culture at our headquarters. Come to think of it, I hate the word "headquarters." I prefer "head office." We called our operations there the Kinko's Service Corporation as a reminder to ourselves that the only reason we existed was to serve the field. Try as I might, I just could not persuade myself to relax while I was there. I never saw any cash registers ringing. I didn't like the overhead. It was a love-hate relationship. My discomfort while I was at the office was a constant source of tension between Dan and me. I fought overhead from day one at Kinko's. It was an uphill battle all the way. Everywhere I looked, all I saw was unnecessary expense. I knew we needed a head office, but I hated it at the same time. As Tim Stancliffe put it, "Kinko's Service Corporation turned into the federal government." I remained convinced during my time with the company that the expansion of this bureaucracy could easily kill us by snuffing out our culture of innovation and push us over the financial brink. Often, when I was introduced to a new hire at the head office, I would ask the more senior coworker later, "Do we really need someone to do what this person is doing?" I was on the constant prowl to ferret out unnecessary expenditures.

The problem with bureaucracy at most "headquarters" is that there is so much passing the buck. No one takes the sort of responsibility people shoulder as a matter of course out in the field, where achievement is comparatively transparent and measurable. I also began to notice that often the people who survived and received promotions at our head office were the cautious ones and not the creative, audacious thinkers. The culture was

> **I fought overhead from day one at Kinko's.**

upside down. At most companies, the headquarters is a notoriously uncreative place, separated from reality. It is a danger to the health of many companies.

That said, I think I was wrong in my passionate dislike of our head office. I just couldn't keep my feelings in perspective. I was like a caged animal when I was there. Dan, by contrast, was comfortable in that environment. I have to give him credit for trying to keep me in line, even when I wasn't inclined to go along with him.

Mark Madden remembers that, at times, I would point to a group of Kinko's middle managers and say, "See those guys? Those guys are red meat." Or, as Tim Stancliffe recalls, I would say, "Those guys are prey." From time to time, I would make the lives of our middle managers miserable. It was simply too easy for them to hide behind excuses or to hide behind the actions of others. When I met our frontline coworkers in the stores, I told our partners, "I work for these guys." But the head office was a place that, by the very nature of the environment, became distracted from the needs of the field. It was constantly churning out obstacles to smooth working in the field. I passionately disagree that—in any organization—just because you work at the so-called headquarters you are any more important than the lowest guy on the totem pole out in the field. In fact, I think it's just the opposite.

Blaise Simqu was one of our coworkers who tried to talk me out of my animus for, as he puts it, the "suits." As Blaise remembers it, "The culture at the head office was one that, in his heart and soul, Paul simply did not respect. I said to Paul, 'I know you like me, but I know you don't respect my type.' Then I said, 'You know, Paul, believe it or not, you need people like me. As the company gets bigger, you need policy guys like me.' You saw his disdain for this idea. You felt it. The only reason I didn't get lumped into that group was because he cared for me personally."

Dark Side, Upside

The upside to my dark side, I'd have to say, is passion. In life, to create anything, a business, a friendship, or a child, passion is the necessary ingredient. I may have overdone it, but I can see that my rages absolutely fueled my drive to help others by creating such a large and enduring company from scratch. If there's one thing I can't stand, it's someone with a milquetoast attitude in life. Passion can be quiet and thoughtful, or foul and loudmouthed, but as a leader I need to see it in the people around me. It took passion to serve our multitudinous customers and their ever-changing requests. It required passion to grow from the ground up as rapidly as we did at Kinko's. When I fought with our partners, I got a chance to see whether or not they (like my cousin Rose) would fight for themselves. If they would, I knew I could count on them to fight for me, too. I saw a lot of this in my family. If you were meek, you didn't stand a chance. My partners' ability to fight for themselves, for me, was another litmus test.

Todd Ordal, a partner of ours in Michigan, says, "Paul can be a scary guy. If you don't fight for yourself, he'd run right over you and he'd do it repeatedly. Not a lot of people figured out that he wanted you to fight back. When I did, it became easier for me to deal with him." It's true that I seemed to fight frequently with coworkers who didn't show a spine. Maybe I was hoping they would develop one. With my insistence on relying on others, you better believe I needed to be surrounded with passionate people. Otherwise we were dead in the water.

Mark Madden is a passionate guy, which is why I tapped him to run my own company. One day I lit into him more severely than usual.

As Mark remembers it, "One time Paul was nagging me about something. Then he started sending me voice mails. He left me about three or four in a row—all personal attacks. It was his nature to just go after you. I can't explain it, but, then, there were a lot of things about Paul I couldn't explain. But I'd had it. I hit reply and I said, 'Hey, Paul, fuck you.' And I sent the message.

"Then, I sat there and I thought, 'That probably wasn't a good idea.' I ran around to Paul's assistant, CiCie, because I knew she could stop the message, but she wasn't in. I called the VMX guys [who ran the Kinko's voice mail service, KVMX]. A few minutes later, the phone rings. I figured I better pick up and it's Paul. He goes, 'Hey, buddy, how are you doing?'

"I wasn't sure what to say. Then he goes, 'Hey, hey, that message. That was *great*. The passion was there. Hey, thanks buddy.' I was completely relieved. Then he calls back a few minutes later and says, 'Hey buddy, one other thing. Hey, don't ever do that again.'"

As long as a person had passion and gumption, I could forgive a lot. And I guess I expected that same sort of understanding from our coworkers.

There's one virtue of my dark side that I haven't mentioned. My struggles with my own dark side have made me especially sensitive to this aspect in others. We experienced our first "constitutional crisis" at Kinko's in the eighties when one of our partners quietly turned on us. In 1978, my partners Tim Stancliffe and John Thysell and I had joined up forces with a new partner, whom I'll call "Bob," when he decided to leave his career as a professor to become a partner in Nebraska. We structured our partnership split just about evenly among Tim, John, and me. We gave the remaining 40 percent to Bob. The precaution of retaining a majority stake, in this case, turned out to be a saving grace. Later, Bob went to North Carolina and, while still working for us, opened up a competing company under another name with different friends. He didn't tell any of us at Kinko's, but word got out.

Dana Jennings, our partner in North Carolina, called me repeatedly to urge me to do something about Bob. All our partners were watching to see how I would handle the situation. Jimmy was especially alarmed. On a trip to North Carolina, Dana suggested that she, Jim, and I just drop in on Bob's store since I'd been unable to reach him by phone. We pulled up and who do you think we bumped into right there on the sidewalk? Bob, of course. When he saw us, he looked like he'd seen a ghost. Dana recalls that I said, "Hey, how are you doing, buddy? Let's go have a cup of coffee." I didn't want to fire Bob, but that afternoon, I did.

I've always liked renegades, extremists, and nonconformists.

The truth is that I liked Bob because he was a renegade. I've always liked renegades, extremists, and nonconformists. We needed renegade thinkers and doers in our midst. There is nothing eccentric about my regard for guys like Bob. A healthy dark side, properly channeled, can be a good thing. They say that what doesn't kill you will make you stronger. Left to his own devices, Bob could have killed off a location or two of ours. But, brought into the fold, he also could have made us stronger. I needed people on our team who would be willing to rock the boat. I tried to convince him to let us buy 50 percent of his operations in North Carolina. I might have even let him keep the name he used for his company. But he didn't go for it.

There were plenty of times at Kinko's when I did a good job of managing my own dark side. This was one of them. I could have gone to anger with Bob, but what would that have accomplished? We never took any further action against him. For many years after, I would sometimes hear that he was still at it running his own copy companies in North Carolina and doing just fine.

Split Personality

My wife convinced me to see a therapist a while back. He thinks that a part of my personality split off because of the trauma of my struggles in childhood, including the sexual abuse I suffered. He theorizes I took on this alter ego, this "Kinko," who was able to channel all that anger—or most of it, anyway—to positive ends. He suspects I could have just as easily gone the other way and followed some of my high school and college friends along the criminal route they took. Instead, I adopted the attitude that if people couldn't help me—with my reading, my understanding, and my trauma—then I would help as many people as I possibly could. As I learned to do when I was a kid, I turned outward. I picked up on the stress of other people. I bent all my energy toward helping them, toward solving their problems. I cajoled and strong-armed lots of people into business careers they would never have contemplated for themselves. Together we built a business that would go on to solve a mind-boggling array of creative and logistical problems for millions of people.

When you think about the business model in corporate America, you can see what was revolutionary about Kinko's. To function, most large companies require the suppression of their coworkers' personalities and of their emotions. We reversed the wiring at Kinko's. Kinko's was born out of and built on emotional extremes. Without the force of all that rage and passion—mine and that of our coworkers and customers—we might not have had the positive energy to build our way up to 1,200 stores.

Chapter 9

Watch Your Karma

I DISCOVERED KARMA AT BERKELEY. NOT BY LEARNING VIRTUE at the feet of some visiting guru, but by being devious at our first Kinko's in the city. Krishna Copy Center, a competitor of ours down the street, kept undercutting our prices. And I could see why. I believed the owner was hiring immigrants from India and other countries and paying them in cash, off the books, which meant keeping his overall cost of doing business much lower than ours.

I decided I knew how to handle the situation. I called the IRS one day and pretended to be a Krishna Copy Center copy jock. I feigned innocence while asking how exactly I was supposed to pay my taxes. I hung up the phone and the very next call that came in was from one of our partners, Stuie Krause, who was doing the books for our northern California operations. We'd just gone through a sales tax audit. Seems there was a double taxation issue. We didn't think we owed the government money, but we did. Our bill came to nearly $50,000!

No one had to explain karma to me after that. I figured it out right then; somebody up there was keeping score. What you put out to the world will come back to you. In other words, do good deeds. And always pay your taxes. I've always been diligent about rendering the government its due. I cheated on tests in grade school only because I felt I had to, to survive. If I could have done it another way, I would have. After learning my lesson a couple of times, I never cheated in business. I didn't want the bad karma. Now, when I teach kids in my college economics class, I tell them the same thing I told our partners: *Integrity is like virginity*—you only lose it once.

My family, my mother especially, taught me about the importance of ethics in business and in life. One time we were at a store when I was a little kid and I tried to steal something. I don't even remember what it was. When we came home, my mother caught me by the arm and took me to the backyard. When she confronted me, I lied. She held a match to my finger until it blistered. "I won't have a thief and a liar in my house," she said. And this is a woman who rarely struck her kids. But when she did, she got her point across. Mom was determined to instill good morals in her kids. She always told us, "Your word is your bond." She admired my father because he always kept his word in business whether there was a written contract or not. Especially because of my dyslexia, this was a useful practice for me to observe. Much of our business, especially in the early years, was based, of necessity, on handshakes.

As Charlie Wright puts it, "We had a pretty good culture of what comes around, goes around. If you were unethical and dishonest, we had no use for you." I remember, one time, one of my partners dropped a quarter into a newspaper machine and took out two copies of the newspaper instead of one. I can't stomach that kind of behavior. It makes my hair stand on end! I still worked with this partner, but I let him know what I thought about that.

If you build an environment where ethics and morals are valued and encouraged, you'll inspire loyalty in the people with whom you live and work. The antidote to the sorts of scandals that befell Enron and WorldCom (and their unwitting shareholders) is to convince businesspeople that it is in their own self-interest to behave ethically. A study of 1,500 publicly traded companies published in the February 2003 issue of the *Quarterly Journal of Economics* found that firms with strong ethics had higher firm value, higher profits, higher sales growth, and lower capital expenditures. This is no surprise to me. In my personal investing, I pay close attention to the ethics of companies in which I buy stock. This is not a tangential, "soft" issue. It's a central investor and operator concern. People need to understand that they will make a lot more money in the long run if they conduct themselves with integrity.

At Kinko's, we regarded the care of our coworkers as an ethical matter. If we had a coworker who fell on bad times, we did what we could to help, whether it was providing time off, loans, or outright monetary gifts. One time, Charlie Wright hired a single mother who was going through a rough patch and we paid the rent on her apartment for a time. When our medical insurer disallowed coverage to another single mother in our Torrance, California, store on a technicality, we yelled and screamed until she got insurance. We helped send some of our managers into rehab for alcohol or drugs. It worked out better for them and for us in the end. When one manager had an anger problem (I could relate), we hired a counselor to work with him in much the same way we brought in a counselor to work with Dan and me. We loaned money to our coworkers all the time and found they never defaulted on their loans.

Finding the Cockroaches

How did we make sure all our coworkers behaved ethically? Talking about integrity is great, but you need good controls. Trust, but verify. Kinko's was a reasonably easy business to police. All our machines had internal counters so we could keep pretty close track of how the number of actual copies squared up against the income every day, week, or month. We developed a system of checks, such as doing our partners' bank reconciliations and bank statements, but there was no way we could scrutinize every line item streaming in from each of our stores. Instead, in the early days, CiCie took a close look at maybe 10 different items out of 1,000 that our partners expensed.

Occasionally, we found transgressions. One time a partner charged us for some new clothes he'd bought. Later, this same partner ended up falling into a pattern of compulsive gambling and we had to fire him. Often, a seemingly minor transgression points to a far deeper problem. I call this phenomenon a "cockroach." Whenever you see one cockroach, it's not a lone bug. You must assume there are many, many others. When I see a cockroach in a company I'm considering investing in—arrogance on the part of the CEO, a small scandal, or a telling accounting error—I assume the worst; I don't invest. The same was true with our stores. If a manager didn't make his daily deposits in the bank, I knew there were many more problems. We just hadn't seen them yet.

One strategy we employed to keep our stores in line was the use of "mystery shoppers," an idea that came out of Kinko's Service Corporation. Posing as customers, these individuals went to stores around the country, looking for several things: Were coworkers cordial and honest? Did they "upsell" by offering them other services when it came time to pay? Did anybody offer to complete the order with higher-priced color or bordered paper? Whenever a store received consistently high scores over a 12-month period, the coworkers there were awarded a plaque.

When I visited stores around the country, I took an entirely different approach. I eliminated the "mystery" from the experience. No matter where I was, I always called ahead to forewarn managers that I was on my way. Some of our partners complained about this habit. They wanted me to make surprise visits. "You aren't seeing the real stores," they said. I disagreed. I trusted that most stores looked and operated pretty much as they usually did even with a little "heads up" that the founder was on the way over. I still stumbled onto lots of problems that needed correcting—in addition to lots of good ideas, too. I believe my approach, by conveying trust, respect, and courtesy, compensated for any flaws I may have missed.

> **I told her to go ahead and fire some people.**

One time, I remember, I sat down with our head of human resources and asked her how it was going. "Great," she said. "We haven't had any lawsuits." She thought I would be pleased, but I didn't want her using that as a barometer of success. I told her to go ahead and fire some people. The fact that we hadn't had any wrongful termination lawsuits wasn't comforting to me. To be effective in our human resources work, we needed to make sure we were letting go of coworkers who were poor performers or bad fits for us. If we had zero termination lawsuits, we weren't being vigilant enough with our employees. When my brother, Dickie, was a banker, before he came to Kinko's, it was expected that a certain percentage of his clients would default on their loans. If he had zero bad loans, it was a sign that he was being too strict. It's all about ambiguity. Sometimes what passes for integrity really isn't integrity at all.

I observed this phenomenon often when we were hiring people. I've hired countless people for a wide variety of positions. Instead of offering salary ranges, I usually ask potential new coworkers what they would like us to pay them. Invariably, they name too low a figure. People don't know how much they are worth. They underestimate themselves. We had to fight this tendency from within our own ranks. One day I was talking with one of our partners, Glenn Carter, and I asked him, "Are you losing any customers on pricing?" He said he wasn't, and I said, "Well, start." The only way we were going to get out of the commodity business was to offer better, more highly customized services, and charge a premium for them. It's OK to lose a few customers if it's part of the process of getting your pricing in line. I read once that J. Paul Getty said, "The meek shall inherit the Earth, but not the mineral rights." We had to be willing to ask for higher prices in order to grow.

On the other hand, I never admired people who bragged about gouging their customers. I didn't want to work with them. Overcharging runs contrary to the Kinko's Philosophy, which emphasizes building long-term relationships with customers. The value of a long-term relationship is so much higher than what you reap from gouging customers and losing all their future business. How do you tell the difference between being appropriately aggressive on pricing and gouging your customers? You provide superior or added service and you ask what the market could or should bear. But, beyond that, like so many ethical questions, it's ambiguous.

Timeliness is Next to Godliness

Taking care of customers while charging high prices. Trusting your coworkers, but checking up on them. Life is paradoxical.

It's filled with sets of opposing values that seem to cancel each other out but, in actuality, both are needed to keep a business afloat. Running a business is nothing more than learning to go to sleep at night with unresolved issues. In business—as with any other endeavor—you have to come to grips with the fact that life is uncertain. I often ask people whether they think business is an art or a science. College students often say it's a science, whereas older people say it's an art. With experience, people figure out just how much art is required to manage all the ambiguity in the science of business or life. Our Philosophy expresses a series of values, many of which seem contradictory, like taking care of our customers while also taking care of our coworkers. Some customers were so rude we had to fire them in order to take care of our own people! At Kinko's, taking care of the field while attending to matters at the head office caused unending conflict. Why? It's ambiguous.

There are ethical arguments on both sides of the equation. As your business grows and you mature, you begin to find you live ever more in the gray. The justices of the Supreme Court could tell you about this. All they do every day is try to tease out the best

> **Running a business is learning to go to sleep at night with unresolved issues.**

decisions from a thicket of ambiguity. Do you really want to live in a black-and-white world? It's your choice. I've found it's much more exciting in the gray.

Our partner Todd Ordal remembers that trying to serve opposing values, like prudence and ambition, could send him reeling. After negotiating lease contracts and incurring legal expenses, he sometimes found that one of his other partners wanted to hold off and not open new stores so quickly. He felt he'd wasted both time and energy.

"I'm a rigid guy," Todd says, "so Paul would just look at me and laugh and say, 'Toddy-boy, you're just going to have to deal with the ambiguity.' I wanted to say, 'What do you *mean*, asshole?' But sometimes life just really is not black and white."

David Vogias: "Everything was so transient you had to be a freak to handle it. And Paul was a freak. But then, I was a freak, too."

While the business was in constant, sometimes maddening, flux, we clung to some practices that kept us on an even keel. I remember that when the psychiatrist Pierre Mornell came to help Dan and me, he was startled to find a bunch of ex-hippies who were so fanatical about punctuality. Even if it promised to be unpleasant, we were never late for a meeting with Pierre. As far as I'm concerned, being on time is a matter of ethics and honesty. I strive to be perfect, or excellent, with my follow-through. CiCie's diligence afforded me the luxury of my high standards in this area. I was always maniacal about returning phone calls as well as written correspondence as promptly as I possibly could, often within a day or two, if not within the hour. Much of this work I farmed out to CiCie. For 20 years her follow-through has been so perfect that I've never had to worry about keeping my word to others.

I believe that if you want to succeed in life, you can't be late. Despite our free-to-be-me, free-to-be-you culture at Kinko's, we had our "Republican" side. Sometimes when I was bored at Kinko's I would grab Mark Madden and we'd go stand at the main entrance to our Ventura offices at 8 A.M., the start of the work day. We'd greet late arrivals until 8:10 A.M. and ask them for explanations.

I have a lot of fun with the students in my economics course at the University of California at Santa Barbara. If they're late, they don't get away with it. I grill them. I make them sit on the floor. I call them lepers. If they don't show up at all, I call them right there in class to find out why. I have all their cell phone numbers. ("Hi, Joey, it's Paul. How come you didn't come to class this morning, buddy? What are you doing? Are you still in bed?") The ones who trot in a few minutes after class starts at 9 A.M. must stand up and tell the rest of us exactly why they kept us all waiting for them. If their excuses or their presentations are vague or muddled, I send them outside and tell them to walk back through the door, greet all of us again, and rephrase their excuse making. It's like an acting class. Those excuses better be good if they're going to win me over. On the first day, I let everyone know that the last person to class every day will be stuck cleaning up all the left-over bagels and cream cheese strewn all over the table. It sometimes seems like a big game, but it isn't. Too many professors let students get away with this stuff. I award students grades lower than an A only if they are consistently late or if they don't show up at all. If you're going to participate in life, first and foremost, you have to show up for it. Being on time is a matter of respect. There's no worse way to disrespect another person than by making them wait for you.

Blaise Simqu knew I treated the people I worked with—whether they were vendors or coworkers—as if they were members of my own family. When someone came to visit, I didn't just walk out to my assistant's desk to greet them, I met them down in the lobby. Often I walked them out to their cars. It used to irritate me to no end when somebody's secretary came out to escort me to their office.

As Blaise remembers it, "Paul would grind the Xerox people on price, but then he would walk them outside. He explained this by asking, 'What would you do in your own home?' He would not send his assistant. Paul is also an absolute stickler on punctuality because it is a sign of respect for another human being. He will not be late for anybody under any circumstances. One day, I was walking into the building at 8:10 A.M. Paul saw me.

Being on time is a matter of respect.

He tore into me. He just unleashed. And Paul liked me. To him, being on time was a sign of respect to the culture of the company."

Even when I felt I had to chew on somebody, I couldn't help feeling badly about it later. Blaise says, "At lunch that day Paul kept asking me over and over, 'Hey, buddy, how's our relationship? Are we OK?'"

Common courtesy these days has become uncommon courtesy. Most of the students I teach haven't been taught how to behave in class or in social settings. They can barely put together an articulate sentence when you ask them a question. They either freeze up or they ramble on and on when they talk, never making their point. Here's a simple rule of thumb in business: If they can't say it in plain English, don't work with them! Universities everywhere used to offer a major called "Rhetoric." About 100 years ago, many students made it the focus of their studies. Maybe this is because there was less communication technology back then and people were compelled to rely on their own verbal communications skills to get things done. Today, only a very few institutions of higher learning offer Rhetoric as a major. It's a shame. I think we've lost much of the art of speaking to one another. In my class, no one goes to sleep, because they don't get a chance to. I force them to interact with me. I was the same way with our partners at our annual meetings. I homed in on the quietest ones and compelled them to tell all of us how things were going in their stores. At colleges and universities, most professors talk *at* their students. They don't engage them in any dialogue. That is not how the real world works.

Out here in the real world, we need to be able to speak to one another, clearly and succinctly. When our partners sent me long-winded voice mails, I sent the message back to them so they could hear what their messages sounded like. Then I'd add the message "Too many words!" They called back and summed up their ideas more succinctly. There's so much emphasis throughout our educational system on the written word, up to and through college, that while students learn to write long essays nobody reads, we've practically lost the ability to speak directly. If you've got learning opportunities like I do, verbal communication is the way you get everything done. I place a high value on the ability of people to clearly and quickly articulate what they want. In my view, this is also a sign of respect. They aren't wasting my time! If someone tries to give me a pitch for a business that lasts more than five minutes, I begin to feel they haven't really thought their idea through. Despite myself, I stop listening.

In my class, the kids catch on quickly. They have to. I draw them out. They wake up, sit up, and talk to me and to each other. I expect it of them. When we began the process of looking for a buyer for Kinko's, I walked away from deals when I found that bigwigs we had traveled to meet kept us waiting in their lobbies—and then didn't come out to greet us. If they couldn't extend us that common courtesy when we first met, what could we expect from the rest of our relationship?

I have a bone to pick with any person or institution that strikes me as elitist. Kinko's was built on a determined populism. It springs out of a grassroots spirit of democracy and antiestablishmentarian-ism. As Charlie Wright puts it, "Paul didn't allow any elitism and that affected me a lot." The greatest advantage of our populist view toward our business, our customers, and our coworkers is that we built a truly democratic system. And that, in the end, was part of the prob-lem, too. When we hired people, we got—and embraced—the whole enchilada, the good and the bad.

When you live or work with human beings, ethical crises are going to happen. You can't avoid them. Whenever partners or coworkers opened up competing copy shops—like our wayward partner "Bob" in North Carolina—we got mad, of course. But we always ended up deciding that the best route was to do nothing about it. Most of the people who cheated us or took advantage of us ended up struggling later, down the line. Years later, Bob opened a store in Iowa and we took great pleasure in kicking his butt there, fair and square.

"All we did was leave cheaters alone," Jimmy Warren remem-bers. "It seemed like the laws of karma were at work."

As my Dad used to ask, "Why would you want to waste time trying to go after someone else when there is always so much gold underneath your feet?"

Chapter 10

Fail Forward

N OT ONLY DO I NOT BELIEVE IN THE TERM "learning dis-abled," I also don't believe in the concept of failure. I don't think there really is such a thing as failure. The whole idea is not particularly helpful. When you "fail" at something it actually means one or more of three things: 1) You're a risk taker and (within reason) that's a good thing—you know how to take initiative; 2) you've learned something about yourself or the world along the way; and 3) there is another, probably better, opportunity elsewhere. People who study entrepre-neurs, like my friend Tom O'Malia, the former head of the Center for the Study of Entrepreneurship at USC, have found they have an abundance of two qualities that enable them to capitalize on failure: optimism and perseverance. Dyslexic entrepreneurs have even more. They have to. As Sally Shaywitz, an author and a dyslexia expert from Yale University, writes in her book *Overcoming Dyslexia,* "Adult dyslexics are tough: Having struggled, they are used to adversity; hard work and perseverance now come naturally. Having experienced fail-ure, they are fearless, undaunted by setbacks." Given my track record as an entrepreneur, given all the jobs I "failed" at as a kid, I have a healthy respect for what it means to face setbacks. I discovered early on that optimism and perseverance are their only effective antidotes.

What do I mean by failure? I'm talking monumental screwups, bad lapses in judgment, or a garden-variety inability to meet the task at hand. I'm also talking about those unexpected blows of fate: the surprise volley from an adversary, a change in the tax law, a death, a disaster, or an abandonment. In my experience, rejection is the hard-est of all. Failures can also spring from an unexpected quarter: our past triumphs. My parents told us constantly when we were kids that *the biggest cause of failure is your past success.* Success too often goes to your head. Whatever the reason, in the wake of every setback, we're left to claw our way up and out of adversity. We rethink our business strategies or our love lives. We rebuild our self-esteem brick by brick. It may be hard to pick up the tools of optimism and perseverance, especially if we are unaccustomed to using them. But we must.

The Chinese have a saying: "Crisis is opportunity." It's a truism that every failure contains the seeds of a new opportunity. This is because loss, especially loss in business, does produce something of exceptionally high value: information. And, though it may not seem so at first, raw data can be even more valuable than whatever it is you lost in the first place. Why do you think the U.S. economy is so resilient? Chalk it up to our bankruptcy laws and our forgiving investment climate. So many companies fail so quickly in this country that we produce a surfeit of information about the markets in which they are born and then die. Our entrepreneurial economy then grows startups out of the graveyards of the old ones. It's a fertile, data-rich climate we've cultivated. We learn as we grow.

Happily, Kinko's avoided bankruptcy. We recreated ourselves so rapidly we were spared that pain. We fundamentally repositioned the business over and over. We started off as a multifaceted company selling stationery, photo developing, printing, and copies. Then we were a campus-based copy chain. Later we sold packs of academic coursework on college campuses nationwide, becoming a sort of sub-academic publisher. Next we abandoned academics altogether (more about that in a minute) and turned to the commercial market. With the rapid rise of information technology in the mid-nineties, we started calling ourselves "The Soup Kitchen for the Technologically Homeless" internally after Dan Frederickson coined the phrase. Today, partnered with FedEx, Kinko's is expanding its ties to the corporate marketplace.

Our official policy at Kinko's was that our mistakes cost us nothing. We enshrined this idea in our Philosophy. We did our best to take our setbacks in stride, to see the unhatched opportunity inside of the crisis. That wasn't *always* possible, but more often than not it was. After all, we weren't running nuclear power plants. By encouraging mistakes, we rewarded experimentation and innovation. We created a culture of risk-taking. How do you think babies learn about gravity? They drop things. They learn where something is by grabbing at it willy-nilly and discovering where it isn't. They learn through failure.

We struggled against daunting obstacles at Kinko's right after we got started. In 1973, shortly after we opened our second location, my accountant tried to convince me to shutter the business. "You are not going to make it," he told me. I sold the sailboat. I put the $8,400 in proceeds into the business. That was a difficult time. My father chipped in with loans to help out. But I was always afraid to ask and it was never enough to pay our bills on time.

The reason? This was the time I mentioned earlier, when Xerox threatened to sue us. They demanded about $100,000 in compensation. We didn't have anywhere near that amount, nor was I about to pay them a cent. Had we been compelled to, it would have easily bankrupted us, since the suit came right in the midst of our first push to expand, when we had a negative capital account. The timing couldn't have been worse. Thank God it was dismissed. In its own way, though, the threat of that lawsuit did help us. It expanded our view of our marketplace and of our vendors. We quickly learned that we could use IBM copiers if we had to. We could survive without Xerox, if necessary.

Family Squabbles

We weren't just fighting with a vendor. We were fighting amongst ourselves, too. In the following decade, I ran into problems with at least a half dozen of our earliest partners. In each case, relationships had soured or simply weren't working anymore. As our partner Craig Redwine remembers it, "That trust thing came back to bite Paul constantly. How did some partners come to be a partner? He anointed them entrepreneurs indiscriminately, especially in the beginning. He partnered with some real lulus. It was brilliant on the one hand and it was amazing that it worked on the other."

Believe me, cultivating loyalty among our family was not an easy job. For instance, after many years with Kinko's, our hot-tempered office manager, Dottie Ault, convinced me to make her a partner in the original store on Pardall Road in Isla Vista. Big mistake. Eventually, she and I struck a deal. She paid me a modest sum for the original Kinko's. Though it was still called Kinko's, we no longer owned it. (Afterwards, without notifying us, Dottie went ahead and opened other stores on her own in Lubbock, Texas, and in St. Louis, Missouri.) I had to let go of a lot of partners as I simultaneously found new ones. At about the same time Dottie bought me out, Brad and I sold the print shop, too, for $100,000, which enabled us to expand our operations in the Northwest. We also let go of our second location in Irvine, where I wasn't getting along well with my partner. I let her buy me out for another $15,000. In later years, I persuaded our partner in Hawaii to buy me out, too. We sold her the rights to the use of the Kinko's name anywhere on the Hawaiian Islands for $25,000. Much later, when Brad and Charley Williams opened stores in Hawaii for us, they had to come up with another name for the stores. They called them Ditto's. For a time, it was Ditto's versus Kinko's.

> **For a time it was Ditto's versus Kinko's.**

Or, in actual fact, Kinko's versus Kinko's. It was pretty confusing. As we got closer to selling all of Kinko's, we were able to go and buy back the name and reclaim territories that were previously lost to us. But for many years there, we left some scorched earth behind us.

I'm not proud of all these failed partnerships. However, many setbacks may litter the path to success. As my best friend, Danny, puts it, "If you're real anal like I am, you respect people like Paul who can screw around and be messy, because you realize you don't have to be perfect to succeed. Paul didn't mind failing to become more successful." Most tennis greats have far more unforced errors than aces on their way to a championship win. I was glad to be rid of these stores. In each and every case, I got rid of headaches. When a personal relationship or a business relationship goes bad, it's a draining thing. That doesn't mean it didn't affect me to think we no longer owned the very first location. After I sold the first Kinko's to Dottie, I stopped driving down Pardall Road. For a brief time I was a partner in a Chinese restaurant, Wok 'n Roll, directly across the street. That venture didn't do so well either and we closed the place. Pardall stopped feeling lucky to me. I still walk past the old location all the time to have a burrito at Freebirds, the restaurant that my cousin Mark Orfalea owns nearby. I just haven't driven down Pardall Road in 30 years.

We had trouble with coworkers, too. One of my earliest coworkers was Walt Wilson, who ran the first Kinko's for me when I traveled to Europe. For a time there, Walt and I were the two young entrepreneurs of Isla Vista. Both in our early twenties, Walt owned and operated a corner gas station, while I ran the first Kinko's just down the street. We were even roommates for a spell. After he closed his gas station, he came to work at Kinko's. A couple years later, Walt and I had a falling out. He became a direct competitor, opening a print shop directly across the street from the original Kinko's location (also on Pardall, of course). Fittingly, he called it the Alternative. He owns three other Alternative locations in California and one in Arizona. My friends tell me Walt's business is modeled largely on what he learned from his time with us. They are all still in business.

As you've seen, one of the most important ways I've learned to deal with setbacks is by letting go. I might have hung onto any of those early locations, for sentimental reasons. But to move forward required us to take our losses and move on. Acceptance is another huge lesson of failure. To the extent that we fight our failures, they control us and keep us from moving forward. But that doesn't mean acceptance is an easy thing. It's a process and often a long one. And, as with optimism and perseverance, it's not optional. Not if you want to move forward in your life and be happy. You've got *no other choice than to accept.* To an outsider looking in, it might seem surprising that I so willingly parted ways not only with so many early partners but with so many early locations. I've found that too many people, when faced with frustrations or setbacks, dwell on them for unreasonable lengths of time. I learned to focus my sights ahead of me, to accept what went wrong, and to move on from it. We used the proceeds from the sale of the earliest stores to open new locations elsewhere. After partnering with so many difficult people, I got better at picking partners.

It's easier to accept a flub, of course, if you have great faith in the future. And I had great faith in the future of Kinko's. When you stack up the losses of those early stores with what we all went on to build, they were trivial.

The Death of a Golden Goose . . .

Perhaps the single most difficult setback we were forced to accept at Kinko's was the loss of our Professor Publishing business in the early nineties. This was the business through which we sold anthologies of academic materials to college students. The coursepacks consisted of Xeroxed copies of book excerpts, articles, and other materials assembled by professors at colleges around the country. For our first two decades, selling coursepacks was the largest single driver of growth at Kinko's.

First, a little background. In the mid-seventies, I was doing my favorite thing—wandering and observing. I happened to walk through the library on campus one day when I hit upon an idea. Professors at every university were putting a number of books, articles, and other research materials in the reserve room at the campus library every semester or quarter for their classes. To study from them, students went to the library and checked them out. The problem is that students couldn't get access to the same materials simultaneously. Nor would it make sense for the professors to ask students to shell out hundreds of dollars for books from which they needed only a page or a chapter. Some of the devious, more competitive students would slice or rip out the materials they needed and steal them.

I hit upon the idea of copying these materials and assembling them into reading packs for professors. As soon as we began to stick flyers into professors' boxes offering the service, professors took us up on it. It really hit a nerve. We sold coursepacks in droves to students. Our coursepack division was the main reason we opened stores for nearly two decades on or near college campuses. Dave Vogias' store near Penn State sometimes brought in $30,000 in coursepacks a day. On a given day, other stores could do as much as $50,000 to $80,000 in coursepacks.

We expanded around the country, but I delayed opening a Kinko's in New York City, the capital of the publishing industry. I knew we risked calling down on our heads the ire of publishers by opening in their backyard. It was the late eighties before we opened our first Kinko's in a great location in Greenwich Village, near New York University.

Sure enough, a lawsuit arrived in the mail in 1989. It was filed by eight publishing houses: Basic Books Inc., Harper & Row Publishers Inc., John Wiley & Sons Inc., McGraw-Hill Inc., Penguin Books USA Inc., Prentice-Hall Inc., Richard D. Irwin Inc., and William Morrow & Co., Inc. It came to be known as the Basic Books Copyright Infringement Suit. In it, the publishers alleged that we were violating the so-called fair-use portion of the copyright law. This section of law allowed professors to copy materials used for educational purposes so long as the copies didn't constitute a substantial amount of work. They argued that, under copyright law, our sale of coursepacks was illegal.

> **Sure enough, a lawsuit arrived in the mail.**

At the time I felt strongly that selling coursepacks did not materially infringe on the rights of publishers. Coursepacks enabled a free exchange of intellectual property and ideas at our universities. (Although we are no longer in the business, the demand remains. Other smaller copying companies still do a brisk business selling coursepacks as do most universities.)

We fought the suit with all we had. The National School Boards Association and the American Association of Libraries backed us, as well as other organizations with a strong interest in the free flow of intellectual ideas. There I was, basically illiterate myself, fighting for education. Still, that wasn't enough to persuade the best law firms in New York to represent us. Those we approached cited conflicts of interest with publishing clients. The law firm we retained turned out to be a big disappointment. We were not aggressively represented. Against our better judgment, we were persuaded to forgo a jury trial. I still wonder what the outcome of that suit might have been had the fate of Professor Publishing been in the hands of a jury instead of a judge. In 1991, after a frustrating year, we lost the lawsuit and agreed upon a settlement. We ended up paying $3.5 million in damages and legal fees, which included fees for our opponents' lawyers.

To hang onto the business, while compensating publishers in compliance with the law, we instituted a laborious procedure for obtaining copyright clearances on each and every excerpt in all of our coursepacks. Forward-thinking publishing houses, including Harvard Business School Press and Sage Publications in Thousand Oaks, California, permitted us to use their published materials, without having to wait for clearances on individual excerpts. It was a financial boon for them; suddenly they had a new income stream that didn't demand any new work from them at all. But there was little we could do to reduce the six-week waiting times for clearances from other, less-agreeable publishers. The paperwork became onerous. The whole process began to bog us down.

Although we lost the suit, many partners, especially those with stores bringing in upwards of $250,000 a month in coursepack sales, naturally wanted to stay in the business. We felt that Kinko's was born through Professor Publishing. Blaise Simqu came to work with us from the publishing industry to see if the program could be brought into compliance. He remembers, "Coursepacks were the fabric of the culture. They drove the other business. It was a very emotional issue: Do we stay in or do we get out?"

. . . And the Birth of Another

Some partners had begun making changes even before the lawsuit was filed. At the same time, fortunately, we all had started noticing a new trend: The percentage of commercial customers we were serving was on the rise. But we couldn't adequately serve them because we were so tied to the annual boom-and-bust cycle of the academic calendar. When summer ended, the flood of students cramming the stores made it nearly impossible to focus on our commercial customers. Twice a year, we might as well have put up a sign saying, "Not open for business." Brad Krause quietly opened a couple of commercial stores in the mid-eighties. Todd Johnson, in Tennessee, stopped opening stores near colleges in the late eighties. While his first 9 locations were largely on college campuses, the subsequent 26 stores he opened were almost entirely commercial. The lawsuit reinforced the commercial direction Todd had embarked upon. In the Northwest, Brad was one of my first partners who said out loud that it was time to get out of the coursepack business entirely.

It was by no means an easy decision. It wasn't until I went away on a long vacation in 1992 that I came to agree. I gradually came to see the paperwork involved with trying to comply with so many slow-moving publishers had become unmanageable. We had to let go. Still, the business dwindled for several years until we formally announced its closure at our 1994 summer picnic in Hilton Head, North Carolina.

Our president Dan remembers the anguish we felt at the time: "We had a copyright clearance department of 25 to 30 people that did nothing but try to pay publishers. But the publishers were not cooperative and didn't seem to care about the students. I don't think they were doing what they should for education. Professor Publishing was truly ingenious and important. It gave teachers the means to teach students their own curriculum and not the publishers' curriculum. It set the teachers free. They could become sculptors of their own class curricula. The other big deal was those materials could be current. They were also cost-effective for students. Every college student in America suffered when we lost that suit. Because of a few publishers in New York, these kids weren't allowed to get the materials they needed."

At the time, the loss of the business felt like a huge failure. As far as I was concerned, I'd gotten my ass kicked. I wasn't sleeping nights. Finally even I had to admit that it was time to let go. All of sudden, we needed to rethink our business model once again. We needed to get away from college campuses. Focusing on the academic market was precluding us from doing what we should have been doing, which was serving our growing base of commercial customers. So much new technology was coming out—color copiers, blueprint copiers, and high-speed faxes—that we had yet to exploit. I realized —once again—that sometimes you have to make painful decisions to separate yourself from the past.

I read a statistic somewhere that in 1970, at the time I opened the first Kinko's, there were an estimated 7 million people who worked out of their homes. By the time my partners and I sold our shares in the late nineties, that number had risen to an estimated 42 million. That's a huge shift. At the same time, the number of small businesses with fewer than 20 workers was exploding. In 1992 we started calling ourselves "Your Branch Office."

Looking back, I realize that, while lucrative, Professor Publishing actually had been obstructing our ability to make much more money. With hindsight, it became obvious that losing the lawsuit was the best thing that could have happened to us. Our revenues mushroomed from $500 million to more than $2 billion between 1990 and 2000. We opened hundreds and hundreds of new stores for our new commercial clients. We started our international division, which my brother, Dick, ran initially. Brad Krause had opened the first international store in British Columbia in 1991. Our international division bought out that location and opened the next Kinko's abroad in Japan in 1993. Later we brought in Michael Cohn, formerly of Baskin-Robbins, who expanded our operations abroad at a fast clip. Soon we were operating Kinko's stores in the United Arab Emirates, Australia, Canada, and Europe. Virgin founder Richard Branson (a fellow dyslexic) became our partner in Great Britain. We were becoming a different company— more professional, more adult. We had finally "graduated" from college. We took advantage of our failures. We failed forward.

Succeeding with Our Kids

With all lessons in business, there is a corollary lesson in life. When I think of failure, I can't help but think about our kids and how they suffer and struggle to grow during their schooling years. Shouldn't we have the same attitude toward our kids who fail as we at Kinko's had toward each other? Parents ought to lighten up. I think we celebrate all the wrong things with our kids. We should celebrate their failures! Not just their successes. This is a radical concept, I know. Follow it through to its logical conclusion and it would mean revamping and reorienting our entire educational system towards experimentation and practical experience and away from the old carrots and sticks.

At Kinko's, when our partners did well, I pushed them to work even harder. I knew they had the capacity to grow so I didn't let up on them. When they stumbled, I encouraged them and gave them kudos. At those times, they were stretching themselves and frustrated. They needed the support so they didn't lose heart. Think about our kids. We give them awards when they do well in their studies, in sports or in performances. But what better time in life is there to fail than during school, while they are still at home? Kids don't have to worry about paying the rent or going out of business. They should be encouraged to try as many new and different things as they can. Most important, they should learn to go through the experience of failure. Most straight-A types live in abject fear of failure. They rack up all these perfect grades and think they will die if they come home with a B or a C. That's no preparation for real life. Out in the real world, failure—and benefitting from it—is the name of the game.

Straight-A types unaccustomed to failure enter the marketplace and take their first belly flops especially hard. They're so shocked they don't know how to react. Why do you think so many of them go back to graduate school? It's a huge relief to return to the safety of a system through which they can navigate like trout. Our schools are producing test takers, not creative thinkers. My brother once told me that studies have shown a trout will bite at a hook and circle back and bite on the same hook 17 minutes later. They're automatons. They aren't using their imaginations. Too many straight-A kids enter the real world primed to fall and to fall hard. They don't know how to roll with the punches in either the workplace or life. They don't know how to work through their setbacks. What we really want to produce in our kids is resilience. I may be sensitive, but I learned to be resilient, too.

With so much emphasis on high SAT scores and 4.0 grade point averages, I think our schools and universities are selecting out the resilient kids, eliminating all the students like me. We've created a system geared to advancing the test takers and the trout. If George W. Bush ever truly succeeded with his "No Child Left Behind" program, I'd still be in the third grade. Some kids just aren't ever going to grasp the Pythagorean theorem. But they shouldn't be stigmatized for the rest of their lives. We need to ask ourselves: Is this what we really want for our society and for ourselves? Do we really need all this eating-your-alphabet-soup-alphabetically perfectionism? Do we really want to learn how to do well on multiple choice tests? Or do we want to do well in life?

I think the five-year-olds have it right.

Let me ask you a question. How do you respond when a child comes to you with a painting that she did that day in kindergarten? If you're like most people, you say, "That is beautiful, Sarah!" I don't want to break your heart, but that is the wrong thing to say. Why not say, "Why did you paint that, Sarah? What does it mean to you?" Otherwise, you teach kids to please others, instead of pleasing themselves. It's been observed that when five-year-olds draw trees, they draw messy, green blurs. By the time they are eight years old, they draw round circles with sticks. They've learned to draw like other people expect them to. I think the five-year-olds have it right.

In college, I once took yet another stab at trying to please others, a bunch of straight-A types at USC. I rushed a fraternity and scrambled to complete all the assignments my would-be frat brothers had given me as a pledge. But I couldn't keep them straight. I went through

Hell Week and thought I'd survived. Instead, the next day, the other guys held a secret meeting when they knew that my best friend, Danny Tevrizian, wouldn't be there to defend me. They expelled me. It was a crushing disappointment. That is, until I realized I was being a big phony trying to fit in with them. I wasn't me. It was a good failure to have. I became a little more resilient. Wouldn't you prefer a resilient kid to a straight-A kid?

Sometimes I look back on my life and wonder if I shouldn't go back and thank my erstwhile frat brothers, former grade school teachers and all those principals whose doors I darkened for so many years. Would Kinko's have come to be if I hadn't gone through so much disheartening failure? I really can't say. Kids who are familiar with failure, like all of us who built Kinko's, know each setback is actually a step in the right direction.

Chapter 11

Make Money
While You Sleep

I'VE NOTICED THAT I'VE GOT A DIFFERENT VIEW OF MONEY than most people do. I was so stingy that, in the early days at Kinko's, I sometimes hand delivered my mail in order to save on postage. I slept on other people's couches for $50 a month rather than pay full rent. When I lived in Santa Barbara I waited to change the oil in my car until I was two hours south in Los Angeles. Why? Because it was so expensive to park in downtown L.A. that I wanted to save the parking fee by getting my oil changed there. I was always working angles. Any new strategy to save a nickel delighted me. I believe you can either earn your way into a fortune or save your way into one. Take your pick. Or do both, like I did. Both ways are valid. As my mother used to say, "*it's not how much you make in life, it's how much you save.*" I took this advice to heart.

All my life I wanted to be wealthy. Many people suffer from what I call the Poverty Complex. They don't really want to make money. They think it's some kind of sin. I've never understood that attitude. I'm glad I wasn't raised with it. We learned a lot more in our household about money than about grades. I like to ask college kids, "Don't you think you might get a little farther in life with savings than with grades?" This question shocks them. Aren't they supposed to pull all-nighters to get straight A's on their finals? I like to tell them what my dad said when he saw my brother Dickie up late, cramming for a test in high school once: "Go to bed," he told my brother. "Why bother memorizing it when you're going to forget it right after the test anyhow?" My parents were much more interested in my savings account and my critical thinking skills than they were in my grades. I remind college kids that they're really in school not for the degree but to discover their passion. They shouldn't let grades kill their passion.

As a dyslexic, I never lost sight of the fact that savings were going to get me much farther along in life than any report card ever would. I wanted to grow up to be like my uncles. When they were older they had fancy cars. They spent their days polishing them. The hardest decision they had to make was where to go for lunch that day. They were also free to take care of their kids, to spend time with their families. They never missed a dinner at home. People often equate wealth with immorality, but that's not what I saw as a kid. I saw people who both made and then saved enough money to have the leisure time to devote to their hobbies and to their families.

One time my friend Alan Porter told me *your integrity is directly related to your liquidity,* and I never forgot it. You sure don't hear *that* in schools. Especially on college campuses, where it's fashionable to look down on wealth-building. But if you've saved enough money, you can afford to have higher values. Sure, some wealthy people don't choose to have higher values. That's their problem. And some people without money have exquisitely high values, often at great personal cost. How many of us are really cut out for martyrdom? But if you have some savings stored up to live on, you don't have to keep working for an unethical boss. You don't have to work so much that you can't be there for the people in your life.

I've always found that the Kinko's stores that made the most money had the happiest coworkers and did the best work. It was like the atmosphere in our family's home, where there was enough money to go around and plenty of laughter. I really liked having prosperous partners. By the time FedEx bought Kinko's, more than 100 people connected with the company—most of whom were our former partners—had become millionaires. Several of them are double-digit—and a handful are triple-digit—millionaires. I'm extremely proud of this fact; I only wish more of our former coworkers and partners had done even better. When I teach college kids and budding entrepreneurs today, I spend a lot of time discussing making, saving, and growing money. It's amazing to me how little they know. College kids today don't know the first thing about financial planning or staying out of credit card debt.

The first secret I share with college students, and with partners for that matter, is one-word long: Save. Savings was the cornerstone of my life. I knew damn well I wasn't going to make it in life if I didn't have money. When I was in my mid-thirties and still not married, my mother kept harassing me to find a wife. When I told her to give it a rest, she said to me, "OK, honey, I won't ever bring up marriage again. But when I look at you, you'll know what I'm thinking." By the time the first class is over with my college students, I say to them, "Now, when I look at you, what am I thinking?" They say, "Save your money!" That's right! You can still be a socialist, I tell them, just "save your money."

> **I knew damn well I wasn't going to make it in life if I didn't have money.**

Let me ask you a simple question. What sorts of checks do you prefer? Rent checks, dividend checks, or paychecks? Believe it or not, college kids are often stumped by this question. The answer is rent checks and dividend checks, of course! If you're getting a paycheck by the time you are my age (or at any age), you have very little say in your own destiny. If a boss treats you unethically, you can't flip him or her off and walk out the door, especially if you have a spouse and two kids. All of a sudden you've lost your independence and, with it, your dignity. If you've saved enough so that you've made investments in real estate or equities, you've got rent checks and dividend checks coming in. My whole life I've opted for rent checks and profit checks over paychecks. The greatest thing about real estate is that not only are you getting rent checks, the value of the property continues to rise. When I was 26 years old, I bought an apartment building with 4 units for $125,000. I sold it years later for $450,000. That made an impression on me, believe me. I was finally getting to the place where I was making money while I slept.

I'll let you in on another little secret. Before I sold my stake in Kinko's, I made more money as a landlord in some years than I did selling copies. As my Kinko's "bank account" grew stronger, I tapped into my profits to buy properties. My rule was that if the monthly rent was 1 percent of the purchase price, I'd buy the property. By 1980, I had bought about four or five properties. I started by putting money into apartment buildings and, by 1985, I owned ten or twelve. My period of greatest real estate expansion during my Kinko's years was between 1985 and 1990, when I acquired another 50-odd properties. Wherever I could, I bought the buildings that leased commercial space to our Kinko's locations.

I brought our partners in on these deals whenever possible. When we bought the building that housed our head office in Ventura, we gave all the Kinko's partners a chance to buy in. It was a large building and a multimillion dollar deal. We offered pieces of it at $25,000 a share. About half the partners—or 50-some people in all—bought in personally or they bought in through their businesses. "It was a good deal because in southern California real estate is so expensive," Denny says. "When we sold the building, we each got back a good return on our investment."

The reason I was so keen to diversify into real estate goes back to something I heard from my mom. She once met a diamond merchant who sketched out the following diagram of lifetime wealth creation. I've reproduced this sketch on countless napkins in countless bars with countless partners and coworkers over the years. Many of our partners bought into it completely, and they are wealthy people today as a result. It's pretty simple and it goes like this. When you're in your twenties, you don't have excess money to stick into real estate, stocks, or savings, so the bulk of your net worth is concentrated in your business. The allocation of your wealth looks something like this:

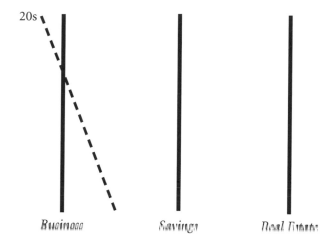

When you're 30, you've started to diversify and you're diverting some of your assets into stocks and bonds. You're becoming more liquid. Your portfolio looks like this:

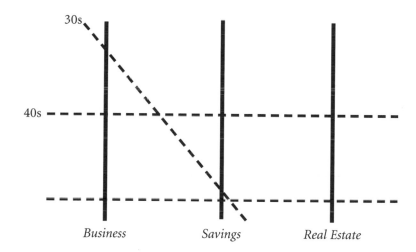

By the time you're 40, you've begun to spread your resources evenly between your business, your savings, stocks and real estate. By the time you're 50, you've shifted your assets out of business and primarily into savings and real estate.

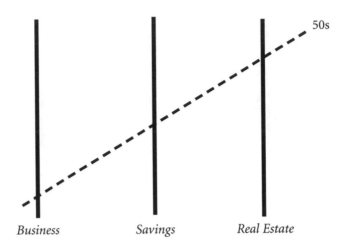

If you want to hang onto a little aggravation (like me), you keep a chunk of your money in business. The idea is you want multiple income streams. You want to be bulletproof, with interest, dividends, rent, and liquidity. This is not a new idea but, strangely enough, in our capitalist system, not too many people know about it. Look at the amount of credit card debt we have in our society. We're raising sheep in our educational system, not independent thinkers and doers.

As far as I'm concerned, the definition of owning your own business is *making money while you sleep*. If your business is so dependent on you and on your presence that you have to be there every minute of the day to make money, you don't really own your business—your business owns you. Greg Clark, who started as our corporate counsel at Kinko's, remembers a conversation we had along these lines years ago.

"Paul would say, 'I'm making money sitting here talking to you. You have to charge me $100 an hour because that's the only way you get to make money.'"

Nobody had put it to him quite that way before. It helped motivate Greg to change his line of work. A couple of years later he became a Kinko's partner in Utah. Today we own real estate together and a statement-printing business called The Data Center. The goal of every entrepreneur, of every financially astute investor, should be to make money while you sleep. Your savings and your ideas work for you 24 hours a day, 365 days a year. I love going to sleep knowing that my investments are making money for me all night long. I felt much better about Kinko's once I knew all our stores were spreading their overhead and serving customers 24 hours a day. The same goes for the real estate I own and for all my different investments in companies. I may no longer have 126 Kinko's partners, but through an investment company, my partner Phil Smith and I own stakes in a lightbulb company, a chain of Italian restaurants, a document processing concern, and an alternative health magazine—each of them a great business. I'm invested in other companies elsewhere, such as a chain of coffee shops in the Midwest and our bowling center. The true value of all these investments is that, on most days, I don't have to do a thing to keep them running because I invest in and with fabulous people.

When I was 22 years old, with one Kinko's location, I didn't yet have the assets to make investments. I didn't even have a savings account. But, looking back, wouldn't you say that Kinko's was my savings account? When we were younger, our mother used to tell all of us, "In your twenties, try everything. In your thirties, figure out what you're good at. In your forties, make money off what you're good at. And in your fifties, do what you want to do." That's what my uncles did. As it happens I was 50 when I sold my first stake in Kinko's.

Learning Young, Earning Young

When I was younger, I was lucky to be able to compensate for my poor reading skills with an unusual facility with numbers. Back in second grade when I was stuck in a school for kids with mental retardation, my teachers noticed that I was a little too good at math to justify my placement alongside classmates with Down's syndrome. In yet another attempt to teach me to read, one of them said, "To get you good at reading, we're going to have to make you bad at math." Good thing that plan failed.

In my family, people talked about stocks and investing incessantly. I listened to my father and my uncles as much as I could. When I was about 12 years old, I started ditching school and taking a bus into downtown Los Angeles to see a family friend named Charles "Chuck" Doud who was (and still is) a stock broker. I'd turn up at Chuck's office, at the top of a high-rise building, and ask him to teach me about stocks and investing. Mom got wise. While Chuck was going over stocks with me, Mom would call and say, "Chuck, is Paul in your office?" Chuck would wave me out in the hallway and say, "No, he isn't, Mrs. Orfalea."

When my dad discovered what I was up to, he didn't want to discourage me, especially since I was facing so much discouragement elsewhere. So he told Chuck to let me trade some stocks in his account if I wanted. Sometime later, Dad opened one of his statements from the brokerage and he discovered that I'd made a bunch of stock trades. The good news is that I'd actually made him a profit. The bad news is that was the end of trading in my father's account. I got better and better at picking stocks over the years. One time, while I was in junior college racking up credits so that I could enroll at USC, I entered a stock-picking contest. Out of 500 entrants, I won! The ten stocks I'd picked outperformed everyone else's. I was given five shares of a mutual fund as a prize. It was the only time that I can recall when a performance at school—though it didn't involve class work—drew praise from my extended family.

My desire to invest my money drove my interest in savings. My mom took me to the bank when I was about five years old. I had $6 saved and we deposited it. I remember the guard who would tell me about bonds and interest rates. I would deposit 17 cents at a time. Mom would say, "You've got a lot of nerve to deposit only 17 cents. Wait until you've got a dollar." I always had a piggy bank at home. One time, after I'd dipped into it to spend $2.50 to buy a slingshot, I suffered badly from what I would later learn was buyer's remorse. I wished I'd kept the money.

Two times before I was 21, through scrimping and saving, I managed to save $5,000, which was a lot of money back in the sixties. Both times I lost all of it in bad investments in the bond market. The first time was through highly leveraged convertible bonds. When the Federal Reserve started regulating the convertible bond market, they lost all their value. I remember riding on a public bus one day when I heard a radio broadcast about the change. With a sinking feeling, I knew my entire investment was worthless. I lost my second $5,000 on highly leveraged junk bonds. Turns out I got burned by bonds long before the future "junk bond king," Michael Milken, who, as it happens, was in my class at Birmingham High School. (When we met later in life, he rattled off a bunch of names to see if I recognized any of his friends. They must have all been straight-A types because I didn't. I asked him, "Were any of them in woodshop?")

I'd made my second $5,000 from a vegetable stand that a friend and I ran on a street corner in La Cañada, California,

> **By selling vegetables I learned a lot about what I did not want in business.**

not far from my sister Marlene's house. I haven't mentioned this before, but it was my one true business success—albeit a qualified one—before Kinko's. At 3 A.M. every morning my friend and I would drive into downtown Los Angeles to buy vegetables and then we'd drive back to sell them to people in the suburbs throughout the day. My mom gave me the idea for the business. By selling vegetables, I learned a lot about what I did *not* want in business. Having an inventory-based business, I discovered, caused a lot of headaches. Talk about mundane. Even more so than when watching my father's apparel company, I learned what a tremendous burden it could be to shoulder all the busywork yourself by trying to sell vegetables with your own two hands. It was a big epiphany. I was forever procuring those vegetables, arranging them in displays, and trying to sell or dispose of them before they rotted. I got completely caught up in the tedium of the work. I was so busy I forgot to put an ad in the paper. And then, when I did remember, I'd kick myself because my business would triple. I never had time to think about the big picture. What big picture is there for a vegetable stand, you may ask?

Good question. I could never answer it because I was simply too busy to think about it.

I was 21 when I lost the money I'd made selling vegetables on highly leveraged junk bonds. I was engaged to my girlfriend at the time and suddenly out of cash. My best friend Danny's older brother Dickran told me, "Orfalea, you're so poor that if you get married now you'll be eating leftovers." I knew he was right. I postponed the wedding and my girlfriend broke up with me. While at the time I wished she hadn't dumped me, in retrospect, losing the $5,000 was a good experience. I was starting to get cocky. I count myself extremely lucky for those two $5,000 reversals. They humbled me. By the time I got to college, I knew that the market wasn't some two-dimensional board game. You could take real losses that caused real pain.

For a college-age investor, those losses matured me pretty quickly. They also contributed to one shining moment in my school career. During my senior year at USC, I was taking an investing course taught by a professor named Dr. Kenneth Trefze. Unlike my other teachers, Professor Trefze wasn't an academic by nature. He was a mutual fund pioneer on the West Coast. He was retired at the time and teaching college kids just because he liked to. I had tremendous respect for him. The feelings were not mutual. When Dr. Trefze saw how poorly I wrote, he snatched up one of my reports and took it to the admissions office. He demanded to know how a student like me was ever admitted to a place like USC. He hassled me constantly about my spelling.

One day we were sitting in his class when Dr. Trefze asked all of us to calculate the dividend return on an IBM stock. Sitting next to me was one of those straight-A types. He and the other students pulled out their slide rules and started crunching numbers. I was accustomed to working out figures like dividend returns on the fly, so I did the calculation in my head. I called out the answer.

"You're wrong, Orfalea," one kid near me said, quoting a much higher number; it was off by a factor of ten. If he'd ever actually invested in stocks, he would have known he was wrong.

"No, I'm right," I said softly.

From the front of the room, Dr. Trefze announced, "Mr. Orfalea is right."

After that day, Dr. Trefze started to appreciate talents he'd overlooked. One day he pulled my best friend, Danny, aside and, within earshot of other students, said, "Tell Mr. Orfalea I won't bother him about his spelling any more. Tell him I hear he's on the brink of brilliance."

"You're a diamond in the rough, Mr. Orfalea," Dr. Trefze said to me later in his office. "You can sit behind any business desk in America that you want to." This was extravagant praise, especially from someone like Dr. Trefze. The support I received over the course of my life from supportive teachers like him (and several others at USC, including my finance professor, Professor Stancill) really helped turn my life around. They gave me confidence when I had none. That day Dr. Trefze told me about his work. He urged me to plan for my future wealth and to be sure that I gave back to my community. He told me to remember the enormous responsibility I would have to others, especially the people who would work with me. I suspect that part of the reason I teach college courses today is because of what I learned from him. For my part, I've already found other "Paul Orfaleas" in my classes. Two of my former students, Mark and Eric Jones—identical twins who were not even 30 yet—convinced me to invest in an Internet company several years ago. It made a huge return for everyone involved. Keep your eyes open. There are great ideas everywhere.

It's the Cash, Stupid—and the People

Especially in the early years, I ran Kinko's like a peddler. I didn't follow a corporate model. In fact, I did just the opposite. I paid attention to cash flow, and I also paid attention to marginal cost—the cost required to produce one extra unit in any business. Say a steak costs a restaurateur $7 and he or she sells it for $21. That's a tremendously high marginal cost—about 33 cents of every dollar. And the food is perishable to boot! At Kinko's, I sold copies for about 5 cents, but the weighted average cost of goods was only about 1/2 a cent. If we screwed up, it didn't cost us much. I wanted to encourage mistakes and our cost structure made that possible. Believe me, $100,000 worth of gross income business at Kinko's generated a lot more in actual profit than $100,000 in gross income at that restaurant. Marginal cost is a very simple concept, but most businesspeople have no idea what theirs is. When scrutinizing any business, this is one of the first figures I nail down. It tells me something crucial about its viability.

I've found that corporate types don't understand cash, either. Why? you ask. Aren't they whizzes at reading financial statements? The thing about financial statements is that reported net income doesn't have anything to do with how much money a company actually has on hand at any given moment. I'll give you an example of a corporate view of money. We used to sell passport photos at Kinko's and we advertised the service in the local Yellow Pages. It would cost

> **There is a lot of corporate dyslexia going on out there.**

us 75 cents to make a passport photo. I calculated that price jumped by $1 to $1.75 when you added in the cost of the Yellow Pages ads. We'd sell those photos for $13 a piece. You think this is a nice business? Shortly after we sold a controlling stake in Kinko's, the new budget people came in and, to make their numbers, they got rid of the Yellow Pages ads. They saw it as an advertising expense and didn't take into account how it affected the rest of our business. I used to go to the office and think, "Are they deliberately trying to be idiots?" These straight-A types drove me nuts. Then, like a self-fulfilling prophecy, we abandoned our passport business. That is corporate dyslexia. There is a lot of corporate dyslexia going on out there.

As Kinko's grew, one of the things which I became proudest of is that I learned to manage our cash flow—as far as I'm concerned the most important financial measure of any business. When it comes to managing your personal finances, what is the first thing you look at? It's your bank statement, isn't it? Cash flow is the first thing I look for in a financial statement. I don't really care where the money was yesterday. I want to know where the money is *today* and where it's coming from tomorrow. At Kinko's each partner gave me cash flow statements every month. I may not have read novels, but I poured over all of these statements as if they were *The Da Vinci Code*. I checked my revenue every day. Accountants can mess with line items like net income or net earnings, but cash flow statements don't lie. A wise person said that he couldn't understand the cash flow statements from Enron, so he didn't buy the stock. Makes sense to me. When we were a decade old at Kinko's, we were still running the business out of the cash drawer. My strong intuition about the role of cash in the company kept us going. As John Davis once observed, "Paul paid attention to two things: people and cash."

There is only one other company that I know of that used a partnership structure that was similar to ours to grow. That was the Sambo's restaurant chain. It turns out that the co-founder, Sam Battistone, lived in Santa Barbara, too. After Kinko's was a couple of years old, I went to talk to him. "Always do your arithmetic," he told me. It seems like obvious advice. But, at that point, the business was going so poorly that we didn't yet have good financial controls in place. I was emotionally afraid of doing my arithmetic. When I started running the numbers, it was depressing. We were always short on cash.

We had only six or seven locations at the time. Our cash flow was so dicey that, especially during the slow summers, we didn't have the money to pay our vendors. One day, I remember coming into the office and discovering that we had about $8,000 on hand to cover about $32,000 in bills. My bookkeeper and his assistant were born-again Christians. They started speaking in tongues over the books. They told me if we would just have faith, the money would appear. They were going to send out all these hot checks in the name of God. "You know," I said to them, "let's just sleep on this tonight." I went to bed and barely slept a wink. All night long I was thinking, What am I going to tell the banker? The next day I went back to the bookkeeper and said, "We're just not going to rely on God in this way." Eventually he couldn't handle the stress from the ups and downs of our cash flow and he quit.

In later years, I got much better at handling the dips in our cash flow. Dave Vogias remembers how hard it was to navigate our way through the summer lows when classes weren't in session. "For the first ten years," Dave recalls, "we were tied to the university, so we were very cyclical. I wanted to pay my vendors on time. I would pull on my line of credit in the summer and pay it off in December. I would pull on it over Christmas break and pay if off in the spring."

The main strategy we developed to contend with summer lows was the creation of Kinko's Financial Services (KFS), the in-house financing arm that Jimmy, Dan, and I owned together. We started it to lend money to our partners when they needed funds to open new stores or improve their existing ones. We also used it both to pay all our bills to vendors like Xerox on time and to leverage our massive collective buying power. Many of our partners were such small operators that, in the early days, securing bank loans was simply not possible. We became the lenders of last resort, loaning at higher rates than the banks. The payments flowing in from all our partners gave us an extra income stream when we needed it. KFS wasn't a tax-sheltering organ, but it did help us to pay our quarterly tax bills by giving us reliable cash flow. It's very difficult to pay taxes and manage your cash flow when you're a growing business and you need resources to expand. The government takes away all your liquidity every April 15, June 15, September 15, and January 15. To make sure we didn't overextend ourselves—a constant risk—I made sure that we grew no more than 30 percent a year. I knew intuitively that the only way I could both keep our culture intact and manage our cash flow was to grow no faster than that. I knew if we didn't have enough liquidity, we couldn't throw loose nickels at all of our new ideas. In the rapid growth years at Kinko's, I had insomnia a lot. I spent a lot of night-time hours calculating our cash flow. It captivated me.

Although our partners didn't always like the high interest rates we charged through Kinko's Financial Services, they were highly motivated to pay off their loans quickly. Dana Jennings from North Carolina remembers, "Paul got me to expand because he lent me money, but my goal was to get off the KFS chow line as soon as I could. We had to fight tooth and nail to get lines of credit from banks." Partners like Dana were motivated to get out of debt, and fast. That bolstered our cash flow while KFS enabled lots of partners to expand when they couldn't have done so otherwise.

Buy the Toppings

One difference between the way other people see money and I see money is evident in my view of large public companies. I've got a pet peeve with these companies where the atmosphere is so cozy. I've noticed there are two types of people: those who deduct and those who capitalize. Big shots, like the managers of some of these companies, are out to bulk up their revenues, often at the expense of good money management. They want to impress their accountants, so they don't take the sorts of losses that can significantly reduce their tax bills. They are hamstrung by shareholders who are always looking for increasing returns. It's different when you own your own company; I never cared how we looked to our accountant. I didn't keep much money in the company because we didn't have to impress anyone and I wanted to save on the tax bill. In my family, every other word I heard as a kid was "deductible." I may be dyslexic, but I can deduct. For the privilege of being a corporation, the government charges you 40 percent in taxes and your money is taxed twice: first as corporate income and then again as personal income. As a Subchapter S corporation, you pay only personal income taxes. The downside is that the owners shoulder tremendous personal liability. The upside is that your income is taxed only once.

> **In my family every other word I heard as a kid was "deductible."**

I liked having high expenses. It may not have looked pretty in the books, but it helped at the bottom line. Take the free lunch we served every Friday at our head office in Ventura. This lunch wholesale cost us only two dollars a person and our coworkers loved it. Now think about it. If we're going to *pay* somebody two dollars, it costs us three dollars to write the check—with payroll and Social Security tax added in. But, as a service, it really costs us only one dollar because I get such a good break from the federal government. Not only do I save those additional taxes, I can expense it to lower my overall tax bill. The marginal benefit this cheap lunch generated—the goodwill and the loyalty—was tremendous. I always wonder why companies don't give these sorts of freebies more often to their workers. To me, it's like making the trip all the way to the pizza parlor and then refusing to pay for extra toppings. Don't pass up the orthodontia coverage, the daycare, and the pension benefits. You get a 35 percent discount *after* you deduct.

Don't be stingy! Get the toppings—they cost you nothing! And your kids will appreciate it! Think of it this way: When you date a woman, do you get more mileage out of the steak and lobster dinner or the little flower you give her when you show up at the door? A little act of appreciation, a thank you, costs you absolutely nothing.

And it can save you money in ways you might not imagine. In nearly three decades in business at Kinko's, we never faced a serious union threat. I remember one time Dave Vogias learned that some of his workers in Philadelphia, where unions are phenomenally strong, were making noises about organizing. He went out and had a talk with them.

As Dave remembers it, "I had to explain, 'If we go union, this is what we get. We won't have parties. We won't get flex time. And you're not going to get profit sharing.' People realized it wouldn't be a good thing. This is where the Philosophy played in to our money management strategy. The Philosophy says, 'We take care of each other.' By profit sharing, we are taking care of each other. Profit sharing is the most brilliant thing we ever did. So, we were never unionized."

I think the only reason we've got so many unions in this country is simply that big business became too selfish. The only reason we have Social Security and Medicare is that business didn't realize we have to take care of the whole worker, so the government was forced to come in and impose regulations. The result is that the whole system became much less efficient. If businesses don't voluntarily provide daycare or adequate medical coverage, odds are that the government will start to force them to do it.

Like I said, buy the toppings! I guess you could say I've come a long way from my penny-pinching days.

Chapter 12

Know When

to Fold 'Em

FUNNY, ISN'T IT, HOW GOOFING AROUND CAN BE a good way to learn? Ask Bill Gates. When he was a freshman at Harvard, Gates spent more time playing poker than attending his classes. I can relate. Eventually Gates dropped out of Harvard and put the principles he was practicing in his poker games to work in the marketplace, and we all know what happened next. You won't find a wilier outfit out there than Microsoft (nor many fortunes larger than Gates's). Love it or hate it, you've got to admit that Microsoft, and Gates, know how to play the cards to their advantage. Other well-known business, political, and legal minds play poker to sharpen their negotiating and deal-making skills—or just to make money. Richard Nixon paid his way through law school with his poker winnings. Other savvy players include Carl Icahn, the Wall Street financier, and Supreme Court Justices William H. Rehnquist and Antonin Scalia, to name a few.

Not long ago, the head of the Chicago Board of Trade told me that the biggest predictor of success for future traders was not success in academics, but the amount of time they spent playing games as kids. I do my best to make up for this hole in the educational system in my world economics class at UCSB—I make poker and Monopoly part of the coursework every quarter. Typically, we divide each class into four to six subgroups. Each group picks a particular night to meet and I give them pizza money. We spend our subsequent classes discussing everything they learned (more on this later).

Poker is such an engrossing game because it teaches players so many things at once. Whether they know it or not, when friends like Gates and his crowd gather to play poker, they are honing their skills in at least ten different areas simultaneously. Have you ever wondered why poker players look so intent when they're deep in a game? It's because their minds are working on so many different fronts at once. Among them:

1. Emotional control

2. Intuition

3. Circle of competence

4. Risk analysis

5. Human nature

6. Adaptability

7. Perseverance

8. Management of ambiguity

9. Luck

10. Patience

Arguably, one of the most important lessons you learn while gambling, whether in a friendly game at home or at the casino, is how to manage your emotions. It's so essential that, if you can learn to master them (something I've never done all that well), you've got a better chance of tackling all the other nine principles. Once your emotions fly out the window, your game goes with it. The only way to truly learn about emotional control in games of chance is when the risks that you assume are real. If you've ever played for crackers or matches, you know it just isn't the same as playing for cash. With crackers, everyone can stay in each hand just to see what happens. With real money at stake, you are forced to make tough decisions and live with the consequences. It's the same with the stock market.

My younger cousin Lance Helfert and I, who run a money management company together called West Coast Asset Management LLC, both know people who study the stock market but don't invest. They fancy themselves brilliant stock pickers, but they don't have a clue how they might behave when their own money is at stake.

One of my earliest gambling adventures with Lance came at the craps table in Lake Tahoe. At the time, he was barely gambling age. As with all my friends who come gambling with me—I like to fly to Vegas with upward of a dozen friends at a pop—we formed a corporation at the tables. (As my friend Jacques Soiret describes it, "Paul gets down on his knees. We pray. We blow on the dice. We do the oogie boogie dance around the table.") This time, Lance and his sister Michelle put in $20 a piece for a 10 percent stake each and I put in about $200 for the remaining 90 percent. I always find that when I gamble with others, especially virgin rollers, I win. If I gamble alone, I get my butt kicked. After an hour or so at craps, the kids' shares of the pie had grown to $1,000 each. It was a huge win for them, but I wasn't entirely thrilled about it.

> **When I gamble with others, especially virgin rollers, I win.**

As Lance remembers it, "All night and all the next day Paul was saying, 'I wish you had lost that money. It doesn't always work that way. I wish you had lost that money.'" Part of me was happy for Lance and Michelle. He ended up buying a used Bronco with his winnings because his parents had promised to match any money he earned toward his first car. But I didn't want either of them to get the wrong message. I wanted them to experience a little losing. That's an important experience to have, all the more so when you're young and you can afford it.

Keeping your emotions in check *during* a card game is one thing, but taking defeat in stride *afterward* is another. Gambling is like being married. When you've got a family, your wife humbles you and your kids humble you even more. In life, you have to be careful not to believe your own hype. You've got to learn to be adaptable. In Vegas and at the poker table, I've been known to win, but I've also been known to lose and to lose big time. When I gamble I don't start small and build up my winnings. Instead, I go out big on the first roll and hope for a huge payoff (ergo all the praying and dancing). While gambling may seem at odds with my strategy of savings, it isn't. I head out to every gambling date knowing what my cutoff point is; when my losses hit that number, I do my best to quit. (That's where the emotional control comes in. I don't always have it!)

I like to gamble against the house. Once I win, then I can relax. I play with the casino's money. While I love winning, the losses have been better for me, ultimately. They bring me back down to earth. When I lose, I have a tendency to brood. You see this phenomenon in the stock market when people can't believe the value of a particular stock has dropped. They hang onto losers instead of cutting those losses and investing in winners. I think most people are brooders from time to time. I try to snap myself out of that state. Painful though it may be, losing kicks me into a healthy bout of reflection. My parents told me *most fortunes are lost in the good times.* People tend to overinvest in the good times. It's just like when I lost all my money as a kid—twice. I thought I was invincible. It's called hubris. The problem is that, in the good times, it's hard to remember how bad things can go and how quickly they can go bad. Gambling refreshes the memory. Playing games of chance with money, like craps, poker, or betting on sports, checks your ego.

Know When To Go with Your Gut

Everything taught in our schools is so rational, so linear and logical. Kids don't get a chance to learn about an exceedingly valuable skill: intuition. It's the name of the game in Vegas or at the poker table. You could argue that learning about intuition is more important than many of the core subjects in schools today. When you fall in love, for example, you might fall in love in a number of different ways. You could fall in love with your head and not with your heart. Or you could fall in love with your heart but not with your head. Then you've got a problem. There's a war underway between two different parts of your body. You'll find the answer to the conflict down in your stomach, home of the "gut instinct." That's where you learn intuition. And playing games is as good a place as any to practice and develop the use of this part of your anatomy.

The best players, like the best investors, minimize their emotional swings and maximize their intuitive strength by staying within their circle of competence. In poker, in the stock market, and in life, you can't win if you don't play. But how and when to play is your choice. In friendly poker games, players take turns dealing and calling the game. As a result, you can't always pick the game, but you *can* pick which game to bet on. And you can always choose to sit a game out. How well you choose will affect your ability to keep your emotions in check. If you only know how to play classic five-card draw, you better sit out the hand of Omaha, stud poker, or Pirate's Booty (deuces, one-eyed jacks, and suicide kings wild). In a friendly game, you might be inclined to learn new variations by playing and betting conservatively. But there's always plenty of opportunity within your own circle of competence. Stick with what you know and you'll improve your odds.

> You can't always pick the game, but you *can* pick which game to bet on.

The copy business appealed to me because it fell perfectly within my circle of competence. It was a simple business, at least in the early days. It didn't take extraordinary genius to figure out the fundamentals. And it wasn't an inventory business. I took an aptitude test once in high school and discovered I had all the makings of a good social worker. Selling copies may not have been social work, but it had some of the hallmarks of that profession, especially its focus on trying to help people and assuage their anxiety. I learned how to stick within my circle of competence. I didn't—God forbid—take over my dad's business or go into a complex inventory industry like department stores. If I had trouble controlling my emotional nature at Kinko's, I don't think I would have stood a chance juggling the purchase, distribution, and sale of millions of shoes, handbags, and cosmetics.

In order to conduct risk analysis in both business and in life, you've got to remember that *your eyes believe what they see and your ears believe others,* as a Chinese fortune cookie once told me. In *The Prince,* Niccolò Machiavelli takes this even further: "Generally men judge by the eye rather than by the hand, for all men can see a thing, but few men can come close enough to touch it. All men will see what you seem to be; only a few will know what you are."

That's a sad commentary. I talk about this constantly with my partners. As you already know, this is a big drawback suffered by the readers of the world. They read reports or listen to others instead of seeing for themselves. One legendary story in my family concerns the time my Uncle Nick bought some shares in Beckman Industries. He happened to be at a local print shop and watched a humongous job being done for Beckman. He checked them out further and bought in. Beckman's stock skyrocketed in the following years. That's the way we invest in my family. We use our eyes. I mean, come on, with the advent of digital cameras, who out there didn't know that Eastman Kodak was going to be struggling? Just pay attention. If you use your vision, the world is a fun place. To be a good investor, a good card player, or good in business, you've got to look past the four-to-a-straight cards showing and notice the nervously tapping finger. You must become a rigorous student of human nature. You've got to look beyond financial reports and analysts' recommendations. Meet directly with the coworkers and customers of a company. Take them to lunch. Hang out with your kids. Talk to them.

Give the glory and take the money.

In other words, get the dirt. Poker is about both ferreting out another player's truth and simultaneously hiding your own. It's a truism about gambling, and life, that sometimes you need to keep your own cards close to the chest. While playing poker, you learn to show others only what you want them to know while at the same time observing them very closely. My mother, who was a fanatical poker player, always told me that whenever the business was going poorly, I should brag, and that whenever the business was going well, I should complain. It's a peddler concept and a poker concept through and through. During our years of most rapid growth at Kinko's, I made a policy of not talking to the press. What would I have stood to gain by doing so? I kept my personal profile intentionally low when it came to my relations with the outside world. When *Forbes* published its first piece on me back in the mid-nineties, I wouldn't let them take a picture of me. I always told my partners to *give the glory and take the money.* There's no point in bragging in good times; as my mother used to say: *"Your friends don't need to hear it and your enemies won't believe it anyway."*

Going Head-to-Head with Xerox

When I play poker with my kids or with friends I'm trying to teach, I pounce on them if they happen inadvertently to show me their hands. I'd never do that, of course, in a serious game when you expect your opponent to know better. Experienced players never show their cards during negotiations. We didn't tell Xerox why we always tried to negotiate our annual machine leases or purchase agreements with them near the end of the year. This is because we knew that Xerox—being a big, public company—needed to book as much revenue as it could by the end of the year. Its salespeople, who were paid by commission, were obsessed with short-term earnings. We got a lot better at our Xerox negotiations when Dan Frederickson, who had been a financial manager at Xerox, came to work with us as president. In some years, if we waited long enough, Xerox would actually come to us and say, "Hey, could you take these 100 machines?" Usually we took them, knowing we could negotiate comprehensive, three- or four-year service contracts with them so late in the year.

We also strategically neglected to tell Xerox exactly what those service contracts meant to us. As far as I was concerned, they were more valuable than the machines themselves. Some years we leased and some years we bought. It didn't matter all that much to me. All I ever wanted was to rent out time on them. I figured that with approximately 800 hours in a month, it would cost us about $20 an hour to run them. But we could make as much as $100 an hour, ideally, if we ran them 24 hours a day, seven days a week. That's a profit of 400 percent! Believe me, that's a figure we didn't mention either.

You might think that the agendas of Xerox and Kinko's were aligned—that both companies, in the end, wanted to sell more copies. In one sense that was true. But, the reality was far more nuanced. Because it was beholden to shareholders, Xerox was interested primarily in revenue. They wanted to sell those machines. I wanted to sell what came out of them. That's a fundamental distinction. Whereas some of our coworkers felt that Xerox and Kinko's were on the same page, I disagreed. I took note of the difference in our motives. And I exploited it to our advantage. They wanted to show revenue by the end of the year and I wanted to rent by the hour. It was a total mismatch. And it worked for us. That's the poker of business.

Every time we negotiated, I relished the back-and-forth. I would toss out possible scenarios and then rethink them. I was ruthless, but

Being a skeptic is different from being a cynic.

I had a great deal of fun during each and every one of our annual negotiations. The Xerox guys picked up on my excitement. I gave them a hard time, but I think they enjoyed the game because we made it fun for them, too. Our meetings were never boring. Dan now says I "controlled the situation by keeping everybody off balance. It's called management through chaos." Dan and I played good cop, bad cop with our friendly rivals. I think you can guess which part I got.

We also had fun playing our various vendors off each other. When Kodak began to make high-quality copiers, we wanted to get them into the stores. But Kodak didn't have a history with the partners, as IBM and Xerox did. We needed to create an incentive for our partners to clear some floor space. Dan convinced Kodak to lease us machines without our paying a cent up front. Instead we paid them "per click"—per copy—as we used the machines. We'd never done a deal like that before. But we knew what Kodak wanted and found a way to make it work. And another thing: Working with Kodak threw Xerox off balance. It bought us leverage the next time we sat down with the guys from Xerox or IBM.

Just as gambling and poker teach you to keep your cards close to the vest, they also teach you to be a skeptic. Being a skeptic is different from being a cynic. Skeptics are careful in their investments. Cynics are too jaundiced (or scared) to take any risks in business or in life. They can't trust. My mother always told me that *you can't make money while you're running scared* and I've found it's true. You can't let fear or cynicism guide you. But a healthy skepticism is a good thing to develop. When you've been duped in cards, you find out quickly and pay immediately for your lack of perception. You develop a finer insight into human nature. You grow in your ability to manage ambiguity. You begin to trust your intuition. Every time you get a new card, you readjust your hand. You learn to adapt. And to look beyond appearances.

One sobering lesson of life, business, and poker is this: Relationships that start out friendly do not always end up that way. Whenever possible, I avoid playing poker with hotheads and cheats. As I said before, I always look for "cockroaches." Whenever there is a problem with a potential partner's ethics or with a potential investment's financials, there are bound to be other problems you can't see right away. The same principle held at all the different Kinko's stores we used to visit around the country. A slovenly appearance meant there were other problems elsewhere. I could tell if it was a good or a bad store by the way workers looked me in the eye, by their demeanor. My intuition told me that. I apply the same standard to business and investing. Another way we don't invest properly is when we don't take a company's culture into account. For example, Johnson & Johnson, which I mentioned earlier, is a good company because of both its research and development and its marketing prowess. But J&J's company credo and selfless culture make it a great company.

Sometimes a potential partner and I will sit down and play games together. As much as anything, gambling gives me insight into a person's strengths and weaknesses. On a business trip not long ago, my cousin Gary Safady and I played cards with a recent graduate from USC named Chris Shane who had a business plan for student housing he wanted me to look over.

As we got off the plane, I turned to Gary and said, "He's sharp. I like him. He knew how to manage his risk. He knew how to play to his level." Gary and I went ahead and invested in Chris's plan.

Respect Your Luck

Games of chance give people the chance to experiment with the influence of luck. Though I'm a great believer in building skills, I'm also tremendously superstitious. I have a healthy respect for Lady Luck, especially beginner's luck. That's why I took chances on so many inexperienced partners at Kinko's. When at the craps table, I try to play with virgin rollers (like Lance) whenever I can. I believe their good luck will rub off on me. In fact, without it, I'm a bad bet at the tables. Or, as Dan puts it, "Paul *never* wins." Now *that's* an exaggeration! But if I bet on myself alone, it's more than half true.

Sometimes virgin rollers lose faith before I do, like when I persuaded my operations vice president Karen to come gambling with me in Vegas. Here's Karen: "Paul says, 'You're going to be my lucky charm.' So he gets me to stand next to him at the craps table. He has me touch the dice. He gets on his knees and prays. He starts losing money having me standing there. He loses *a lot* of money. I couldn't take it anymore so, finally, I left. Paul was like, 'No, no, you're my lucky charm.'" I still think our luck would have turned if Karen had stuck it out.

Here's an interesting side note as to why Karen might have walked away. Researchers observing kids on the playground found that when a conflict arose, the girls stopped the game because the relationships were more important than the game. The little boys, on the other hand, worked the conflict out because, to them, the game was more important. I think we need both perspectives in life to be successful.

When gambling, whether at the tables or in business, I figure I've got to do everything I can to enhance the luck of both our partners and myself. I won't let a black cat cross my path. I don't step on cracks in the road. I'll drive in circles to avoid driving down Pardall Road in Isla Vista. My partner Mark Madden used to empty out his left shoe after each of our long rambling walks that served as our business meetings. All the loose change we found on the ground went into that shoe. ("It became normal for me," Mark recalls.) Or I stuck coins into my own shoe. My foot would hurt from all the change because I made sure to keep it in that shoe for the rest of the day. My left foot was screwed up for years. Whenever I found a coin and it was showing heads, I'd have to switch it to tails before picking it up. Don't ask me where I picked up these habits because I can't remember and now I can't stop myself. When Mark and I walked together, we were forever running around obstacles like fire hydrants or street signs so that nothing divided us. I got this from my parents. I do the same thing in Vegas. Say a group of my friends and I are in a casino and headed up a flight of stairs with a handrail running up the middle, and I start up the opposite side by mistake. I always catch myself. A couple steps up, I'll stop, run back down, and run back up the same side of the handrail that they're on. On the street, if a pedestrian tries to cut between us, I'll practically wrestle the person out of our way. Be it a handrail or a passerby, I won't let anything between us. I won't let anything divide us. In gambling, as in life, we've got to stick together.

My left foot was screwed up for years.

And practice, practice, practice. When my students come back from their poker and Monopoly games, I often find that playing together has driven them apart. They want to tell me about the fallout. Sometimes somebody had a fight with somebody else. Maybe one student became the pariah because he or she so dominated the game. Another kid pouted and sat the game out entirely. Conversely, other game nights do more to spark matchmaking than all those blind dates I kick-started combined.

But, back in the classroom, I don't want to hear about it. The games have thrown the students into such disarray that they've missed the lessons they were supposed to learn. I want them to tell me what they observed about the time value of money, about how to manage their impulsivity, their liquidity, and their marginal revenue. Marginal revenue and marginal cost are two of the most important measures in assessing the viability of any business.

Don't Pass Go Without Collecting a Lesson

Monopoly gives you a chance to watch marginal revenue in action when you build houses. If you buy Boardwalk, for instance, you pay $200 to build each house. For the first house, you get back only $200 in rent—not a great return. But the second and third houses pay you $600 and $1,400 respectively. Your marginal revenue on those two homes is the difference between the $200 you paid for them and what they produce in return: $400 and $1,200. You see that an extra increment of expense gives you a disproportionate amount of income. This is a powerful lesson. But, for the most part, the students are too distracted to get it. They're too impulsive. They have a real rough time with the concept. They're "in" Monopoly and not "on" Monopoly. They haven't yet learned how to focus.

As with life, it's so easy to become distracted—by the details, the drama, the ups and downs—that you can simply miss the lesson. Games of chance compress life into smaller moments. They distill the lessons for us if we can just pay attention. It's no surprise that so many of the principles and aphorisms that guided our time at Kinko's came directly from my mother. My mother taught me how to pay attention. She wasn't a business owner herself, but she was raised by one and married to another. And she played games obsessively. When she played poker, she and her friends often played straight through the night to breakfast. When Mom couldn't get a game together, she would sometimes drive to casinos, in City of Industry or Gardena, for example, and spend the night at the tables. She played obsessively, but she never pushed the envelope financially. She knew how to manage her risk.

After my father died, Mom was still playing poker with the same friends and relatives with whom she'd been playing for 50 years. One night in 1988, during a game, Mom had a stroke and, a short while later, died. One minute, she was gambling with her sisters; the next minute she was gone. She was the first of her seven siblings to pass away. We consoled ourselves knowing she left us while doing something she loved. After she was gone, one of her sisters came to me and handed me something. "These were her last chips," she told me. "I think she would have wanted you to have them." In her final gesture, Mom, who, like me, was a huge joker, made me laugh. She may have "cashed in her chips," but it was as if she was urging me to keep playing.

So many people suffer from a tendency to get stuck in ruts. I wonder if the nongamblers of the world fall into this category. All that adjusting and readjusting can be too rattling for them. But the thing about poker is that, at the same time that you need to change constantly, you need enough patience and perseverance to see the game through to the end. During a typical poker game, over the course of several hours, stacks of chips large and small will travel around the table. One person's stake will rise and fall just as a stock's value will rise and fall over time. And if you can't manage your emotions, you won't last. It does no good to play well all night, only to let hubris take over at 5 A.M. as you bet it all on a possible straight flush.

In her final gesture, Mom made me laugh.

It's like life. Near the middle of the nineties, it was becoming time to choose a new circle of competence for myself. It was time, after three decades. But, compared to knowing when to hold 'em and knowing when to fold 'em, knowing when to walk away is sometimes the hardest thing of all.

Chapter 13

Know When to Walk Away

NO MATTER WHAT ANYONE SAYS, WALKING AWAY from something you've spent 30 years nurturing, whether it's a child, a company, or even a hobby, is going to take a toll. How can it not? How is it humanly possible to say goodbye to something that contains so much of you and your love and devotion? When my father shuttered his business in 1981, a part of him died along with it. It wasn't that he stopped living after closing Charm of Hollywood. He even came to Kinko's for a time to jointly run the division—which still exists—that made banner signs along with David Vogias. But it was hard on him. I don't know if closing his company took the life out of him, but he died too soon, five years after it went out of business.

This phenomenon doesn't just affect company founders, by any means. I see it constantly in business people, especially when I give talks on one of my favorite subjects: balancing work, love, and play. Men are worse than women. Dan Frederickson recalls: "When the Kinko's thing ended for me, I almost felt like I wasn't anywhere anymore. When the job was gone, I was gone." He went into a severe depression. Most of us men identify far too personally with our work. It's only human, of course. But it's unhealthy. My personal belief is that we've all got to do whatever we can to draw our sense of self out of something much larger than just our careers. Otherwise, it's simply not possible, psychologically, to survive those inevitable workplace setbacks or transitions. Retirement is only one of them.

At Kinko's I did my best to avoid going through that kind of trauma. I tried to safeguard as much of my personal life as I could. My wife will tell you I didn't do the best job at this, but it certainly could have been worse. To get a visual image of what this separation should look like, I picture a Venn diagram in my mind. It's one of the few things I remember from my high school algebra class. They are used to visually represent complex, overlapping concepts. In my diagram there are two circles. Kinko's represented one of them and Paul represented the other. I tried to keep both of these circles separate.

This goes back to staying "on" your business, not "in" it. Relying on talented people meant I could more easily hold those circles apart. I could leave work in enough time to have dinner with my family every weeknight when I wasn't traveling. I never worked weekends. I was so preoccupied with business during our peak years that I wasn't there mentally half the time when I was with my family, but at least my body was there. Other times, like during the annual picnic, it was worse; the circles converged despite myself. During the picnic, I spent whole days talking and handing out hats to thousands of people. By the early 90s the picnics grew so gigantic that it was increasingly hard to focus on the fun. So many people were trying to kiss up to me all at once. I wasn't raised to be a mascot, but once you become one, it's hard to drop the role. Even on those days when Kinko took Paul over completely, somewhere deep within myself, I tried to remember that I was Paul long before I became Kinko. One day, I would become just Paul once again. Business schools mostly teach students how to build businesses, but they ought to offer a course on how to let them go, too. I've harped a lot on the importance of staying "on" your business and your life. The ultimate expression of this idea is knowing when you are ready to let it go, not just for a day, a weekend, or a vacation, but for good.

I didn't figure this out all at once. It crept up on me over time. By my mid-forties, as you may recall, I was having increasing trouble managing my emotional nature. I was getting tired of playing the father figure to so many people and worrying about their individual and collective welfare. Every workday, I was battling our partners more and more. As Todd Johnson remembers, "Some partners didn't want to invest in the future. They didn't want to put in new signs or counters. They just wanted a cash cow. That is probably why over the years Paul got more and more irritable. What can a man do?"

Take our largest partners. If I told Tim, "This is a great machine," he wouldn't buy any of them, but Brad would buy 20. I'd have to encourage Tim and slow Brad down, like a parent who knows he has to parent each child slightly differently. Out in Ohio, I'd have to loosen up Dave Vogias. Dave would analyze any machine purchases to death. And he was too authoritarian. He acted like he was doing someone a favor when he paid them. That's a bad attitude for everyone. I was better at this juggling act when I was younger. I just hit a point where I couldn't continue playing the cop for 126 partners.

Democracy's Downside

A dd to that the fact that our democratic structure that gave birth to Kinko's and fueled our growth, started to work against us once we grew to a certain size. In the mid-90s, we tapped our coworker Blaise Simqu to set up a national accounts division for customers like General Electric. Big clients expected standardized service nationwide. But with so many partnerships, it was a tough proposition to bring the different factions of the company into agreement. While trying to set up a nationwide account for G.E., Blaise felt like he was running a political campaign for national office. One day he fielded about 30 voice mails with questions and requests about the program, but he couldn't properly answer any of them.

"It was a time of great despair," Blaise says. "I realized there was nothing I could do. The corporate structure, the way it was before we merged the partnerships, was the antithesis of what it needed to be to roll out a national accounts program. This was an unmanageable situation. It had to change. It absolutely had to change for Kinko's to go to the next level."

None of this was change I particularly wanted to be part of. When we were smaller and growing, there was always room for individuality and for fun. But as we grew bigger and bigger, we grew more technologically complex. We needed something I've never been fond of: homogeneity. In my experience, homogeneity isn't much fun. Mom used to hold up her hand and tell us, "You have five different fingers for a reason." Then she'd close her hand into a fist and say, "School and life want to make us like this." At Kinko's, we had an expression that got at the same idea: "One size fits all means a poor fit for everybody." I was never interested in the lowest common denominator.

In addition, the dynamics of the industry had changed so much that, increasingly, I found I could neither explain the business to myself or to others. What did we stand for in the eyes of the customer? Were we a jack-of-all-trades, but a master of none? I was always looking for the guy out in left field who could wipe us out. I feared that the emergence of personal laser printers and digital photography could render Kinko's obsolete. I've mentioned that at five, seven, 50, 200 and 800 stores we had a problem. Actually, at 800 stores, the dynamics of the industry were new all over again. We were too small to be big and too big to be small.

"Our big problems came when we reached the top of the mountain and we had no one to rattle our sabers at," says my coworker Dean Zatkowsky. "We did become a little self-obsessed. We just didn't see ourselves very clearly. You can see a lot when you're on top of the mountain, but you can't see the mountain."

Tim Stancliffe remembers it this way: "We were really good at being the underdog, at focusing on our competition and just going after it. Once we became fat and lazy and an 800-pound gorilla, we were miserable. The erosion happened way before the partnerships merged."

At the same time, while growth was still clicking along at about 30 percent, the earliest partners were starting to slow down. We weren't in our twenties anymore, or even our thirties. Some of us could see retirement approaching. Others had kids nearing college age. Because of our partnership structure, we didn't have succession plans in place. We needed to find a way to turn our holdings into cash. We needed an equity event. My brother Dick and a couple of our partners thought we should consider going public and selling a controlling stake in the company. I agreed.

Cashing In the Chips

It was 1995 and our annual revenues had just topped $1.5 billion. We formed a team that was composed of myself, my brother Dick, our president Dan, and our largest partners—Brad, Tim and Jimmy. Our general counsel Stuart Blake headed up the team. With the help of advisory firms, including Bob Montgomery of the law firm Gibson, Dunn & Crutcher, we began interviewing private equity or venture capital firms. Under the auspices of Goldman Sachs, we talked to the Private Equity Group at Merrill Lynch, The Blackstone Group, Apollo Management, Forstman Little, and Clayton, Dubilier & Rice, among others. We also talked with a couple of companies, including Alco Standard, Moore Business Systems, and International Paper, about buying Kinko's outright.

From the start, it was obvious that our federation of 127 partnerships (including my own) presented a stumbling block. There was nothing remotely traditional about the way we were structured. Our chief competitive advantage, our unique structure, had suddenly become our major drawback. Prospective buyers and investors had no idea how to value us. Goldman Sachs recommended that we work with a venture capital firm that had "management depth and experience."

Brad: "We were all on the edge between Apollo and Clayton, Dubilier & Rice. Apollo Group, in Los Angeles, wanted to let us run the business. They liked our culture. CD&R wanted to bring in corporate management. But we were ready to turn over the reins. That's the reason we went with them."

Although Dan and I liked Apollo, the team voted to go with CD&R. And I didn't protest. They seemed like good people when we met them at their New York offices. We knew a newly formed corporation would require substantial funding to provide working capital for ongoing operations and projected expansion. At the same time, we needed equity. We estimated that CD&R would need to invest between $200 and $250 million for 25–30 percent of the company.

The idea was to merge all 127 independent partnerships that comprised Kinko's to form a single legal entity, a C corporation. After some time, the newly formed company would be ready to go public with an IPO. Don Gogel and Andy Pearson, of CD&R, explained that partners would be compensated for their own companies with shares in the new company as part of the merger of the 127 partnerships. At least this was the idea. We all knew it would take a while to get from concept to the reality. It had taken years for all our partners to agree on far simpler matters. When we presented to the partners the idea of merging the partnerships, a good many of them—Dan says it was about half of them; I say it was less—were flat against it.

> **Our imaginations began to work overtime.**

Rich Kraus was one of them. A partner in five stores in California's Inland Empire, Rich was eager to keep building. Unfortunately, his timing didn't mesh with that of the founding partners. Like everyone else, Rich would be compensated for his stores, but was disappointed that he didn't have the chance to build a much larger business. I was disappointed for Rich, too, and for our other partners in similar predicaments, especially those with even fewer stores. (Later I invested with Rich in a new company, Shred Force, that provides secure document destruction.)

The biggest selling point for all of us was the promise of a substantial initial public offering. Don Gogel, of CD&R, along with Rob Pace and Suzanne Nora Johnson of Goldman Sachs, heightened everyone's expectations on this account. This was 1996, right after the Netscape IPO had ushered in an era in which companies with little or no revenue were raking in hundreds of millions of dollars in the public marketplace. What would a cash rich company like Kinko's bring in a public offering? Our imaginations began to work overtime. Still, it was a tough sell.

Our lawyer Bob Montgomery oversaw the transaction from the legal end. And what a transaction it was. Here's Bob: "Throughout the 127 Subchapter S corporations, there were close to 200 different owners involved. Each company operated differently. Some pulled hard while others sat back on their oars. Some partners had not been oriented as much to bottom line profitability and had been focusing primarily in building up their revenue bases through rapid expansion throughout their territories. Many partners left very little money in their businesses. When I began working with Kinko's in 1996, no one could say exactly what the company's overall revenues were nationwide. There were so many inter-company sales and charge back transactions that while we knew sales exceeded $1 billion, we could only guess at the actual number when all the financials were consolidated. Initially, people didn't believe we could come up with a fair and equitable means of valuing each partnership for a merger. My own partners told me it couldn't be done.

"One of the beauties of the transaction was that Paul could have done something called a 'cram-down merger.' He and his large partners had enough control of each Subchapter S Corporation that they could have compelled everyone else to sell. Instead, Paul decided to make it volitional."

It wasn't easy. We spent the better part of 1996 embroiled in heated meetings with different partner groups around the country. Because we'd always treated each partner and coworker as an individual, we recognized the individuality of each of their companies as well. We gave them four different options for valuing their companies: using 1) 15 times pre-tax earnings, 2) 1 times revenues, 3) $1.50 times the number of residents in their areas, or 4) $300,000 times the number of stores. We knew that adding up all these valuations would result in a total greater than the real world value of a consolidated Kinko's. So we cut back everyone's final valuation 50 percent across the board. Bob has been doing mergers and acquisitions for 30 years and still hasn't seen anything like it. As Bob puts it, "I thought the formula we came up with was really ingenius." We also guaranteed our partners a salary for the three years following the sale. We made the sale as democratic and as compelling as we possibly could. In return for selling their companies, our partners received stock in the newly merged, or rolled up, Kinko's. To be honest, none of us thought we could persuade 100 percent of the partners to sell, but in the end, they all did.

To complete the deal before January 1, 1997, Bob's working group in his law firm took over nine conference rooms in their offices in downtown Los Angeles. Eight lawyers and fifteen paralegals were assigned to the project. No one, including Bob, got more than a day or two off for Christmas that year. The finished transaction gave CD&R a controlling stake of the company at the board level, at 29.6 percent. Like me, most partners sold a percentage of their shares while holding onto some shares, too, but we gave up control of the company to the minority shareholders. The day the sale went through was a momentous one for each and every Kinko's partner, for all of us who had once valued our independent operations.

As our general counsel Stuart Blake remembers it, "People were trading in their lives and their lifestyles for some stock." We relinquished control of our individual Subchapter S corporations together. It was the beginning of the end of an era.

The Trials of Transition

The first decision CD&R's Don Gogel made after the sale was to name himself interim chief executive officer. This was not what we were expecting. We thought Dan Frederickson might continue in the position or that it would go to one of our larger partners. Brad Krause was interested in the job. But CD&R swiftly began to set about creating a new company on its own terms. Very quickly relations between the old and the new guard disintegrated. "It was startling how quickly they stopped listening to us," Dan recalls.

I retained the title of chairperson with an office at our head offices in Ventura. But, increasingly, I was cut out of decisions. I should have left right then. Yet, in truth, I wasn't yet ready to let go. In the search for a permanent chief executive, CD&R offered the job to W. Alan McCoullough, the chief executive of Circuit City. Dan was asked to sign the offer letter to Alan himself, which was a very humbling experience. But officers at Circuit City talked McCoullough out of it. John Antioco, the chief executive officer of Blockbuster, was another candidate. Finally, with my approval, CD&R hired Joe Hardin, the president and chief executive of Sam's Club.

Joe stayed with the company for about three years, and my presence didn't help him. The founder of a company should never sit on the same board with a new CEO. Later, CD&R partner George Tamke stepped in as interim chief executive and replaced Joe. Finally, in 2001, Gary Kusin, an entrepreneur in his own right, replaced George. Gary had started and took public Babbage's, a national chain of software stores, and had started and sold Laura Mercier Cosmetics to Neiman-Marcus. He still holds the job of leading Kinko's today.

I respect Gary. He's a smart businessman. But it was painful to watch the Kinko's headquarters moved from Ventura to Dallas, Texas. Eventually some 700 local people in Ventura lost their jobs. Watching the daycare center at our head office shut down and seeing all of our coworkers' infants and babies displaced was especially wrenching for me.

Prior to the move to Dallas, I left the company and became the honorary "chairperson emeritus." Dan was no longer with the company. Only a very small handful of our original partners survived all the change. I sold a full half of my shares in March of 2000 and left the board. I cashed my check and, on the very same day, had my kinky hair cut after all those years. I stopped coming to the office.

In December of 2002, CD&R, J.P. Morgan Partners, the buyout division of J.P. Morgan Chase & Co., along with Kinko's itself, made a final investment to buy out the former partners. I sold the last of my shares at this time. A year later, in early 2004, FedEx, our former vendor, bought Kinko's for $2.4 billion.

I sometimes bump into or speak with Kinko's coworkers, past and present, who describe in vivid detail how the company has been gutted, how the unique culture we built is gone. But Render Dahiya, until recently the last high-ranking member of Kinko's old guard at FedEx Kinko's, tells me this isn't entirely so.

At one meeting, Render says, Kinko's store managers were complaining that there wasn't enough consistency from store to store. What a change a few years can make! Managers and partners in the old Kinko's typically fought more for their rights to act as individuals and not as part of a collective. "We've gotten so large that our biggest competitive advantage is our consistency," Render says. "I think we had to do the merger not just for the partners, but for the customers."

That said, FedEx Kinko's has retained some of Kinko's best qualities from our early years. "When people from other large corporations come to work here," Render said when he was still there, "they constantly talk about the lack of bureaucracy, compared to where they've come from. There are many aspects of the culture that Paul helped create that we have retained. This includes our care of the customer, the high value we place on integrity and our commitment to conducting business in a way that is sensitive to the environment. Kinko's is not like it once was, but it's a much better place to work than in many other large corporations."

Staving off Tycoon's Disease

I'm glad to hear it. I haven't been able to substantiate any of Render's views directly because I haven't been in a store for years. For emotional reasons, I just can't go inside the stores anymore. I don't know if I ever will again. It's too difficult for me. When I see Kinko's coworkers today, they naturally want to tell me about their problems. I can't blame them. I spent three decades browbeating them to confess every niggling grievance about their work lives to me. But I don't want to hear their complaints anymore. I heard once that people suffer nervous breakdowns when they are expected to control situations that are uncontrollable. My former coworkers still treat me as though I have some influence over the work environment at Kinko's. I don't.

The truth is, for everything I've just told you about keeping Paul separate from Kinko, it's been excruciatingly difficult for me to let go. One of our partners, Keith Lawrenz, and I have had our differences of opinion over the years. He used to paint a bleak picture of my coming retirement. "At some point you're going to lose your identity at Kinko's," Keith would say, "and you're going to go down. It's going to be ugly." I didn't like to hear it, but I knew that Keith could be right. I had a dream that Kinko's would one day become the anchor of all-night commercial centers around the country. I envisioned all-night pharmacies, laundromats, coffee shops and Kinko's stores clustered together in attractive strip malls. When I let go of Kinko's, I let go of that dream, too. I just think letting go emotionally is a difficult thing to do for a human being, even when we know we're making the right decision.

**The truth is
I never liked
being called
Kinko.**

My personal physician Bill Morton-Smith once said to me that, by selling my stake in Kinko's, I staved off a severe case of Tycoon's Disease, and possibly saved my own life. I still have the same heart condition (paroxysmal tachycardia) that kept me out of the draft during the Vietnam War. Given my prodigious temper, I'm sure I was a real candidate for a heart attack. I didn't want that for myself or for my family. If I hadn't always *tried* to maintain a healthy distinction between Paul and Kinko, leaving the company would have been all but impossible, psychologically. I'm not sure I could have done it.

The truth is I never liked being called Kinko. Or Mohair, Brillopad, Pubehead, and Carpethead. "Kinko" wasn't exactly intended as a compliment when my friend Tim dreamt it up. But I can't deny it's been good for business. In the early days, Kinko's and I were synonymous. Later on, I got to feeling like the composer, Ravel, listening to that same refrain of Bolero, over and over and over again.

My friend John McGrath used to tell me that sometimes in life you have to forget who you *were* and learn to be happy with who you *are*. I'm trying to do that now. I want to get past the anger. Although I still have my lapses, now that I'm no longer with Kinko's, I think I have a better shot at it. Ten years ago I had bad gas, I couldn't sleep at night, and my neck hurt constantly. Now I don't have gas, my neck doesn't hurt, and I sleep like a baby. Getting to this point hasn't been easy, but it was necessary. Though none of the founding partners is with Kinko's anymore, we're glad to see the company move back on track. We finally took our chips off the table and let the game move on without us.

Chapter 14

Repurpose Yourself

Y BIRTHDAY OFTEN FINDS ME CROUCHED behind a tree, scanning the landscape around me for assailants. I'm wearing so much protective face gear that I look like a space alien. I'm trying hard not to laugh, but it's almost impossible because I suddenly spy one of my cousins or business partners similarly attired and, more important, unaware of my presence. I slowly creep up on him, point my gun, and blast off a couple of rounds. He's hit! I see yellow "blood"—alien blood!—spread across his back and I'm off, dashing madly after my next victim.

As many as 40 of my friends and I gather for these birthday bashes (or clashes) at huge paintball complexes that resemble industrial wastelands. We often bring our sons along with us. Because it's my birthday, I get to set the rules, which are pretty simple: kids against adults. With one exception. My best friend, Danny Tevrizian, and I play on the kids' team. It's just like when we were eight years old and Danny and I would tease our local barber until he chased us out of his shop. In paintball, my favorite strategy is to abandon all strategy, leap out from behind a tree, and attack five or six of my opponents at once. I think it's funny when they retaliate simultaneously, creaming me! It's a great way to release a lot of pent-up energy.

Have you ever noticed that some men, after they retire, stop being funny? They don't laugh as much or crack as many jokes. Something about leaving their jobs or selling off their companies can leave them stuck—permanently—in the doldrums. When the work goes away, something vital leaches out of their systems. Without noticing it themselves, they start to withdraw like nightshades. It's a sad thing to see. If they don't have wives to keep them involved in life, they die young. I always tell my friends to be grateful they have wives who nag because they'll live longer. If they stay involved in the world, they live as long as women do. In the film *About Schmidt,* Jack Nicholson plays an insurance executive who retires and then tries to go back to his old office to help. He sits there with his coat in his lap. The young guy who replaced him is polite, but doesn't need him. After we sold Kinko's, just *talking* about the company on the wrong day made me feel like Schmidt.

I like to think I didn't retire. I don't believe in it. Add "retirement" to the long list of terms (including "learning disabled" and "failure") that I don't believe in. Think about the word "retire" for a moment. That's a sad, Schmidt-like concept, isn't it? It sounds like the horse abandoned to the proverbial pasture. I never wanted to withdraw from life.

I've got a better word:"repurpose." I'm in the process right now of repurposing my life. Life should be a constant process of repurposing. Leaving a job is really no different, fundamentally, than all the other times in our lives when we have to repurpose. You get married, you repurpose. You have kids, you repurpose. Even graduating from college, high school, or grade school, for that matter, requires another death and rebirth. Another repurposing. Through each of these transitions, you have to reassess everything. The cards in your deck change. You reappraise.

After my friend Dan Frederickson emerged from his depression, he found he had a whole new outlook on things. Dan says, "I started to figure out that the job wasn't even a part of me. I think that Paul is finding out some of that, too, that he's more important as a person than as Kinko. People pulled on him all the time and never really cared about him for what he is. He's getting more satisfaction out of life now. He's finding out that life is much better after Kinko's."

Make That Change

That's absolutely true. That's the thing that's great about repurposing. On the professional front, more and more people these days are getting to repurpose their work lives over and over again. You certainly don't have to hit "retirement age" to do so. Hopefully, in the process, you get back in touch with something essential in yourself. That's one of the great things about this combination of longevity and a strong economy that we have. Even if you're stuck in a job or a profession you don't like, you've got a better shot than ever in human history to end up doing something that really satisfies you. Remember, it's all about your imagination. Stop trying to please people the way you did back in school when you were chasing those meaningless A grades. Think about how many professions that would have seemed bizarre or overly specialized years ago are supporting people and families today. Pay attention. Look for opportunities.

The great thing these days is that when I wake up every morning, I get to choose what to focus my energies on. It might be teaching, which is one of my all-time favorite pastimes. Or speaking publicly. I love talking with young (or old) entrepreneurs, students, families, or whomever else wants to listen to me ramble and pontificate. I love spending time with our family or thinking about philanthropy or investing. Even though I rarely trade (I'm a long-term investor), I love monitoring every little hiccup in the stock market. On a given day, I might check on my investments a dozen times. It's a challenge that absorbs me mentally and emotionally. A few years ago, as I told you earlier, my cousin Lance Helfert and I started a money management firm called West Coast Asset Management. A couple of my closest Kinko's partners and friends came on as nonoperating partners (Jimmy, Denny, and my childhood friend and lawyer, Jacques Soiret). They took board seats. A year after the company got underway, we hired on our first coworker, Atticus Lowe, only 22 at the time. He later bought in and became a partner when he was only 23. The three of us, Atticus, Lance, and I (ages 25, 32, and 57), are on track to bringing our total assets under management to $1 billion in the next couple of years. Since inception, and at the time of this writing, we are up around 23 percent while the market is down around 30 percent.

If there is one area of my life that I've always been controlling about, it is this one. For the entire time that I was with Kinko's, I didn't let other people invest my money for me. I did it all myself. I'd trained myself over the years to be much more of an investor than a businessman. I had no desire to partner with another investor. But Lance talked me into it. Like most of my other partnerships, somebody else gave me a pitch and I thought it through and then went with it. I still rely on others for the best ideas.

I lavish West Coast Asset Management with love. I'm still the 12-year-old kid who ditched junior high to learn how to trade stocks in his father's account. We eat our own cooking at WCAM. We invest our own money alongside our clients' money. (To see our newsletter, go to www.wcaminc.com). Though I monitor our every move, we rarely trade because we invest for the long term. The great thing about investments is that they are like grandkids. You can love 'em and leave 'em. Because I trust Lance and Atticus implicitly, when I want to go on a vacation, I can.

In addition to the money management company, my cousin Gary Safady and I develop real estate through our company O&S Holdings (which stands for Orfalea and Safady). We build large commercial properties all over the country. Some of them are beautiful, like the mixed-use commercial and business complex set on three man-made lakes that we are building in Huntsville, Alabama. I feel so creative when I'm working in real estate. My friends Phil Smith and John Davis (a different John Davis than our former philosopher-in-chief at Kinko's) and I operate a small business investment company called Stone Canyon Venture Partners. Sometimes I zoom out to Michigan to look over new locations of the coffeehouse chain, Espresso Royale, in which Jimmy and I have invested with our partner Marcus Goller. I've invested with other former Kinko's partners in several other businesses, too, including a data services company called The Data Center with Greg Clark and DataProse with Glenn Carter.

Education Without End, Amen

Equally absorbing—maybe even more so—is the work I now get to do in education. Having spent the bulk of my grade school years in the principal's office, it's an extraordinary, validating thing as an adult to have the avid ear of educators. Through the Orfalea Fund and the Orfalea Family Foundation, my wife and I have made grants to educational and mentoring programs. We support programs in the areas of "learning opportunities" (we do not call them "learning disabilities"!). In fact, royalties from this book will go to support this cause. We also support what we like to call "experiential" education in which kids learn not through tests but through the real world. We also support learning differences expert Mel Levine, who helps to promote understanding of conditions like dyslexia, ADD, and ADHD through his best-selling books and his organization All Kinds of Minds. I spend many an afternoon huddled over lunch at the faculty clubs of different universities talking with professors like Mark Juergensmeyer, director of the department of global and international studies at UCSB, with whom I coteach my world economics class. We discuss coursework, education, the professors' views of international affairs, and their budgetary challenges.

It's an extraordinary thing to have the ear of educators.

The president of both of our foundations, Lois Mitchell, and her colleagues Solveig Chandler, Lauran Eastman, and former Kinko's vice president Adrianna Foss, do a superb job running day-to-day operations for us. Each year we run a retreat for a group of innovative teachers and educators whose jobs are as thankless as they are important. We try to inject a little of the Kinko's family spirit into their lives. We give directors of child care centers a chance to get together with each other, to brainstorm about the various problems they face at work, and to share ideas and solutions. We also do our best to make them feel appreciated. The last retreat was held over a long weekend at the Renaissance Hotel just off Sunset Boulevard; one night everyone went to see the musical *Mamma Mia!* together. It's not unlike the Kinko's picnic—minus the booze and late-night carousing.

During the retreat, we urge them to make friends and establish relationships with each other. At the last session, my wife, Natalie, took to the podium to inspire them all to care for themselves better—to make sure not to work so hard that they miss their own doctor's appointments and to balance work, love, and play in their lives. When I spoke, I told them what it was like for me as a kid with dyslexia, trying to navigate my way through a hostile educational system. I urged them to reconsider some of the ways they teach and treat their children. I told them how something called "sensory integration" can help kids with learning opportunities like dyslexia. Although science has yet to prove the theory's efficacy, these days some educators believe that developing children's upper body strength, posture, and coordination can possibly improve their reading comprehension. The fact that I was a skinny kid with little upper body strength probably worsened my own condition; even now, as an adult, I have bad posture. I believe parents can help their kids develop strength and coordination through simple exercises like holding their feet while they walk around on their hands. My wife and I are eager to spread the word about sensory integration.

As best we can, we try to give kids the "toppings." We contribute to programs that bus students to museums, run after-school programs, and provide playground equipment. We strongly advocate for Universal Preschool so children entering kindergarten are "ready to learn." We just finished piloting a summer camp outside of Bozeman, Montana, for middle and high school students from Montana and California. It gave kids who would never otherwise have the opportunity the chance to backpack, raft, and live in nature. For three weeks, they bonded with other kids and became more self-confident. You should have seen the change in them at the end. Our own two kids, Mason and Keenan, got involved in the program. We wanted them to have the experience of creating something from the ground up to help others.

Our foundations also support high quality child care, including a program called ONEgeneration, based in Van Nuys, California, that brings together old folks, toddlers, and babies. All you have to do is watch older people at play with young children to understand how the generations need each other. Old people need the spirit of young kids and studies have shown that little kids grow up with better views of aging when they've had the chance to spend time with their elders. Kids become more empathetic and older people get a sense of purpose. One of the hardest things about getting older is living without the people we grew up with. I still keenly feel the loss of so many people in my own family, including Mom and Dad. It's a crime the way we separate the generations in our society. A recent study by the Federal Reserve of Minnesota estimates that for every dollar we spend on quality child care as a society, we save another nine dollars in other costs like operating funds for prisons. I believe quality early care can save society and that the only way we will break the chain of poverty is if we educate the children and their parents, especially single moms.

We have also donated to many institutions of higher learning, especially colleges and universities. Even though I wasn't a good student, I loved college. USC is the first place where I started to feel comfortable with and confident about myself. That's one reason I still spend so much time on college campuses after all these years.

All I've had the good fortune to build came out of nothing.

My mother motivated us to go to college, not by telling us we had to, but by asking us questions like "Doesn't college look like fun?" We donated funds for the Orfalea College of Business at Cal Poly, San Luis Obispo in honor of my parents, Al and Virginia. Mom was right about college. Even when I was failing my classes, I never ditched. And, of course, I never forgot it was colleges and universities that gave birth to Kinko's.

I'm not telling you all of this to impress you. I want to give you a sense of how fun it is to stay engaged in the world and to be able to give back to the community. (See how much you can do when you've invested and saved your money?) When you think about it, all that I've had the good fortune to help build came out of nothing. The best thing in life is making something out of nothing. The imagination is your only limiting factor.

In the philanthropic world, you often find foundations positioning themselves for perpetuity. This is not my view at all. In fact, we intend to complete our donations over the next twenty years, so we can enjoy the giving while we're still here. I've already warned my sons not to count on a huge inheritance. My younger son Keenan's reaction was, "That's fine, Dad, but could you do me one favor?" "What's that?" I said. "Please put an ATM machine on your grave!"

I learned from my parents about the importance of keeping my imagination fresh, no matter what the obstacles. Inspiring others was perhaps my central job while we were building Kinko's. In life, I've found that if you want to succeed you've got to spend time helping people build themselves up. Most people haven't yet learned how to do this on their own. It's not the sort of thing we tend to do well for ourselves. Now that I'm not with Kinko's anymore, I have the liberating opportunity to speak to an even broader cross-section of people, to businesspeople, as well as students, parents, and educators. In as many ways as possible, I try to tell them that the art of life is to rediscover who they are every day. I urge them not to be limited by their own preconceived notions about themselves, other people, and the world.

Flashback

Sometimes, it feels like I'm right back where I started. Not long ago, Charlie and I (along with two other partners, Steve and Terri Davis) opened the high-end bowling center that I told you about earlier, just a couple of miles away from the first Kinko's. We named it Zodo's after Zodo, aka Tim, who first bestowed the name Kinko on me. With 50 different brews, we've got the most beer on tap of any establishment in central California. We've also got a nice restaurant, a pro shop, and a full strength deejay box. (You know the joke about bowlers, don't you? Workers bowl. Managers play tennis. And executives play golf. So the higher up the ladder you go, the smaller your balls get.) For part of each day, we leave the lights up for the older bowlers who come to compete in the weekly leagues. When college kids bowl late into the evening, we hit the black lights, crank up disco music, and puff fog out over the lanes. Just like Kinko's, Zodo's stays open round-the-clock.

One day, to drum up business, I went walking all over the campus of the University of California at Santa Barbara. A couple of our Zodo's coworkers came with me. We stuffed professors' boxes in every academic department with flyers announcing the Zodo's opening. We handed flyers out to kids left and right. (Me: "How are you doing?" Girl: "I'm very tired" Me: "*Why?* Next time you're tired, go bowling instead!")

It was 1971 all over again, when I used to spend my days carrying around a backpack of Kinko's flyers and handing them out to passersby. Handing out a flyer seems like such a simple thing. But, like lots of simple things, it's deceptively effective. I used to walk around telling myself I was making $100 an hour. "We're trolling for dollars. We're trolling for dollars," I'd say. We built each of our Kinko's locations around the country, one by one, through flyers. While passing out Zodo's flyers, I spent part of the day on my stomach, stuffing the lowest professors' boxes against the wall. I could hear a couple of professors nearby talking about sending off a project to be printed at Kinko's. I needed to get them talking about bowling, too!

As for myself, I'm still letting my soul catch up with my body.

The day Zodo's opened, we threw a party. A couple hundred friends and family members came to play and to celebrate before we opened the doors to the public. Many of them used to work at Kinko's. Natalie ordered a giant bowling-pin cake. (It stood up straight just like a real pin!) At one point, we turned on the black lights and the fluorescent designs over the lanes started to glow. Fog wafted out over the lanes. The deejay cranked up Chubby Checker's "Let's Twist Again." In a minute everyone was up dancing together in the lanes in their bowling shoes. Couples and friends. Whole families. I could pick out all the former Kinko's coworkers. For a moment, it was like being back at one of our annual picnics.

We've all moved on by now. But many of us still try to live and work by the same principles that we used to build Kinko's. Looking at all those families dancing together at Zodo's prompted another thought. Today I tell Mason and Keenan, "My job is to market to you now." That's because I've always believed that *the definition of success in life is when your kids want to spend time with you after they've grown up.* I can't imagine anything more painful in life than if my sons rejected me in adulthood. That afternoon, I saw a lot of families at play together. My own kids were running around somewhere. I expect many of those folks will get along great with their kids once they've grown up.

As for myself, I'm still letting my soul catch up with my body. How long will it take? I can't answer that question, but it's a good one to ask. Do you know why children finally outgrow their tendency to ask millions of questions? Not because they've got the answers. They figure out that it irritates the grown-ups. If you've stopped asking questions, start asking them again. Learn to be immature, at least some of the time. It's taken me my whole life to figure out that I don't have the answers. All I've ever had was a bunch of questions. When you think about it, Kinko's started with a question: How come there's a copy center here at USC and not up at UCSB? Why is that? The most important thing is to keep dreaming, keep playing, and keep asking.

Staying "in" or "on" my business is no longer a fight. It's a choice. Every morning I start by asking what I want to do with this particular day. I'm still scheduled up to my eyeballs (because I like it that way), but when I first get up, I think about what I want to think about. That's freedom. I'm surrounded by nice, competent people. They are all far more capable than I at juggling a lot of details that require precision. They are so good at what they do that I no longer have to worry about busywork. With their help, I can get into as many, or as few, of the details as I care to. My life is still built on partnerships. And it still runs on trust.

It's a dyslexic's dream.

The Cast of
Recurring Characters

Gerry Alesia—Former Kinko's partner in Las Vegas

Dottie Ault—One of Kinko's first office managers

Dave Bolton—Former Kinko's regional manager in Bay Area

Glenn Carter—Kinko's partner in a division called DataProse, now DataProse Inc.

Greg Clark—Kinko's partner in Salt Lake City, Utah

John Davis—Former Kinko's board member

Mike Fasth—Former president of Kinko's Northwest

Adrianna Foss—Former Kinko's vice president

CiCie Frederickson—Paul's longtime colleague and former Kinko's partner in Southwestern Florida

Dan Frederickson—former president of Kinko's, 1986–1999, former Kinko's partner in Missouri

Don Gogel—Partner in Kinko's buyout firm Clayton, Dubilier & Rice

Joe Hardin—Former president of Kinko's, 1999–2002

Lance Helfert—Paul's second cousin and partner in West Coast Asset Management

Ken Hightower—former president of Kinko's, 1980–1986, and former Washington, D.C., Kinko's partner

Dennis Itule—Paul's cousin and one of his four largest partners, ran Kinko's of Thousand Oaks, California

Dana Jennings—Former Kinko's partner in North Carolina

Eric Johansing—Paul's nephew

Harry Johansing—Paul's nephew

Todd Johnson—Former Kinko's partner in Tennessee

Brad Krause—One of Paul's four largest partners of Kinko's in the Northwest

Stuie Krause—Former Kinko's partner in the Northwest, married to Brad Krause

Tim LaBrucherie—aka Zodo; Paul's college friend who first called him Kinko.

Karen Madden—Former Kinko's vice president for operations

Mark Madden—Former president of Paul's partnership, Kinko's Graphics Corp.

Annie Odell—Former Kinko's partner in Louisiana

Al and Virginia Orfalea—Paul's parents

Todd Ordal—Former Kinko's executive in Colorado and partner in El Paso, Texas

Dick Orfalea—Paul's brother and former Kinko's executive

Craig Redwine—Former Kinko's partner in Arcata and Eureka, California

Mazen Safadi—Kinko's partner in Western Pennsylvania

Gary Safady—Paul's cousin and partner in his real estate company, O&S Holdings

Blaise Simqu—Former Kinko's executive

Tim Stancliffe—One of Paul's four largest partners, headquartered in Colorado

Dan Tevrizian—Paul's childhood best friend

Dickran Tevrizian—Dan Tevrizian's older brother

Dave Vogias—Paul's fifth largest Kinko's partner, headquartered in Ohio

Jim Warren—One of Paul's four largest partners, ran Kinko's in the Southeast

Charlie Wright—Former Kinko's partner in Long Beach, California; former cousin by marriage

Dean Zatkowsky—Former marketing manager for Kinko's Northwest

Stories That Didn't

Fit in the Book

When Tom Parrish was 19, he was the shipping manager at Kinko's head office:

Paul says to me, "Hey, do you want to come out with me? I need some local information about rental rates in Isla Vista." He grabbed me because I was a student and could give him some feedback about the student perspective on renting near UCSB. So I'm driving with him and Paul is just a *terrible* driver. There are two sets of realtors trying to follow us. Suddenly, he sees this black cat about 300 yards ahead of us. He screeches on the brake, pulls a U-turn, and goes the other way. He will not let a black cat cross his path. Then we're driving along and he sees Pardall Road, the site of the original Kinko's, which he sold to his partner Dottie Ault. Because of that, he won't drive down Pardall Road anymore.

We screech up in front of these apartment buildings. I follow Paul as he runs inside. In each one, he turns on a faucet, lets it run for a minute while he watches it, then asks me, "How much rent do you think we could get for this place?" I'd say something and he'd say, "Nah," and then give me a number 25 percent above my estimate. We saw eight properties in what had to be under an hour. The realtors are running behind us. We get back in the car. He puts offers on six of them and ends up buying four. Basically, he ends up buying about $2 million of real estate in 45 minutes. As we drive back to the office, we stop at a kiosk where, at that time, you had to pay a 50-cent fee to cross the university campus. Paul accidentally drops a dime between the seat and the door. It must have taken him at least two minutes to fish out that dime. By this time, cars are honking behind us. Paul finds the dime, jumps out of the car, puts it on the concrete, and then stomps his heel on it several times before he gets back in the car.

I'm 19 and I'm silent. I'm completely silent. He knew I was mulling that over. I'm looking at him. I'm thinking this guy just bought $2 million in property and he can't drive down Pardall Road or let a black cat cross the road in front of him. Now what does *this* thing with the dime mean? He says to me, "You know what the lesson in that is? Never lose money." All the way back, I try to figure that one out. I didn't know if he was pulling my leg or if he was extremely superstitious or plain psychotic about this stuff.

Paul had some unusual ways of attracting talent, but it worked. He got my attention. So did the company's financial performance. I was the shipping manager and my job was to send out all the profit-and-loss statements to each of the stores every month. I mailed them to the approximately 80 stores we had at the time so I saw how well the company was doing. I became a partner in the organization with five stores in the Bay Area. I eventually sat on the board of directors. I was with the company for 20 years.

Charlie Wright, one of Paul's longtime partners, owned and operated Kinko's stores in Long Beach and surrounding California towns. He was married to Paul's cousin Gayle, who was also a Kinko's partner:
I met Paul at my wedding reception in April of 1978. Gayle's entire family is Lebanese. They're really close. I was a little unsure of the whole family. My mother-in-law threw the reception after she got over the fact that her daughter was marrying a non-Lebanese guy from East Los Angeles. Paul turns up in a green corduroy coat with his bushy, kinky hair. His pants were all wrinkled. He must have had a rough night the night before. I basically remember saying to Gayle, "Who is *that?*" She said, "Oh, that's my cousin Paul." Paul was just out there. He said, "Hey man, thanks for marrying my cousin." And he handed me an envelope with $100 in it. I was pretty taken aback

by that, but I realized later that, in his own way, he was trying to make me feel at ease.

Before Annie Odell became a partner in Louisiana, she was a store manager in Athens, Georgia. Jim Warren hired her:

I flew out to Athens to meet Jim and Barbara Warren. Barbara had talked me into the job over the phone. My father said to me, "Annie, how can you manage anything? You can't even keep your room clean." But I went anyway. Two days later, Jim and Barbara left to open a store in Colombia, South Carolina. I had one employee and the remnants of a store they'd opened a month earlier. I had to run the store from seven to seven every day. The phone rings one day. This guy on the other line said, "Hi, how are you?" I said, "I'm fine." He said, "Everything OK?" I said, "Yeah." He said, "Well, nice to talk to you." I said, "Well, that's nice." These calls would come in from time to time. Finally, I told Jim, "This weird guy named Paul keeps calling here." Jim told me, "Oh, he must be hitting the wrong button on his speed dial."

Craig Redwine was one of Paul's earliest partners. Paul set up Craig and Paul's first-ever partner Brad Krause in a print shop in 1972:

Paul set us up financially. He paid the rent. We ordered all the printing supplies and equipment. Brad and I were running the place. Pretty often, Paul would stop by. He would be very intense, talking a mile a minute. Stuff was coming out of him that was brilliant on the one hand, but on the other hand, it was very disruptive. We couldn't get any work done. Finally Brad and I told him to leave. Paul would put his head down and his hands in his pockets and he'd slink out of the store. A few days later, he'd come back with a big smile on his face. He'd say, "I've got a new attitude, can I stay?" We'd say, "Sure, man, you can stay." Sometimes he'd maintain. Sometimes he'd lose it and we'd kick him out again.

Blaise Simqu worked as an executive in the Kinko's head office for a number of years in the 1990s. One day, in 1995, he was walking down the hall and Paul poked his head out of an office door:

He goes, "Buddy, you want to go to the UCLA-USC game tomorrow?" I say, "You have tickets?" He says, "We'll get some." He says, "Meet me at the Tommy Trojan" [a landmark on the USC campus]. I'm thinking he's going to call in some chits. I'm picturing we're going to be sitting in a box with the president of USC. I'm also thinking, "Blaise, don't *ever* socialize with anybody who's not in your tax bracket." I didn't have much money at that point, but I go to the bank and I take out $500. I meet Paul on campus. Some guy walks past and Paul says, "Hey, you remember me? We were in a psychology class together, remember? I wanted to cheat on this test and you wouldn't help me out." This guy is looking at Paul as though he's crazy. Paul says, "What are you doing now?" The guy says he's a doctor and Paul says, "Oh great, you're a doctor. So that really worked out for you. Hey, nice to see you." This guys walks away and I'm thinking that Paul might have said, "Gee, things worked out for me, too," but he never did. Another guy comes up to Paul and offers him tickets for $50. Paul waves him off and says, "That's too much." It's Paul, his cousin, and I. We end up buying three tickets, not together, for ten bucks apiece. Paul sat about ten rows in front of me. About every ten minutes, throughout the whole game, Paul would stand up and yell back at me, "Hey, how are you doing, buddy?" I went home with $480 in my pocket.

Jacques Soiret is a longtime lawyer and friend of Paul's:

Talking with Paul is like playing conversational roulette. People say he has ADD—attention deficit disorder—but I think it should be called AAD for "accelerated attention disorder." He's so quick that he appears not focused when in fact he knows where you're going before you've said anything. You think, oh, he's not interested. But in fact he's got four conversations going on in perfect synchronization. I'm not a bad trial lawyer, but I can't do that. He's the most economical thinker I've ever seen.

Mark Orfalea is Paul's cousin:

One of Paul's classic tricks is to throw cold water on you in the shower. It pisses you off to no end, but there's not much you can do.

Another one is to set off firecrackers in the middle of the night. One time we were following some friends back to Paul's place. They didn't know we had another garage door opener in the car. We were 100 yards off or so and we weren't sure it would work, but it did. Everytime they clicked the door to open it and started to drive in, we would click it to shut it. This went on forever. Later Clarice comes up to Paul and says, "You've got some screwed-up garage door." You know what it's like when you laugh and you can't stop laughing?

Mark Madden was the president of Paul's company Kinko's Graphics Corp.:

I would tell the managers, "Forget it, let's not have a meeting. We're going to go bowling for an hour." We were a cult. We didn't have a secret handshake. It was, "Go out and have fun." Two or three of my regional managers were Mormons. With their soft drink buzzes, they ended up being some of the craziest people we ever had.

Karen Madden served as vice president of Kinko's Service Corporation:

In the early eighties we had a really big contract with Xerox come up. All of our guys went out and bought a nice shirt and suit. Xerox had been told that this is a very laid-back company so they all showed up in Hawaiian shirts. It was pretty funny.

Blaise Simqu recalls a costume party at one of the annual picnics:

It was a nautical theme party. Paul shows up in this costume. He looks like the land shark played by Chevy Chase on *Saturday Night Live*. It's this huge black rubber thing. He looks hysterical. He can barely move. All you can see is his little face. He comes up to our table. The spouses were invited to this dinner and somebody's husband looks over his shoulder and says to Paul, "I don't know how much they pay you at this company, but it ain't enough to wear that costume." I turn to the guy and say, "Buddy, it's enough."

Kinko's Partner Tim Stancliffe:

There was a period when Paul got involved in so many food fights. One was at Chuck's Steakhouse in Santa Barbara. He'd just get this mischievous little twinkle in his eye. Within a few minutes the air was full of mashed potatoes and steak. I remember him paying everybody off with the large wad of bills he always had in his pocket and skulking outside. Then, out in the parking lot, we started playing this game of kick the can with a crushed soda can. Paul started persuading the waiters to bring drinks outside. As other patrons left the restaurant, he got them to join us. There were like 50 of us. The manager came out and he was all pissed off again and Paul paid him off again. It was just a blast. That was part of the culture—the anarchy of it all.

Dana Jennings was a Kinko's partner in North Carolina:
Within six months I was an assistant manager, then a manager of both the stores in Athens, Georgia. When I was 23, I was one of five or six regional managers in the country. By the time I was 24 or 25, I had invested my life savings in Kinko's and opened a store with my own money. I was an English major with a political science double major and a minor in Spanish, not a business degree. Let's just say that making mistakes was part of the culture.

Terra Reynolds worked in FedEx Kinko's telecommunications department:
I was single for most of my career at Kinko's and no person worked harder than Paul to find me a husband! I really got a kick out of the attention Paul gave to that task. Of course his first choice was another Kinko's coworker. He worked hard during the annual picnics to make a match. One time, on a bus ride from the airport to the hotel he asked all the single men on the bus to raise their hands and then pointed to me and Nancy Caldwell and notified the men that we were also single. We turned bright red and cracked up. Over the years when Paul saw me at work he would check in to make sure I was at least happy in my current relationship even if, to his dismay, it wasn't with a Kinkoid. Finally Paul lucked out, or maybe his years of hard work paid off, because I ended up marrying a fellow Kinko's coworker after all! I remember being very excited to give the news to my parents, but I also couldn't wait to tell Paul.

John Davis is a longtime Kinko's outside board member and a Professor at Harvard Business School:

Business to Paul is not mystical. He speaks in a nonliteral, rather circular or creative way, but his thinking about the basics of business is actually very clear. You start to appreciate how clearly he thinks about business. He keeps his eye on the basics at all times. He doesn't get distracted by the dream or even by relationship issues. He's able to cut through that stuff. And he knows how the partners in his companies are performing. That was a strength of his as a leader and it was intimidating to everyone because all the partners knew that he understood the basics of their business at least as well as they did. And he knew them as people as well as he knew their businesses.

Tom O'Malia is former director of the entrepreneurship program at USC and the first professor to hold the Paul Orfalea chair:

Paul continues to be the single most successful graduate of the Marshall School at USC. And he graduated with a D average. I just think that in the dictionary next to the word "entrepreneur" they should put Paul's picture. Every student can learn twenty-five things from Paul's journey. What every culture needs is a Paul Orfalea who says, "The emperor has no clothes." The cognitive experts are asking how did Paul learn. He didn't test well but he sure as hell learned.

Orfalea's Aphorisms

Anybody else can do it better.

Ask yourself if you are "in" or "on" your business—and your life.

Happy fingers, happy registers.

Manage the environment, not the people.

Give the glory, take the money.

The goal of management is to remove obstacles.

One plus one equals three; we're stronger together.

If you work for someone else, you're only as good as your last paycheck.

The biggest reason you fail is your past success.

Your average street peddler has more business sense than the guy walking past in a suit.

Try it all. You never know what will stick.

Kids have to do everything well; adults get to pick one thing.

Learn to please yourself, not others.

It's not how much you make, it's how much you save.

Success is more about your imagination than anything else.

Your mistakes cost you nothing.

Your eyes believe what they see. Your ears believe others.

If they can't say it in plain English, don't work with them.

Beware of your own bullshit.

Running a business is nothing more than learning to go to sleep at night with unresolved issues.

I always figured I wanted a smaller piece of a bigger pie.

The biggest challenge we had was going from a culture of *things* to a culture of *people.*

Happy wife, happy life.

Trust people. If you don't, you have to do everything yourself.

Why would you want to waste your time going after someone when there is so much gold beneath your feet?

All we had going for us at Kinko's was the sparkle in our coworkers' eyes.

The best way to trust people is to leave them alone.

Are we looking *at* our customers or *as* our customers?

Most fortunes are lost in the good times.

There's no point in bragging in the good times. Your friends don't need to hear it and your enemies won't believe it anyway.

You can't make money while you're running scared.

In business, and in life, you have to come to terms with the fact that life is uncertain.

Investments are like grandkids. You can love 'em and leave 'em.

In life, if you want to succeed, you've got to spend time helping people build themselves up.

To men: If you stay involved in the world, you'll live as long as women do.

The best thing in life is making something out of nothing. The imagination is your only limiting factor.

How do babies learn about gravity? By dropping things.

You've got no other choice than to accept.

You can either earn your way into a fortune or save your way into one.

Don't you think you might get a little farther in life with savings than with grades?

You want to be bulletproof with interest, dividends, rent, and liquidity.

Make your customers comfortable and they will give you their lives.

Everything has a place and everything *in* its place.

People rise to the level of trust you give them.

When business is going poorly, brag. When it's going well, complain.

Retail is detail.

Poker teaches you every time there's a new card, it's an entirely new situation and you have to reappraise.

The art of life is to rediscover who you are every day.

Keep dreaming, keep playing, and keep asking.

I never wanted to work with people whom I made money on; I wanted to work with people whom I made money with.

Accountants are in the past, managers are in the present, and leaders are in the future.

You can see a lot when you're at the top of the mountain, but you can't see the mountain.

The mere fact the competition exists means they're doing something right.

You have to base your whole life on trust. You have no choice but to trust.

As a leader, all you do is manage trust.

It's not the things you do, but the things you don't do, that drive you crazy.

The mundane is like a cancer.

The democratic system, despite its flaws, is based almost entirely on trust.

The worker at the counter is the true hero of the company.

I always told people, "*You* will make yourself successful. Not me."

Attack arrogance at its root.

It didn't matter to me if your skin was green or if you were a zebra. If you could ring a register, you could work with us.

You're only as good as your dreams.

If you can't calculate your cash flow on the back of an envelope, you've got problems.

Goal-setting should be like an impressionistic painting.

I've always valued thinking hard over working hard.

In retail there are few secrets. Ninety percent of what we do and who we are is obvious to customers and competitors alike.

If it's your money on the line, you want to find out all the dirt.

The only things we took seriously were taking care of our coworkers, paying our bills, and the work we performed for our customers.

Get out of as much work as you possibly can.

Deal with your dark side.

You can manage people with the velvet glove or the iron fist. Occasionally you need both.

Fight your emotions.

If you work with me, you're family.

Integrity is like virginity—you only lose it once.

If my partners would fight for themselves, I knew they would fight for me, too.

The only true victories in life are victories over ourselves.

Who wants to follow a leader who is tired, haggard, and miserable?

Do you want to do well on multiple choice tests—or do you want to do well in life?

It's taken me my whole life to figure out that I don't have the answers.

My rule was that if monthly rent was 1 percent of the purchase price, then I'd buy the property.

Don't dwell on people's personality problems. Focus on what they can do.

In your twenties, try everything. In your thirties, figure out what you're good at. In your forties, make money off what you're good at. And in your fifties, do what you want to do.

You only do three things in business: 1) Motivate your workers, 2) Understand your customers, 3) Balance your checkbook.

Success in business is making money while you sleep.

What is the most successful book in history? It's not the Bible. It's the Yellow Pages. It's filled with success stories.

The toughest thing in business is managing ambiguity.

The only way we will break the chain of poverty is if we educate the children and their parents, especially single moms.

One of the most important things you carry with you is your frame of reference. Are you in the past, the present, or the future?

Being too busy is being wedded to the past.

Sometimes in life, you have to forget who you *were* and learn to be happy with who you *are*.

Your integrity is directly related to your liquidity.

Keep work, love, and play in balance.

Be perfect, or excellent, with your follow-through.

Let your soul catch up with your body.

Success in life is when your kids want to spend time with you when they're adults.

About the Authors

In 2000, **PAUL ORFALEA** retired from his position as chairperson of the company he named in honor of his college nickname (after his kinky hair). He is now involved in a range of activities, including West Coast Asset Management Inc., Stone Canyon Venture Partners LP, and other business ventures. Through the Orfalea Family Foundation, he and Kinko's have a long history of supporting educational initiatives, including scholarships and child development programs, as well as organizations addressing "learning differences." Orfalea is also involved in increasing public awareness of the need for "family-friendly" work/life policies, including flex time and quality early care for children of working parents.

Orfalea talks to a wide range of educational and business organizations and frequently teaches at the University of California Santa Barbara and the University of Southern California (his alma mater). California Polytechnic State University has dedicated a business school in the Orfalea name in honor of his ongoing contributions. USC plans to do the same, and UCSB has established the Orfalea Center for Global and International Studies.

ANN MARSH first met and wrote about Paul Orfalea in 1997 when she was a staff writer for *Forbes* magazine. Prior to *Forbes,* Marsh spent two-and-a-half years living in Prague, where she chronicled the country's early transition from Communism to a free-market economy. She now freelances widely.

The Big Thank You

One of the biggest regrets in my life up to this point is that I haven't said thank you enough—to my family, friends, and coworkers at Kinko's and my other businesses. It took an army of passionate, smart, and dedicated people to build Kinko's into the international success story it is. We had more than 25,000 coworkers at the time I left the company. Factoring in turnover and three decades of operation, the actual number of people who worked with us is many, many times that number.

Although it is impossible to track down and thank every coworker, we've assembled a sampling here of people who helped grow the business from its first tiny location in Isla Vista, California, in 1970 to an international powerhouse of more than 1,200 locations.

The individuals named here include Kinko's branch managers, front-counter store coworkers, founding partners, and field and office support staff. Others on this list helped Kinko's from their positions at partner organizations such as Xerox. I've also tried to include other significant people who assisted me, my family, and my other business enterprises in critical ways over the years.

I want to thank all of these remarkable individuals—named and unnamed—for helping me create a life story worth sharing.

Aase Johnson	Al Safady	Alex Smith
Adrian Burk	Alan Adler	Alice Malouf
Adrianna Foss	Alan Lerner	Alice Souza
Adrienne Burks	Alan Porter	Alicia Hoskins
Al Jerome	Alex Mock	Allen Prestegard

Allen Yu
Allison Stock
Alyson Alexander
Amber Williams
Amie Krause
Amy Fukutomi
Amy Reinhart
Amy Thompson
Andra Gordon
Andrea Spears
Andree Marie Harmer
Andrew Martindale
Andrew Sanchez
Andy Dahm
Andy Granatelli
Andy Martindale
Andy Schmiess
Andy Smalley
Angela Fisher
Angela Tabarez
Angela Vengel
Angie Walsh
Angie Winter
Anita Brown
Anita Garcia
Anita Peterson
Ann Berna
Ann Centeno
Ann Fitzgerald
Ann Fleet
Ann Gerk
Ann Griffin
Ann Lippincott
Ann Phan
Ann Tobin
Anna Neczypor

Anne Robillard
Anne Smith
Anne Towbes
Annette Lopez
Annette Merrill
Annie Odell
Annie Sparno
Anthony Norris
April Willenberg
Ara Norwood
Araceli Smith
Archie Allan
Ardean Bennett
Aric Fleet
Arlene Bailey
Arliss Namba
Armando Montejano
Art Damiani
Arvind Bhambri
Ashley Kirk
Atticus Lowe
Austin Bettar
Babji Mesipam
Bambi Leonard
Barbara Fleet
Barbara Kreitzberg
Barbara Myers
Barbara Peterson
Barbara Warren
Barry Hadsell
Bart Clemens
Beck Baez
Becky Barieau
Becky Graves
Becky Kolesiak
Becky Swift

Behnaz Kohan
Belynda Smith
Ben Barstow
Bernadette Buzzell
Bernadette
    Pennington
Bernie Glass
Bernie Perrine
Bernie Simon
Beth Brignac
Beth Desautels
Beth Helfert
Beth Mansfield
Beth Rolinski
Bethany Baker
Betsy Hightower
Betsy Korte
Betty Erhart
Betty Lee
Beverly Cain
Beverly Hardin
Beverly Huber
Beverly Snipes
Bill Aaron
Bill Bailey
Bill Barieau
Bill Capsalis
President Bill Clinton
Bill Crane
Bill Doolittle
Bill Gielow
Bill Helfert
Bill Kiefer
Bill Loomis
Bill Madson
Bill Mann

Bill May

Bill McKay

Bill Miller

Bill Morton-Smith

Bill Murray

Bill Pintard

Bill Pratt

Bill Ross

Bill Rowley

Bill Saba

Bill Seay

Bill Shanbrom

Blaise Simqu

Bob Avery

Bob Bartlein

Bob Brebner

Bob Burns

Bob Curry

Bob Gielow

Bob Hurley

Bob Inbody

Bob Largura

Bob Meltzer

Bob Montgomery

Bob Muir

Bob Peters

Bob Ragan

Bob Ranes

Bob Rhodes

Bob Riggs

Bob Ross

Bob Sheeler

Bobbi Markley

Bobbie Boccali

Bobby Parks

Bonnie Orfalea

Brad Krause

Brenda Allison

Brenda Helfert

Brenda Turner

Brent Myers

Brett Thornton

Brian Barefoot

Brian Brandini

Brian Hutchens

Brian McMorrow

Brian Rapp

Brian Ritchie

Brian Santos

Brian White

Brian Wullner

Brock Fisher

Brock McDonald

Brooke Carter

Brooks Dexter

Brooks Firestone

Bruce Hochstetler

Bruce Knowlton

Bruce Murray

Bruce Smith

Bruce Venturelli

Bryan Fleet

Bryan Hegney

Bryan Richardson

Buck Brellhart

Byron Cooper

Cameron Leggett

Cameron Moseley

Candace
    Fotheringham

Candy Cornelius

Candy Widener

Carl Heimowitz

Carl Razak

Carmela Chiurazzi

Carol Clenard

Carol Fell

Carol Gavel

Carol Houlton

Carol Mathieu

Carol Weddaburne

Carolee Warkentine

Caroline Prikosovits

Caroll Barrymore

Carolyn Gehl

Carolyn Vaughan

Carolyn Venegas

Carrie Burns

Carter Hines

Catherine Bourne

Catherine Coady

Catherine Dealy

Cathy Callow

Cathy Gregory

Cathy Reissman
    Perrou

Cathy Rivera

Cecilia Santana

Celeste Emerson

Chad Loomis

Chad Thompson

Charles Smith

Charley Williams

Charlie Monger

Charlie Morrison

Charlie Takita

Charlie Udet

Charlie Wright

Charlotte Huff
Charlotte McGee
Cheri Neathery
Cherie McAullife
Chip Hightower
Chip Stanczak
Chris Benoit
Chris Ching
Chris Coleman
Chris Cutting
Chris Davis
Chris DeYoung
Chris Itule
Chris Jung
Chris Kueny
Chris Lewis
Chris Longo
Chris Maertzweiler
Chris McGinn
Chris Merritt
Chris Ratner
Chris Shane
Chris Sparno
Chris Vogias
Chris Williams
Chrissy Brager
Christie Gilbert
Christina Harless
Christine Knight
Christine Naegley
Christl Baker
Christopher Sparno
Christy Christian
Christy Holz
Chuck Dicker
Chuck Doud

Chuck Hechler
Chuck Lawrence
Chuck Mayper
Chuck Rickenhouse
Chuck Slosser
Cici Morton
CiCie Frederickson
Cindy Howard
Cindy Lawrenz
Cindy Luff
Claire Ferris
Claudia Wyse
Cliff Ruff
Cliff Walkush
Coleen Dominquez
Colette Waddell
Colin Silverman
Conny Swindall
Cora Johnson
Corky Manns
Cornelius Shields
Craig Cerny
Craig Kessler
Craig Marks
Craig Merrifield
Craig Redwine
Craig Reece
Craig Salkeld
Craig Shuler
Craig Solomon
Curt Caldwell
Curt Hoy
Curtis Nelson
Cynthia Hu
Cynthia Kersey
Cynthia Perry

Daehn Steffen
Dale Hightower
Damaris Ruano
Dan Danford
Dan Dellaflora
Dan Frederickson
Dan Jones
Dan Rindfleisch
Dana Fleet
Dana Jennings
Daniel Haier
Daniel Lopez
Danielle Clinton
Danielle Harmer
Danny Ross
Danny Tevrizian
Danny Wilson
Dar Reding
Darlene Halvorson
Darol Josef
Darren Nerland
Dave Allen
Dave Bolton
Dave Everett
Dave Faucher
Dave Gibson
Dave Grokenberger
Dave Hamil
Dave Krause
Dave McClain
Dave Miescke
Dave Morris
Dave Peterson
Dave Russo
David Beerman
David Blanchard

David Cox
David Douds
David Eddie
David Howard
David Hughes
David Key
David Krueger
David Luff
David Muir
David Myerscough
David Raney
David Ring
David Vogias
David Winn
David Winter
Dawn Christensen
Dawn Cushway
Dawn Graham
Dawn Herrin
Dawn Mathon
Dayle Paulson
Dean Hiner
Dean Lomeyer
Dean Zatkowsky
Deana Bartholomew
Deanna Clear
Deanna Gerner
Deb George
Deb Jackson
Deb Stewart
DebAnn Orfalea
Debbie Gately
Debbie Mackall
Debbie McDevitt
Debbie Radley
Debbie Ray

Debbie Seymour
Debbie Strauss
Debbie Young
Deborah Hamilton
Deborah Shaw
Debra Rose
Delores Saba
Dena Valencia
Denise Heesy
Denise Heller
Denise Ishida
Denise Svacina
Denise Vona
Dennis Itule
Dennis Yoshida
Des Rock
Dexter Loeble
Dexter Wiland
Diana Andonian
Diana DeCoste
Diana Rydberg
Diana Scott
Diane Ingram
Diane Merriman
Diane Stewart
Diane West
Dick Hessler
Dick Orfalea
Dick Ostrup
Dick Summers
Dickran Tevrizian
Dilling Yang
Dinah Van Wingerden
Dipanjan Chatterjee
Doc Blanchard
Dolly Granatelli

Dolores Saba
Don DuBeau
Don Gevirtz
Don Harmer
Don Harreld
Don Ozier
Don Sludge
Don Sowa
Dona Knutson
Donna Schey
Dorothy Peters
Dorothy Sandow
Dottie Ault
Doug Deweber
Doug Fell
Doug Gotterba
Doug Jessup
Doug Kempton
Doug Lippert
Doug Moshy
Drew Tevrizian
Dwight Lyman
E.J. Delaune
Ed Birch
Ed Stephan
Ed Togami
Edd Hoyes
Eddie Estave
Eldon Edwards
Elena Rowe
Eliot Nahigian
Elizabeth Armstrong
Elizabeth Frederick
Elizabeth Perez
Elizabeth Ruiz
Elizabeth Shura

Elizabeth Thompson
Ellen Allen
Ellie Ramsey
Elliott Eddy
Ellison Herro
Ellwood Kendrick
Ellyn Friedman
Elton Gallegly
Emily Safady
Emily Thomas
Emma Safady
Emman T. Chapman
Eric Boehm
Eric Davis
Eric Hanes
Eric Johansing
Eric Jones
Eric Joyal
Eric Miller
Eric Peus
Eric Schwartz
Eric Schwarz
Eric Werbalowski
Erica Marion
Erick Hanes
Erin Evans
Esperanza Ruano
Ethna Jackman
Eva Lane
Eva Wolfe
Evelyn Ferris
Father Bob Simpson
Father Martin Connell
Father Maurice
   O'Mahony
Father O'Byrne

Faye Matthews
Fiona Bremmer
Florence Wenzinger
Flynn Dekker
Fran Jabara
Frank Cerny
Frank Perez
Frank Szymanski
Frank Weinmann
Fred Fleet, Jr.
Fred Fleet, Sr.
Fred Herczeg
Fred Kreitzberg
Fred Ouweleen
Fred Safady
Fred Scott
Fred Simanek
Frederic Elias
Frieda Kabbash
Fritz Leiss
Gail Mason
Gail Michalak
Gail Robillard
Gary Applegate
Gary Awad
Gary Fettis
Gary King
Gary Kusin
Gary Safady
Gaurav Gupta
Gay Fox
Gayle Wright
Gene Goehring
Gene Miller (Kinko's)
Gene Miller (USC)
General DeLaune

Genevieve Beeston
Genie Smith
George Cann
George Ellison
George Erhart
George Korte
George Lily
George Stephan
George Stewart
Georgette Herro
Gerald Price
Geri Cerny
Geri Willoughby
Gerry Alesia
Gerry Polansky
Gillian Holmes
Gina Jones
Gina Ruskauff
Glen Miller
Glen Moriwaki
Glenda Lee
Glenn Carter
Gloria Kabbash
Gloria Stewart
Grace Delaune
Grace Stalica
Graham DeVilliers
Greg Anderson
Greg Bloom
Greg Clark
Greg Gebhardt
Greg George
Greg Griffin
Greg Grimes
Greg Hantgin
Greg Jackson

Greg Klausner
Greg Lara
Greg Lowe
Greg Meece
Greg Melheim
Greg Millslagle
Greg Orfalea
Greg Paulus
Greg Safady
Greg Soulages
Greg Taylor
Greg Woods
Gregg Eyre
Gregory Johansing
Guillermo Santana
Gunnar Fredlund
Hal Johansing
Hans Backman
Harjit Singh
Harriet Whaley
Harry Johansing
Harry Waaler
Harvey Applebaum
Heather Hoffmann
Heather Imrie
Heather Lewis
Heather Olmstead
Heather Parafan
Heather Sterling
Heather Tiffany
Heba Gamal
Heidi Lawhead
Heidi Molen
Helen Lloyd
Helena Baum
Helene Sullivan

Helene Winter
Henry Yang
Herb Peterson
Herb Simon
Hilary Lloyd
Senator Hillary
   Clinton
Hiro Izutsu
Holly Palance
Holly Tanner
Holly Wiggins
Howard Jones
Howard Miller
Huey Lang
Hughes Morton
Ike Basha
Isaac Jaffe
Isabel Moropoulos
J.C. Cole
J.T. Teemer
Jack Harreld
Jack O'Connell
Jack Wenzinger
Jack Woodruff
Jackie Torres
Jacque Graves
Jacques Soiret
Jacques Thiebaud
Jacy Neczypor
James Harper
James Hilyard
James McClurking
Jan Leeth
Jan Tevrizian
Jana Kellar
Jane Hartnett

Jane Marshall
Jane Ouweleen
Jane Waters
Janelle Neczypor
Janet Bruner
Janet Hentsch
Janet Pickthorn
Janet Ristow
Janice Teemer
Jarek Neczypor
Jarod Bangs
Jason Harris
Jason Muir
Jason Winters
Jay Prosch
Jay Richardson
Jean Brem
Jean Tibshraeny
Jeanetter Napolitano
Jeanne Boyes
Jeannie Smith
Jeff Abbott
Jeff Bermant
Jeff Davis
Jeff Delong
Jeff Dinkler
Jeff Estoppey
Jeff Fisher
Jeff Frank
Jeff Galluci
Jeff Harding
Jeff Johnson
Jeff Matthews
Jeff Menecci
Jeff Mitchell
Jeff Morse

Jeff Moxie
Jeff Neczypor
Jeff Peyton
Jeff Weiss
Jeff Wilkin
Jen Draper
Jennie Fisher
Jennifer Basha
Jennifer Bowie
Jennifer Clark
Jennifer Neczypor
Jennifer Nunez
Jennifer Smith
Jennifer Speakman
Jennifer Terry
Jeri Lock
Jerome Bohnett
Jerone Jackson
Jerry McGinn
Jerry Phillipeck
Jerry Purdy
Jerry Reissman
Jess Paredes
Jessica Hokanson
Jessie Ellison
Jill Jones
Jill Miro
Jim Cornell
Jim Cote
Jim Downey
Jim Kirk
Jim Lilliefors
Jim Lund
Jim Malouf
Jim McClatchy
Jim Owens

Jim Perry
Jim Thornton
Jim Volpa
Jim Warren
Jim Wilmore
Jimmy O'Shea
Jo Martinez
Joan Baker
Joan Kraus
JoAnn Robin
JoAnn Norris-Robie
JoAnn Wickenhauser
Joanna Dacanay
Joanne Hardin
Joanne Masotta
Joanne Rapp
Jock Cooper
Jodi Thomas
Joe Durdik
Joe Hardin
Joe Heath
Joe Hendricks
Joe Kautz
Joe Kreutz
Joe Ozmina
Joe Piette
Joe Schneider
Joe Vona
Joe Weyers
Joe Wynne
Joel Julian
Joel Maloney
Joel Rayden
John Bellanca
John Bevacqua
John Davis

John Delaune
John Ellis
John Foronda
John Frederickson
John Garcia
John Gavel
John Gladden
John Holbert
John Huffman
John Ireland
John Irwin
John Klink
John Lacagnina
John Leonard
John Lewis
John Lunde
John Mackall
John McGrath
John McIntyre
John McManigal
John Meredith
John Odell
John Ramos
John Ray
John Rinaldi
John Romo
John Rooney
John Thysell
John Trentanove
John Turturro
John Walker
John Wilson
John Wurzel
Jon Cannon
Jon Rowe
Jon Stancliffe

Jon Van Nostrand
Jonathon Ortiz
Joni Marley
   Holmes
Jordan Bender
Joseph Jabbra
Joseph Jacobs
Josh Freeman
Josh Miller
Josie Robles
J.P. LaBrucherie
Juanita Ruano
Judy Bartlein
Judy Burditt
Judy Clark
Judy Menne
Jules Zimmer
Julia Lanphier
Julie Bagg
Julie Holbert
Julie Salazar
Julie Vogias
Justin Stone
Karen Cooper
Karen DiRocco
Karen Hart
Karen Holt
Karen Kelley
Karen Madden
Karen Maranville
Karen Murray Mendo
Karen Pope
Karen Schoof
Karen Shaw
Karen Sloan
Karen Sophiea

Karen Yancy
Karen Young
Kari Martindale
Karl Greer
Karlene Wamhoff
Kasper Allison
Kat Tansey
Kate Firestone
Kate Love
Kathi Alvarez
Kathleen Sullivan
   Alioto
Kathleen Horton
Kathy Bennett
Kathy Briggs
Kathy Hanson
Kathy Kristof
Kathy Muldoon
Kathy Norton
Kathy Oltz
Kathy O'Malley
Kathy Ruckstuhl
Katie Nelson
Keely Cormier
Keith Brooks
Keith Coonce
Keith Jagger
Keith Lawrenz
Kelli George
Kelly Anderson
Kelly Burton
Kelly Coonce
Kelly Ringwald
Kelly Steed
Ken Hagar
Ken Hannemenn

Ken Hightower
Ken Hill
Ken Jaeger
Ken Mays
Kerry Mormann
Kevin Barnes
Kevin Holland
Kevin Kekoa
Kevin McQueen
Kevin Ross
Kevin Saul
Kevin Togami
Kevin Williams
Kim Aguirre
Kim Blievernicht
Kim Briggs
Kim Delledonne
Kim Focht
Kim Helgeson
Kim Konigsberg
Kim Manns
Kim Rowe
Kimberly Boudro
Kimberly Graves
Kimberly Holguin
Kimi Roming
Kipp Harmer
Kirk Adcox
Kit Halligan
Kit Tryon
Korth Ellsworth
Kraig Schexnayder
Kris Ellison
Kris Plasch
Krisi McGrath
Kristen Flaherty

Kristin Loomis
Kurt Koenig
Kurt Sowa
Kyle Foster
Kyoko Gillio
Lacey Davis
Lana Junker
Larry Buckley
Larry Chasen
Larry Dessailly
Larry Ferris
Larry Fettis
Larry Fitzgerald
Larry Fitzgibbon
Larry Gerber
Larry Hardin
Larry Hart
Larry Hay
Larry Holmer
Larry Kapocius
Larry Maltz
Larry Peterson
Larry Raney
Larry Rogero
Laura Bala Adamson
Laura Flowers
Laura Gaber
Laura McCormick
Lauran Eastman
Lauri Laskoski
Laurie Pandich-
    Genevish
Laurie Smith
Laurie Wren
Laurita Franklin
Leah Evert-Burks

Lee Kennedy
Lee Neill
Leila Kabbash
Lenn Freedman
Leo Robidoux
Leslie Maloney
Leslie Veenhuis
Lestlie Prokosch
Leticia Estoppey
Leticia Zavala
Lilette Grant
Lillian Heesey
Lily Ruff
Linda Faciana
Linda Fisher
Linda Mitchell
Linda Mornell
Linda Osgood
Linda Powers
Linda Saba
Linda Schuman
Linda Smith
Linda Solanik
Linda Stancliffe
Lindsey Smith
Lisa Barbee
Lisa Bolton
Lisa Clements
Lisa Fell
Lisa Finerty
Lisa Hattrup
Lisa Henderlite
Lisa Hornbaker
Lisa Lewis
Lisa McGill
Lisa Mundrake

Lisa Schneider
Lisa Trisch
Lisa Warburg
Lisa Winlock
Liz Boscacci
Liz Soprano
Liz Stanczak
Lizz Ladiana
Lois Capps
Lois Mitchell
Loren Beswick
Lori Dahl
Lori Hampton
Lori Kirk
Lori Lynn
Lori Martin
Lori Moshy
Lori Palomino
Lori Pullman
Lori Rose
Lori Zimmermann
Lorretta Ferjo
Lou Moropoulos
Louisa Murray
Luann Alvarez
Luci Orozco
Lupe Conchas
Lyn Luxmore
Lyn Perry
Lynn DeVilliers
Lynn Houston
Lynn Jones
Lynn Larson
Lynn Nuibe
Lynn Robinson
Lynn Suchy

Lynne Helmrich
Lynne Lee
Lynnette Coverly
M. Bruce Johnson
Maggie Cote
Maggie DeLaSelva
Maggie Khabbaz
Maggie McMurray
   Pfeffer
Manou Khabbaz
Marcelle Monahan
Marcus Goller
Margaret Bechtel
Margaret Miller
Margaret Ros
Margaret Stallings
Margaret Velasquez
Margie Williams
Maria Miller
Maria Souza
Marilee Hagar
Marilyn Gevirtz
Marilyn Ross
Marisa Mach
Mark Albion
Mark Barrinuevo
Mark Dean
Mark Dewald
Mark Drennon
Mark Fell
Mark Hjelm
Mark Jones
Mark Juergensmeyer
Mark Little
Mark Madden
Mark McCready

Mark Orfalea
Mark Safady
Mark Sanford
Mark Wynne
Mark Zutkoff
Marla Naysmith
Marla Sandall
Marlena Carlson
Marlene Johansing
Marlene Schiff
Marni Tennison
Martha Aylard
Martha Baker
Martha Schroeder
Martha Zeiher
Marti Aaron
Martin Kircher
Martin Nahigian
Marty Manuud
Marty Simmons
Marty Skrobis
Mary Ann Jordan
Mary Brickenstein-
   Morris
Mary Certo
Mary Chapman
Mary Clark
Mary Cole
Mary Gomez
Mary Hagar
Mary Hamilton
Mary Jane McCracken
Mary Kay Whalen
Mary LaBrucherie
Mary Pat Maloney
Mary Pretty

Mary Ray
Mary Sperling
Mary Spinner
Mary Williams
Mary Wynne
Matt Broch
Matt Faucet
Matt Hansen
Matt Hodson
Matt McDonald
Matt Richey
Matt Scheer
Matthew Leider
Maura Donaghey
Maureen Johansing
Mazen Safadi
Meghan Tevrizian
Dr. Mel Levine
Melanie Cherrey
Melissa Becker
Melissa Harreld
Melissa Lalum
Melody Sadler
Merrill Tevrizian
Michael Allison
Michael Barton
Michael Coady
Michael Cohn
Michael Deeth
Michael Domani
Michael Hart
Michael Hernandez
Michael Jackman
Michael Kim
Michael Lape
Michael McQueen

Michael Thornburg
Michael Towbes
Michael Williams
Michelle Bagdonas
Michelle Harrison
Michelle Hinds
Michelle Howery
Michelle LaBrucherie
Michelle Menzel
Michelle Myers
Michelle Patrick
Michelle Simanek
Mickey McAllister
Mike Adams
Mike Bagg
Mike Drew
Mike Evans
Mike Farah
Mike Fasth
Mike Gadberry
Mike Gorleski
Mike Kari
Mike Koval
Mike LaForge
Mike Medina
Mike Menard
Mike Moropoulos
Mike Nisky
Mike Preston
Mike Safady
Mike Sheedy
Mike Siefe
Mike Takos
Mike Tobin
Mike Whalen
Milt Bowden

Mimi Cote
Miny Willmon
Misty Cross
Mitty Powell
M'Lu Ellsworth
Monique Johansing
Monique Payne
Murray Feig
Nada Safady
Naj Citrowske
Nan Aderholt
Nancy Baca
Nancy Caldwell
Nancy Campero
Nancy Deville
Nancy Ellis
Nancy Hayward
Nancy Hicks
Nancy Lathan
Nancy Lund-Wirth
Nancy Muir
Nancy Pratt
Nannette Alberti
Natalie Cassady
Nathanael Pearson
Ned Emerson
Neil Pappone
Neil Stewart
Nick Brady
Nick Heesey
Nick Heller
Nick Myers
Nick Shauer
Nicole Tries-Botti
Nikki Boone
Nina Beard

Nita Tuvesson
Noah Ruano
O. J. Sutherland
Olga Martel
Olina Muller
Pam Burns
Pam Ferris
Pam Gibson
Pam Hiner
Pam Hood
Pam Tabor
Pat Benson
Pat Madden
Pat McLaughlin
Pat Pagnusat
Pat Walker
Patricia Gordon
Patrick Brennan
Patrick Lewis
Patti Price
Patty Barnwell
Patty Fisher
Patty Julian
Patty Peterson
Patty Stonesifer
Paul Cronshaw
Paul Dore
Paul Freund
Paul Hindrichs
Paul Leibowitz
Paul Mitsuuchi
Paul Parrott
Paul Rauch
Paul Robbins
Paul Rolinski
Paul Rostron

Paul Schlichting
Paul Stephan
Paul Van Waard
Paula Panzica
Pauli Zandona
Pauline Ferris
Peggy Heath
Peggy Hightower
Peggy Van Waard
Pete Centeno
Pete Thompson
Peter Barker
Peter Domani
Peter MacDougall
Peter Premenko
Peter Ranck
Peter Rudenberg
Peter Tanner
Phil Angelides
Phil Morreale
Phil Schlageter
Phil Smith
Phyllis Manning
Pierre Mornell
Polly Monear
Rachel Austin
Rachelle Garcia
Ralph Iannelli
Randall Ford
Randy Barron
Randy Jaramillo
Randy Mitchell
Randy Sadler
Randy Trebs
Rathin Sinha
Ray George

Ray Reveles
Rebeca Quintana
Reed Waddell
Reggie Lathan
Regina Perkins
Rekha Singh
Render Dahiya
Rene Syndergaard
Renee Radar
Renee Thompson
Renee Woodson
Lt. and Mrs. R. H.
   General Groves
Rhonda Bovee Leabo
Rhonda Childers
Rhonda Madsen
Ric Vane
Rich Kraus
Rich Marshall
Rich Peters
Richard Dillard
Richard Hur
Richard Maranville
Richard McCauley
Richard McShirley
Richard Nahigian
Richard Pferdner
Richard Spanjian
Richard Weedn
Rick Curry
Rick Eisen
Rick Hummer
Rip Mason
Rita-Jean Aranzazu
Rob Curry
Rob Hood

Rob Loucks
Rob Pace
Rob Paulis
Rob Reynolds
Rob Tebbe
Rob Tonkin
Rob Welles
Robert Bulger
Robert Dedona
Robert Jackson
Robert Laundry
Robert Nunez
Robert Parks
Robert Sabini
Robert Schaefer
Robert Smiley
Robert Walsh
Robin Anderson
Rochelle Teague
Rocky Rockholt
Rocky Standifer
Rod Lathim
Rod Tryon
Rodney Jones
Roel Aranzazu
Roger Beeston
Roger Coleman
Roger Morrison
Roger Wayland
Roger Whalen
Roger Willmon
Roland Felice
Ron Barrett
Ron Bertoia
Ron Boeddeker
Ron Boehm

Ron Brown
Ron Halpern
Ron Kirk
Ron Kuhn
Ron Levine
Ron Mergler
Ron Naysmith
Ron Pachosa
Ronda Abrams
Rony Ruano
Rony Ruano Jr.
Roscoe Worth-Jones
Rose Orfalea
Rose Tevrizian
Ross Waddell
Rowan Cypher
Roxann Gregory
Roxanne Robinson
Roy Harvey
Roy Saquing
Russ Gillespie
Ruth Anderson
Ruth Pihlaja
Ruth Surry
Ryan Fell
Ryan Schnobrich
Sabrina Dixon
Salle Smith
Sally Douds
Sam Chapman
Sam Fleet
Sam Lee
Sam Reese
Sandi Jonas
Sandra Aylard
Sandy Boyd Griffin

Sandy McElwaine
Sandy Paden
Sandy Swenson
Scott
Sanket Koli
Sara McCune
Sarah Epps
Sarah Russell
Schea Mayfield
Scott Baum
Scott Bogart
Scott Dubak
Scott Genevish
Scott Gerus
Scott Haliday
Scott Hargis
Scott Harvey
Scott Holland
Scott Kennedy
Scott Miller
Scott Santarosa
Scott Sauder
Scott Wattenbarger
Scotty Perkins
Shane Adair-Roginski
Shane McGinn
Shane Parker
Shannon Melick
Shari Carlson
Shari Shoemaker
Sharon Ertel
Sharon Grogg
Sharon Orfalea
Sharon Riggs
Shaun Tomson
Sheila Barnes

Shelley Campbell
Shelley Haynes
Sher Sutherland
Sheri Itule
Sid Castle
Sioux DeFabrizio
Sister Christine
Bowman
Sister Hagen
Sister Kathleen Patrice
Sullivan
Skip Osgood
Solveig Chandler
Sossity Garguilo
Stacey Hooper
Stacy Howery
Stacy Rice
Stan Alpert
Stan Witnov
Starla Sloan
Stefanie Reardon
Stephanie Fasth
Stephanie LaBrucherie
Stephanie O'Neil
Stephanie Slosser
Stephanie Souza
Stephen Schumacher
Steve Averill
Steve Beebe
Steve Cohn
Steve Davis
Steve Dowling
Steve Eden
Steve Fleet
Steve Golgart
Steve Jensen

Steve Keddington

Steve Kellar

Steve Kosakowski

Steve Leider

Steve Lopez

Steve McLaughlin

Steve Nalevansky

Steve Padberg

Steve Ponder

Steve Slyker

Steve Trebs

Steve West

Steve Wick

Steve Williams

Steven Sample

Stewart Bosley

Stuart Bagwell

Stuart Blake

Stuart Winthrop

Stuie Krause

Sue Chartrand

Sue Cline

Sue Coffaro

Sue Kasmar

Sue Murphey

Sue Peterson

Sue Rockholt

Susan Conway

Susan Felice

Susan Larkin

Susan Neighbors

Susan Thatcher

Suzane Pedulla

Suzie Henderson

Suzy Kent-Evans

Suzzanne Fleet

Sydney Fleet

T.J. Cowles

Tamera Harper

Tami Lara

Tammy Gentry

Tammy Spears

Tammy Tudor

Tanya Hobart

Tara Ferris

Tara Rosenthal

Tari Vogias

Tariq Kadri

Taylor Maloney

Ted Fleet

Ted Nagel

Ted Raymond

Ted Swift

Ted Vrahiotes

Teresa Reynolds

Teresa Wann-Davis

Terra Reynolds

Terri Leavitt

Terrie Hamilton

Terrie Longo

Terry Rauch

Terry Solis

Tess Christenson

Thad Jones

The Ferris Family

The Groves Family

The Herro Family

The Honorable
 Judge Davies

The Klink Family

The Marinucci Family

The Moorehart

Family

The Nance Family

Theresa Johansing

Theresa Thompson

Therese Robillard

Thom Birich

Tim Baker

Tim Ball

Tim Bell

Tim Blakesly

Tim Gramatovich

Tim Green

Tim LaBrucherie

Tim Smith

Tim Stancliffe

Tim Weibelhaus

Tim Whitcomb

Timothy Forbes

Tina Killion

Tina Marshall

Tina Slay

Tina Vervoorn

Toby Sevier

Todd Brown

Todd Evans

Todd Johnson

Todd Ordal

Todd Reinert

Todd Trish

Tom Bush

Tom Cole

Tom Dowd

Tom Dunning

Tom Ferguson

Tom Finerty

Tom Gerari

Tom Hale
Tom Hendricks
Tom Haythorne
Tom Lucas
Tom Matthews
Tom Mielko
Tom O'Malia
Tom Palmer
Tom Parker
Tom Parrish
Tom Randolph
Tom Rau
Tom Wagner
Tom Watanabe
Toni Alesia
Tony Abbott
Tony DiFranco
Tony Dowling
Tony Ferris
Tony Kasprzyk
Tony Wynne
Tonya Fossey
Tori Orfalea
Traci Luke

Traci Miller
Tracy Ozmina
Tracy Raney
Tracy Rock
Tricia Brown
Tricia Dueing
Tricia Koenig
Tricia Ugarte
Tricia Wakeford
Trina Grokenberger
Trinidad Garcia
Val Montgomery
Valerie James
Vern Smith
Vic Santiago
Vicki Southworth
Vicki Tosher
Vicky Fliss
Vincent Eubanks
Viran Singh
Vonnie Krekos
Wallis Windsor
Walt Wilson
Wanda Venturelli

Warren Baker
Warren Bennis
Wayne Hammond
Wayne Leggett
Wayne Matthews
Wayne Siemens
Wendell Wilson
Wendy Adler
Wendy Arimura
Wendy Brown
Wendy Clark
Wes Wada
Will Evans
William Crookston
Winfred Van
  Wingerden
Yolanda Desmore
Yvonne Milton
Zach Eccles
Zach Shuman
Zaida Ramirez
Zeke Ashton

Index